Volume 7 No. 2. June 2002

Translations

Issue Editors: Ric Allsopp and Caroline Bergvall

T0314606

Forthcoming Issues

On Fluxus
September 2002

To mark the 40th anniversary of the first Fluxus festival in Wiesbaden, Germany, and the 30th anniversary of Fluxshoe which toured England with a series of performances, concerts, and exhibitions (1972–3), 'On Fluxus' will continue the volume theme of 'textualities, scores and documents' and focus on the relationship of writing and textuality to Fluxus. Fluxus was an international community of artists, architects, designers, and composers described as 'the most radical and experimental art movement of the 1960s'. As a laboratory of experimental art, Fluxus was the first locus of intermedia, concept art, events, and video, and a central influence on performance art, arte povera, and mail art. The issue will be guest edited by Ken Friedman, an active participant in Fluxus, as an artist since 1966, as director of Fluxus West for a decade, and as editor of *The Fluxus Reader* (1997); and Owen Smith, an art historian and curator specializing in intermedia and multimedia art forms, and author of *Fluxus: History of an Attitude* (1998).

On Archives and Archiving
December 2002

Performance is widely regarded as that which cannot be archived – its presentness at odds with the archive's quest for permanence, its disappearing acts resisting the desire to label, stack and store. Yet, at the same time as performance has asserted its radical ephemerality, the demand for documenting and archiving its practices on behalf of performance research and historiography has grown. What then is performance's relationship with the archive? The issue contains contributions that explore this relationship in all its facets, including the role of performance in the culture of the archive and the role of the archive in conceptualizations of performance; the cultural histories and ideologies of archival practices; the future of performance and the archive in the digital age; performance as an archive of its own history; performative interventions into archival culture; the role of forgeries, rumours and lies in the development of performance history; the role of the document in performance research; the practices of performance archives; and performers' archives. 'On Archives and Archiving' will continue the discussion on archiving and performance begun in earlier issues of *Performance Research* ('On Memory' and 'On Maps and Mapping'). Responses to previous contributions on the theme are especially welcome.

Submissions

Performance Research welcomes responses to the ideas and issues it raises. Submissions and proposals do not have to relate to issue themes. We actively seek submission in any area of performance research, practice and scholarship from artists, scholars, curators and critics. As well as substantial essays, interviews, reviews and documentation we welcome proposals using visual, graphic and photographic forms, including photo essays and original artwork which extend possibilities for the visual page. We are also interested in proposals for collaborations between artists and critics. *Performance Research* welcomes submissions in other languages and encourages work which challenges boundaries between disciplines and media. Further information on submissions and the work of the journal is available at: http://www.performance-research.net or by e-mail from: performance-research@dartington.ac.uk.

All editorial enquiries should be directed to the journal administrator: Linden Elmhirst, *Performance Research*, Dartington College of Arts, Totnes, Devon, TQ9 6EJ, UK. Tel: +44 (0)1803 862095; Fax: +44 (0)1803 866053;

e-mail: performance-research@dartington.ac.uk

ISBN 978-0-415-28941-2
First published 2002 by Routledge
711 Third Avenue, New York, NY 10017
2 Park Square, Milton Park, Abingdon, Oxon, OX14 4RN
Routledge is an imprint of the Taylor and Francis group an informa business

Typeset by Type Study, Scarborough, UK.

Abstracting & Indexing services: *Performance Research* is currently noted in *Arts and Humanities Citation Index*, *Current Contents/Arts & Humanities* and *ISI Alerting Services*.

Editorial Translations

At the time of writing, the Nationality, Immigration and Asylum Bill which will aim to enforce stricter regulations for asylum seekers to the UK is being discussed in Parliament. The French Front National finds itself at the heart of the presidential election, and other EU member states are uncovering a widespread and deep-seated escalation of xenophobic behaviour among many voters towards immigrants and EU citizens of non-European descent. At the other end of the Mediterranean, the Israel–Palestine conflict is descending into horror. All this casts an uneasy shadow on this issue on translations.

Indeed, if nothing else, translation implies a potential for cultural exchange and admits to the import–export value of cultural material and cultural influence. It acts as a reminder that cross-cultural and cross-linguistic traffic is one of the ways through which languages and cultures enrich not only one another, but also their own development. As a practical and exploratory manifestation of cross-lingualism, translation makes the point that language is always on the move and always being moved.

Whilst it confirms cultural and linguistic differences, translation also promotes the possibility of bringing such differences to bear on the understanding of one's own culture. It is through the maze of etymologies and unexplained occurrences, the sudden eruptions of borrowed words and phrases that have long since been recontextualized as part of the language, that various divergent histories of influence and cultural trade can be felt. In a sense, translation is in itself indicative of such a traffic. It crosses borders with text, with written language, whilst remembering, or being reminded, that cultural and linguistic borders are there.

Hélène Cixous, meditating on the underlying and widespread return of nationalism and the impulses towards border shutdown, in her book *Three Steps on the Ladder of Writing* (1993), saw in this a renewed need for the 'proper' (country, name) which immediately seems to imply separation and rejection, a distaste for difference or, as she says, 'a harsh, trenchant desire not to be you'. This awareness of separation, this knowledge of boundaries and borders which throw up the question of collective identity, is always at the heart of the process of translation: what gets left out, what gets brought out of the individual text or material, and how and why. In many ways translation can be seen to be providing a 'double vision' on cultural texts. The text or material to be translated is read and apprehended with a home (or target) culture in mind which in turn is seen from the intimate distance of what is coming in, alerting it to itself. Both There and Here. Both One and Other. Both I and You. Or, rather, possibly-You and possibly-I, when taken to mean language instances and, placing the translator at macro distance, at one critical remove. As a partial mediator of cultural texts the translator is positioned across language divides, literary identities and cultural allegiances. Translation defines both the bridge and the divide of this traffic.

For Walter Benjamin, in his still much discussed essay 'The Task of the Translator' (1970), the very fact of translation releases the possibility of what he called the 'pure' language: that which lies in the undercurrent of language, that which manifests all languages differently, yet links them all in language. In many ways, one can imagine that the principle of translation does contain a post-babelian dream of cohesive plurality.

Performance Research 7(2), pp.1–3 © Taylor & Francis Ltd 2002

Yet, as translation theorist Lawrence Venuti has insisted on showing throughout his work, on approaching translation from a more historical and pragmatic perspective, and placing it firmly within the social networks and language ideologies, it is subsumed by, one can see a long history in Europe of how the role of translation has been apprehended as assisting the aims of the homogenization, absorption and assimilation of its officially mono-lingual cultures. Translation has also assisted in an opening up of new language, of language made anew, of critical and subverted language, whilst at the same time acquiring what is desired of the other without shifting ground – exoticizing, excising or assimilating. Examples are countless: how 'English' a text sounds; how this could have been written in French; the task of 'fluency', bending the text to make it fit the translation language or the trans-lation culture; making a translation as homely as possible.

Far from being recognized as a mediating and potentially enlightening or commentating presence at the heart of culture, the translator frequently sees their role relegated to that of an invisible player – one who passes the text on. Such sub-sidiary roles and functions tie in with notions of cultural dominance and linguistic hegemony rather than with dialogue and exchange. They also maintain the idea of the uniqueness and 'untrans-latability' of the original artistic work. As Venuti has written: 'the "original" is eternal; the trans-lation dates'. The assumption is that translations are the victims of the mannerisms of their own time, whereas the work itself breaks through such limitations. This may explain the interest in homo-phonic or procedural translation tactics which attempt to bypass such limitations by setting them-selves up as an aspect of experimental poetics; and which indirectly or directly comment on the ideo-logical base through which translation is made fluent. [For example, see the work of Charles Bernstein, Allan Fisher and Anne Tardos in this issue pp. 90–5.]

It is nevertheless interesting that it is precisely through this point of untranslatability that contem-porary ideas about identity can meet and free up those of translation. As the American poet Lyn Hejinian once wrote, translation 'catalyses one's own otherness'. It is through the catalyst of untranslated cultural detail that identity formations such as hybridity have taken up language. Linguistic and/or language minorities within larger communi-ties have used art as a tactic of resistance with which to explore ways of forcing up an understanding of heterogeneity from within. Writers, artists and activists since the 1990s have attempted to manifest and break open the many linguistic communities within an officially monolingual nation-state, sub-verting monolingual dominance through local detail, the resistant motif, and the untranslatable hiatus of identity. By manifesting an understanding of mixed languages, of mixed cultural backgrounds and allegiances as a way of performing otherness, such strategies provide a recourse to bi-culturalism, to double-vision, to mixed bags of cultural identity which bring up (in both a broad and narrow sense) the endless translation processes that culture grapples with or ignores at any one time. It becomes more pertinent to access incomprehensibility, to display it rather than to cover it over, or erase its edges. In this scenario, 'not-translation' is a dynamic provocation which might show up the non-homo-geneity of any monolinguistic culture, the way it is porous from within even as it attempts to strengthen its own boundaries.

The fact that such tactics are also spread through the Net and that we are now in a culture of intense mediatization, sheds another light on the issue of translation. Whether good or bad, it places mediation more squarely at the centre. Like Douglas Adams's 'Babel Fish', translation is placed at the service of the linguistic supremacy of the new global language – English – increasing its mechanics, its mediations and mediators. The additional programming that has to be typed in order to code any non-standard (ie non-English) signs for use on the internet is a painful (and uncommented on) reminder of the cost of such lin-guistic supremacy. Yet the politics and methods of mediation need to be highlighted and valued.

Mediation increasingly plays a role in dissemination as a way of making work and directs attention to the translative and transformative aspects of cultural performativity. This broadened yet specific disposition of translation as an aspect of electronic and global communications plays out cultural traffic in more ways than one.

It is with all this in mind that we set out to collate and commission work for this present issue. The broad range of work that we are able to present here within a wider thematic of textuality and performance the absence of a 'total project' in relation to translation, and the types of questions that the issue as a site of translations raises, in a sense reflect our own need to question rather than affirm the collaborative potential of translation and its many realities. For example, the five textual 'interventions' that are scattered through the following pages approach the work of artists, critics and researchers in terms of mediation, utilizing translational methods and providing a reciprocal strand for the more overtly graphic and poetic translations of the six sets of 'artists' pages'.

Translation as a performance of passage and of transit can play its part at a time when we are caught between globalization and surges of isolationism. It operates as a play of mediation and mediators, to distort, to report and to inform the shifting intersections of contemporary cultural discourses. Or, as the Cuban poet Octavio Armand wrote: ' the translator's quest is not to silence but to give voice, to make available texts that raise difficult questions and open perspectives.' As editors of the issue, we also hope that we have managed to do that and not lose sight of the essentially collaborative and generous spirit of all our contributors and colleagues which has made this issue possible.

Caroline Bergvall and Ric Allsopp

REFERENCES

Benjamin, Walter (1970) 'The Task of the Translator', in *Illuminations*, trans. Harry Zohn, London: Fontana/ Collins.

Cixous, Hélène (1993) *Three Steps on the Ladder of Writing*, trans. S. Cornell and S. Sellers, New York: Columbia UP.

Translating Humour

Equivalence, Compensation, Discourse

Lawrence Venuti

In what follows I aim to formulate methods of analyzing and evaluating literary translations. To achieve this aim, it is essential to approach a translation *as a translation*, as a text that is relatively autonomous from the foreign text because it communicates that text with a domestic difference, a difference that reflects the receiving language and culture. This idea doesn't constitute a new departure in translation studies, where since the 1970s it has been developed by theorists who emphasize such constraints on the translating process as 'target norms' and the 'skopos' or goal that the translator intends the translation to realize (see Toury 1995; Vermeer 2000). Yet unlike these theorists I want to describe the relative autonomy of a translation without losing sight of its decisive relation to the foreign text: this relation is decisive because it helps to define a translation as a translation, distinct from other kinds of derivative texts. The relative autonomy is more clearly seen, I want to argue, if we return to the concept of equivalence and rethink it on the basis of particular translations in various literary forms and genres. I will draw my examples mainly from poetry, narrative, and satirical prose, making an effort to give theoretical concepts the formal and generic specificity that will enable them to be applied productively to different kinds of literary translations.

By considering particular translations in detail, I want to question the value of any argument or research project that restricts itself primarily to developing the most general theoretical concepts or seeks to validate such concepts by engaging primarily with other theories. But I also want to question empirically oriented projects that collect data without submitting their theoretical assumptions to a searching critique. Translating is a linguistic and cultural practice, and like every practice it is distinguished by specific kinds of materials (linguistic and cultural, foreign and domestic) and specific methods of transforming them (the full gamut of discursive strategies that might be employed in a translation). No practice can develop without an interrogative reflection on the theoretical concepts that make it possible, that inform its selection of materials and its transformative methods. By the same token, however, no theory can develop without the proof of practice, of the specific case. In the end, my rethinking of basic concepts through examples will result not only in a more nuanced theory of equivalence, but in a theory of translating a specific literary form: the literature of humour.

1. EQUIVALENCE AND THE DOMESTIC REMAINDER

Equivalence can be useful in analyzing and evaluating translations only if we avoid understanding it as a one-to-one or univocal correspondence between the foreign and translated texts. This sort of correspondence is seldom possible because the translating process usually involves a simultaneous loss and gain. It is in fact this loss and gain that defines the peculiar second-order status of a translation, its relative autonomy. The loss occurs because translating is radically decontextualizing.

Performance Research 7(2), pp.6-16 © Taylor & Francis Ltd 2002

Translating detaches a foreign literary text from the literary traditions, the network of intertextual connections, that invest that text with significance for readers of the foreign language who have read widely in it. The foreign context is irrevocably lost: an entire foreign literature is never translated into a particular language, so that readers of a translation have no or limited access to the traditions that inform the literature. Even more fundamentally, translating dismantles the linguistic and literary context – a context with varying degrees of subtlety and complexity – that was created within the foreign text and can be said to constitute it, its texture (see Berman 1985). The signifying process of the foreign text often cannot be reconstructed because languages signify in different ways. Translating always effects a loss of the foreign text at various levels: a loss of form and meaning, syntax and lexicon, sound and meter, allusion and intertextuality.

At the same time, however, a gain occurs because translating is radically recontextualizing, actually exorbitant in its creation of another context. It adds formal and semantic features to the foreign text simply by rewriting it in another language with different linguistic structures and different literary traditions. Languages differ, sometimes markedly, in syntax and lexicon. Contrastive linguistics shows that English demands greater precision and cohesiveness than Romance languages like French, Spanish, and Italian (see, for example, Guillemin-Flescher 1981). Thus, the Italian preposition 'da' is rendered more precisely by diverse English words and phrases in diverse contexts: 'by', 'with', 'from', 'through', 'to', 'for', 'at the home of', among other possibilities. Further, different literary traditions take shape within languages: different in the sense of possessing distinctive styles, discourses, and genres, but also different in the sense of following distinctive modes and speeds of development and establishing unique affiliations with foreign and domestic literatures. Translating, especially in the case of a literary text, always effects a linguistic and cultural gain that exceeds the foreign text and signifies primarily in the receiving culture, evoking domestic forms, traditions, and values.

Since equivalence can never be a bi–univocal correspondence, the relations between the foreign text and the translation can take many different forms, and these relations will vary historically and geographically. Some periods, such as the 17th and 18th centuries in England, have been dominated by a preference for free translation, if not simply by an erasure of the distinction that we draw today between translation and adaptation (see Venuti 1995). A typical example is Alexander Pope's version of the *Iliad*, which recast the Homeric hexameter into the heroic couplet and displaced ancient Greek values with those specific to Hanoverian Britain.

Other periods are dominated by a greater demand for linguistic precision or an adequacy to the foreign text. Today, the prevailing expectation in the United Kingdom and the United States, as well as many other countries worldwide, is that a translation will be adequate to the foreign text by containing roughly the same number of words or pages. Although contemporary translators often depart from foreign syntactical constructions, they nonetheless try to maintain a semantic equivalence based on current dictionary definitions, or in other words a lexicographical equivalence. And in maintaining this basic equivalence, they also try to reproduce various formal aspects of a foreign literary text, its plot, characterization, and narrative point of view, its pattern of figurative language and stanzaic structure, its use of stylistic devices like irony. Despite these efforts, translators can never entirely escape the loss that the translating process inflicts on the foreign text, on its meanings and structures, figures and traditions. And they cannot obviate the gain in their translating, the construction of different meanings, structures, figures, and traditions and thereby the creation of textual effects that go far beyond the establishment of a lexicographical equivalence to signify primarily in the terms of the translating language and culture. Translating creates effects that vary to some extent the semantic and formal dimensions of a foreign text. I shall call these effects the domestic 'remainder' in a translation because they exceed the communication of a univocal meaning and reflect the linguistic and cultural conditions of the receptors (cf. Lecercle 1990). The remainder is the most visible sign of the domesticating process that always functions in translating, the assimilation of the foreign text to intelligibilities and interests that define the domestic cultural situation.

Consider, for example, the American translator Allen Mandelbaum's 1958 version of a text by the Italian poet Giuseppe Ungaretti:

Lontano	Distantly
Lontano lontano	Distantly distantly
come un cieco	like a blind man
m'hanno portato per mano	by the hand they led me

Mandelbaum's translation maintains a lexicographical equivalence with Ungaretti's poem while giving special attention to reproducing its line breaks and sound effects. The English version imitates the echo in the Italian text (the repetition of the long vowel 'o' and the rhyme on '-ano') by creating a rhyme (the long 'e' in 'distantly'/'me') and assonance (the short 'a' in 'man'/'hand'). Consequently, the last line of the translation resorts to a syntactical inversion ('by the hand they led me') that deviates from the straightforward, rather ordinary syntax of the Italian line. This deviation, moreover, releases an English remainder: such a syntactical inversion is archaic in English, indicative of older poetries, Elizabethan or Victorian, where it was already seen as a poeticism. Yet it was in fact poetical diction that Ungaretti sought to abandon in his poetry, preferring instead plain, precise Italian that rejected the rhetorical ornamentation favoured by predecessors such as Giosue Carducci and Gabriele D'Annunzio, Giovanni Pascoli and Guido Gozzano. In releasing a distinctively English remainder, Mandelbaum's translation detaches Ungaretti's poem from its moment in Italian literary history and links it to contrasting poetic discourses and traditions in English literature.

2. COMPENSATION AND THE ETHICS OF TRANSLATION

Because of the irreducible differences between languages and cultural traditions, translators often resort to various strategies to compensate for the losses that result from translation. A typical compensation is the insertion of a brief explanation for terms and allusions that are unfamiliar to the readership of the translation, especially those that are deeply rooted in the foreign culture. Compensations may also include free renderings or substitutions designed to produce an effect that the translator could not produce in the translation at precisely the same place that it occurs in the foreign text (see Harvey 1995).

In rendering the Italian writer Antonio Tabucchi's novel *Sostiene Pereira* (1994), the British translator Patrick Creagh inserted some words and phrases that are immediately recognizable to British readers. He turned the expression 'un buon cattolico' into 'a good Roman Catholic', where the inserted word 'Roman' serves as a useful qualification in a country in which the dominant religion is Protestant and Catholics are routinely identified with the city of the Pope's residence. Similarly, the academic expression 'a pieni voti', used to describe the highest grade when a candidate is awarded a university degree, was rendered as 'a First in Philosophy' in accordance with the British university system. In both cases, Creagh's translations compensated for cultural differences and made the text more familiar and comprehensible to British readers. Creagh resorted to similar compensations on the stylistic level. Tabucchi's text mixes standard and colloquial dialects of Italian to endow the narrative with an orality that matches the occasion: it is presented as an official testimony to an unnamed authority. Creagh too mixed comparable English dialects, but he maintained the orality more consistently by inserting colloquialisms and slang expressions where Tabucchi used the standard. Thus, Creagh rendered the Italian colloquialism 'stufo' with the appropriate English phrase 'fed up'. Yet in the case of 'quotidianamente' Creagh chose the expression 'day in day out', which is more colloquial than the most likely alternative, 'daily'. Sometimes Creagh used more figurative renderings that effectively increase the oral quality of the translation. With the Italian phrase 'non sapeva che fare', he avoided the close rendering 'he didn't know what to do', and instead translated freely, using a visual image that conventionally signifies indecision or anxiety: 'biting his pen'. With the Italian phrase 'si trovava nell'imbarazzo', Creagh again avoided a close if prosaic rendering, 'he found himself in the difficult position,' in favour of a more expressive metaphor: 'he himself was saddled'.

In making the translation more accessible to readers, compensatory strategies necessarily increase the domestic remainder and raise questions regarding how much the translator should assimilate the foreign text to the receiving culture or, in other words, inscribe that text with domestic codes. Translating is fundamentally domesticating: its goal is to rewrite linguistic and cultural differences in terms that are intelligible or even recognizable to readers of the translation. Hence, translating enacts an ethnocentric violence that risks a suppression or erasure of those differences.

British and American cultures, among many others, have long been dominated by domesticating theories and practices that prefer fluent translation, an easy readability that adheres to current usage, the standard dialect, the most familiar language (see Venuti 1995). Fluency, readability, familiarity produce an illusion of transparency whereby the translated text appears to be not in fact a translation, but the 'original'. Consequently, the process of domestication is mystified by an illusory textual effect. At the beginning of the 19th century, however, Friedrich Schleiermacher indicated that the literary translator ('literary' is here used in the broad sense to include literature, philosophy, and the human sciences in general) always exercises a choice in regard to the extent and direction of the violence in his work: the translator can choose between a thoroughly domesticating strategy, an

ethnocentric reduction of the foreign text to the cultural values in the translating language, or a foreignizing strategy, an ethnodeviant pressure on those values to register the linguistic and cultural difference of the foreign text.

This isn't simply a discursive choice between different translation strategies, but an ethical choice between different attitudes toward the foreign text and culture. I agree with Antoine Berman that the translator ought to show respect for the foreign, and that substantially minimizing or removing the foreignness of the foreign text is unethical, especially where the domesticating process is mystified by the illusion of transparency (see Berman 1985). In effect, this sort of domestication constitutes a cultural imperialism in which the foreign is not respected for the linguistic and cultural difference that it represents, but instead is exploited merely to serve domestic interests and agendas.

Nonetheless, I depart from both Berman and Schleiermacher in arguing that foreignizing translation should not be understood as mere literalism or the retention of foreign words in the translated text – even if both methods can be useful in certain situations. No, the foreignness of the foreign text can never be manifested directly, in its own terms, but only indirectly, in the terms of a translation. To signal this foreignness, the translator must vary the translating language and culture, must introduce a difference or set of differences in the selection of a foreign text or in the translation strategy, deviations from the kinds of texts already translated from the foreign literature and from the strategies most frequently used to translate it. Through such deviations, the reader can come to realize that he or she is reading a translation, not to be confused with the foreign text. The 'foreign' element in a foreignizing translation isn't a transparent or unmediated representation of an essence that resides in the foreign text and is valuable in itself, but rather a strategic construction whose value is contingent on the current situation in the translating language and culture. Foreignizing translation indicates the linguistic and cultural differences of the foreign text, but it can do so only by disrupting the cultural codes that prevail in the domestic language. In English, as in many languages, the most striking way to introduce such differences in the translation is through variations of the most familiar linguistic form, the standard dialect or the most widely used colloquial forms. The more heterogeneous the language, conjoined with the foreign themes, the more likely the reader will become aware that the text is a translation, a derivative work.

In these terms, Creagh's translation of Tabucchi's novel is foreignizing. The mix of standard and colloquial dialects also includes Britishisms, usually slang. The Italian expression 'in ferie' becomes 'on holiday', whereas the American English rendering is 'on vacation'. The phrase 'non voleva più' ('he didn't want [it] any longer') becomes 'he didn't fancy it at all', in which the use of the word 'fancy' as a verb is typically British. Elsewhere 'sono nei guai' ('I'm in trouble') becomes 'I'm in a pickle', 'pensioncina' ('little boarding house') becomes 'little doss-house', and 'parlano' ('they speak') becomes 'natter'. Creagh's polylingual mixture of Englishes, especially the colloquialisms, alters the characterization of Pereira by suggesting that he is less staid and perhaps younger than the elderly journalist presented in the Italian text. Yet the linguistic heterogeneity will also make an important cultural difference to readers of the translation.

Readers' reactions will of course vary according to diverse factors. But in this case the most important factor may be the linguistic standard in the receiving culture. American readers will notice the difference immediately, not only because they generally expect a homogeneous translation discourse that relies on the standard dialect, but because Creagh's translation contains Britishisms, words and expressions from a dialect of English that remains somewhat foreign to Americans. Yet both British and American readers will also notice the difference because of the theme of Tabucchi's novel: *Sostiene Pereira* is a political thriller set in Portugal in 1938 under Salazar's dictatorship. The mix of dialects in Creagh's translation evokes a

comparable British novel, Graham Greene's *The Confidential Agent* (1939), which is similarly set during the Spanish Civil War. At the same time, however, the linguistic resemblance between Creagh's translation and Greene's novel highlights the thematic difference between Tabucchi's leftwing opposition to fascism and Greene's more circumspect liberalism. The language of Creagh's translation releases a domestic remainder, a reference to an analogous moment in British narrative traditions, yet this resemblance indicates a cultural difference from the Italian text.

3. HUMOUR IN TRANSLATION

The concept of the remainder enables a more incisive consideration of analyzing and evaluating translations of humorous literature. This concept also sheds light on the problems involved in writing such translations. If the task of translation is to inscribe the foreign text with a domestic remainder that compensates for, and at the same time signals, the linguistic and cultural differences of that text, then in the case of a humorous foreign text the remainder must recreate a particular discourse of humour in a different language and culture.

The prose of the Argentine-Italian writer Juan Rodolfo Wilcock can help to develop this point. Born in Buenos Aires in 1912, Wilcock belonged to the circle of innovative writers that included Jorge Luis Borges, Adolfo Bioy Casares, and Silvina Ocampo; during the 1940s and 1950s he wrote poetry and prose in Spanish. Repulsed by Juan Perón's dictatorship (1946–55), he immigrated to Italy where he associated with such writers as Alberto Moravia, Elsa Morante, and Pier Paolo Pasolini. In 1960 he started publishing in Italian and produced some 15 books, fiction, poetry, and drama, as well as many translations from English, French, and Spanish. He died at Lubriano near Viterbo in 1978.

Wilcock's narratives tend to be carnivalesque in Mikhail Bakhtin's sense, suffused with the dark humour that accompanies the collapse or sheer subversion of hallowed truths, official standards, institutional authority (see Bakhtin 1968). Jacket copy that Wilcock wrote for one of his books refers to the 'impossibility, in our culture, of severing the tragic from the ridiculous'. Wilcock's hilarotragedy takes the form of incongruous juxtapositions, irony, and parody in the service of social satire.

Sometimes his humour relies on camp, a gay verbal and literary discourse that emphasizes sexuality and is characterized by heterogeneity at every level (for a useful analysis of camp, see Harvey 2000). Camp mixes dialects, registers, styles, and even languages, sometimes using French as an ironic sign of cultural sophistication. Camp also mixes allusions and genres from elite and popular cultures. And it employs such themes as transvestitism, blurring genders, and the theatricalization of experience, blurring the distinction between art and life. The humour of camp issues from its sheer heterogeneity, its frustration of literary and cultural expectations raised by forms and themes as well as its violation of heterosexual norms.

Since camp is a homosexual discourse, the very decision to translate Wilcock's writing insinuates the difference of a sexual minority. But this decision also signals a cultural difference against a canon of 20th-century Italian writing in English which is dominated by male authors and heterosexual themes. Think of Italo Svevo and Moravia, Ungaretti and Eugenio Montale, Italo Calvino and Umberto Eco. Gay writers who explore homosexual themes, such Pier Vittorio Tondelli and Aldo Busi, have been translated, but they remain marginal, virtually unknown to most readers of contemporary Italian literature in English translation. In addition to the mere choice of Wilcock for translation, a translation strategy can signal the foreignness of his Italian texts by cultivating a camp discourse. As an illustration, I offer my version of an extract from a collection of short texts that Wilcock wrote with a collaborator, Francesco Fantasia. Here camp is frequently used to satirize various mainstream cultural targets, including canonical writers, commercial publishing, and bourgeois sexual morality. Thus a text entitled

'Dante and Philosophy' ('Dante e la filosofia') represents the relation between Dante's poetry and his philosophical themes in an allegorical narrative that is at once culinary and pornographic, parodying Dante's own recourse to allegory in the *Divine Comedy*. Another text, entitled 'Bestsellers' ('I più venduti'), personifies bestselling novels, presenting them as two people engaged in a nonsensical and somewhat obscene conversation. The text I have translated, entitled 'Ask Oscar: A Syndicated Column' ('Posta di Madame, a cura di Oscar Wilde'), features a prudish fiancé who sees his matrimonial courtship as a diabolical masquerade. Typical of camp, the Italian text offers a dense sedimentation of forms: an allusion to an elite literary figure, Oscar Wilde, is combined with a popular genre, a newspaper advice column, while the fiancé's letter itself strongly resembles the repetitive narratives sometimes encountered in jokes.

To maintain the distinctive satiric humour of the Italian text, my translation recreates the camp discourse on various levels (see p. 12).

It contains a heterogeneous lexicon and syntax.

I not only use current standard English, but also introduce noticeable variations, including formal or Latinate diction ('civilities', 'summoned', 'transpired', 'vicinity'), a poetical archaism ('bedight'), and many colloquialisms. Thus, 'Fermo la macchina', which might be rendered closely as 'I stop the car', becomes 'I slammed on the brakes', and 'vedo', or 'I see', becomes 'I spotted'. I occasionally give the fiancé's syntax a punctilious quality by avoiding contractions ('I do not know'), embedding the phrase 'I must confess', and adding the ceremonious 'I can testify'.

The translation also uses language with distinctly sexual connotations.

The recurrent verb 'spogliarsi' is translated more than once as 'stripped', evoking 'striptease'. In line with this sexual resonance, the transvestitism that is subtly suggested in the Italian becomes more explicit in the translation: I expand the feminine

Cara Oscar Wilde,
ieri mi è successo qualcosa di imbarazzante. Premetto che sono del segno della Vergine. La mia fidanzata è Scorpione. Stavo andando in macchina quando la professoressa di francese della mia fidanzata si spoglia nuda e indossa il suo costume da diavolo. Fermo la macchina, scendo e proseguo tranquillamente a piedi. Per strada vedo che pure altre persone si stanno vestendo da diavolo. Arrivo a casa della mia fidanzata e anche lei si spoglia e si traveste da diavola. Devo confessare che lì per lì mi è sembrata un'impertinenza. Entra il padre e le lascio immaginare la scena: anche lui era travestito da diavolo. Scambiati alcuni convenevoli, chiama la madre e questa appena mi vede comincia a spogliersi e infila il suo costume da diavola. Tutto questo avveniva nei pressi dell'università, in via Piero Gobetti. Non so se lei ha mai visto una famiglia vestita da diavoli, è quasi peggio che nuda. Me ne andai confuso e titubante. Ora vorrei chiederle: le pare opportuno che la prossima volta che vado a trovare la mia fidanzata mi metta anch'io il mio costume da diavoletto, che mi sta un po' stretto?

  Oscar Wilde risponde: Che posso risponderle? Si affidi all'istinto. Non bisogna lasciarsi trascinare dai luoghi comuni.

(Wilcock and Fantasia 1976: 42)

Dear Miss Oscar Wilde,
Yesterday something embarrassing happened to me. First, I must tell you that I am a Virgo; my fiancée's sign is Scorpio. I was driving home my fiancée's French tutor when she suddenly starts to undress. She stripped naked and slipped into a devil's costume, all red leather and spandex. I slammed on the brakes, jumped out, and proceeded on foot as calmly as possible. On the street I spotted many other people dressed like devils. When I arrived at my fiancée's house, she greeted me warmly and immediately started to undress, donning a devil's costume, all red lace and feathers. Then and there, I must confess, it seemed rather impertinent. Her father entered, and just imagine what happened: he too was dressed like a devil, sporting a crimson silk smoking jacket and a black cravat bedight with tiny crimson pitchforks. After we exchanged a few civilities, he summoned mother who on arrival started stripping down. She then wriggled into a strapless scarlet sheath and slid her matching toenails into cloven-heeled pumps. All this transpired in the vicinity of the university, on via Dante Alighieri. I do not know if you have ever glimpsed a family dressed like devils, but I can testify that it is almost worse than seeing them naked. It sent me reeling with perplexity and doubt. Now here is the question that I would like to ask you: When next I meet my fiancée, would it be appropriate for me to wear my devil's costume as well (even if it is a bit tight around the waist)?

  Oscar Wilde replies: What can I tell you? Trust in instinct. Don't be enthralled by commonplaces. One must either be a work of art, or wear a work of art.

salutation, 'Cara Oscar Wilde', to include the word 'Miss'.

Allusions are inserted to join elite and popular forms.
The Italian text already combines two popular genres, a newspaper column and a joke. To these I add elite allusions. The street name, 'via Piero Gobetti', is changed to 'via Dante Alighieri' so as to give a Dantesque twist to the theme of the devil's costume. Oscar Wilde's reply contains an aphorism drawn from Wilde's actual writing: 'One must either be a work of art, or wear a work of art'.

The translation increases the precision and cohesiveness of the language according to the demands of English.

This strategy ranges from a more specific lexicon to more explicit syntactical connections to the addition of words and phrases that sketch more detailed scenes. Whereas the Italian words that signify putting on or wearing clothing constitute common choices – 'indossa', 'vestendo', 'si traveste' – my renderings tend to be more vivid: 'slipped on', 'wriggled', 'donning', 'sporting'. I also insert exact descriptions of the devil's costumes, including articles of clothing, fabrics, and accessories.

4. THE ETHICS OF A CAMPY TRANSLATION

In releasing such a distinctively English-language remainder, my translation might be judged as unethical according to the very concept of ethics I formulated earlier, an ethics that depends on the reader's recognition of the foreignness of the foreign text in translation. More precisely, to communicate the humour of the Italian text, I exaggerate its camp discourse and risk the charge of domesticating it too much by fashioning a lexicon and syntax that answer to the English demand for specificity and by inserting allusions that are familiar to English-language readers. British readers might even feel that I assimilate the Italian text too closely to a form of humour that is currently popular in the UK. In fact, the London *Times* runs a parody of an advice column called 'Help! The answer to all your problems' (Mary Wardle of the University of Rome La Sapienza kindly brought this column to my attention). Here is a recent example (9 April 2000: 62) that bears a resemblance to the physical themes and heterogeneous language of the translation:

> *Question.* I am on the horns of a dilemma. Today's luxury quilted loo rolls are too fat for my bathroom fittings. I do not wish to be thought a cheapskate, but the only ones that fit are the 'recycled' ones (an unpleasant concept in itself). What do I do to avoid being a social pariah?

> *Answer.* For goodness' sake, nothing is more lower-middle-class than 'luxury quilted toilet tissue'. If you want to be posh your bottom must suffer. Throw out that ergonomically moulded seat and get a wooden one that digs into your thighs (and will most likely give you splinters in a few years). Make sure the cistern clanks ominously when you flush. And above all, seek out that shiny disinfected paper with all the absorbency of a bucket of razor blades (and a similar texture, it feels, as it slides over your softer regions).

The humour in this parody comes partly from breaking the social taboo against discussing bodily functions and partly from mixing lexicons and registers to refer to those functions. The language is colloquial ('loo rolls', 'cheapskate', 'posh') and technical ('recycled', 'ergonomically', 'cistern'), politely euphemistic ('bottom', 'softer regions') and even faintly literary ('the horns of a dilemma', 'clanks ominously').

Yet 'Ask Oscar: A Syndicated Column' is obviously much more heterogeneous than this newspaper parody, and herein lies its ethical significance as a foreignized translation. More generally, the foreignness of a foreign text can be signalled in translation most forcefully by upsetting the hierarchy of values in the receiving language and culture. An exaggerated camp discourse tampers with this hierarchy through its multi-levelled heterogeneity: the mixture of dialects, registers, styles, and genres runs counter to the English-language reader's expectation that the preferred language for translating is the current standard dialect, the most familiar form of English. The translation is laden with effects that work only in English, in terms of the history and current state of the language, in the incongruity – for example – of a poetical archaism like 'bedight', a foreign borrowing like 'cravat', and fashion-industry jargon like 'spandex'. Even if a British reader should recall the parodic newspaper column when encountering 'Ask Oscar: A Syndicated Column', upon further consideration the resemblance will ultimately indicate a cultural difference: camp is a more complicated discourse of humour than a journalistic parody, and homosexuality continues to be a more taboo topic than going to the bathroom.

To perceive my translation as foreignized, the English-language reader must not only keep in mind that it bears two foreign authors' names and a translator's by-line; this reader must also allow the heterogeneous language to play havoc with the linguistic and cultural expectations that today are usually brought to literary translations, especially English translations of Italian literature. For some readers, the language may seem so heterogeneous as to compel them to glance back at the authors' names, incredulously wondering about the cultural identity of the writer who produced the text. Reading a translation as a translation, then, is not to detect an unpleasurable awkwardness of language, otherwise known as 'translationese'. On the contrary, it is to appreciate the writerly qualities of the translation, the textual effects that work primarily in the translating language and culture and distinguish the translation from the foreign text.

To test the effect of my translation, I surveyed the responses of approximately 150 readers, using audiences who subsequently listened to this paper as a lecture. I presented them with two English translations of the Italian text: a very close version and the elaborated version I have reproduced above. And then I asked them to judge which was the more humorous. Although the readers didn't see the Italian, I identified the translations as such and provided the names of the Italian authors as well as the bibliographical data concerning their text. The readers who participated in my experiment were very diverse. They included literary critics and translation scholars as well as translators, undergraduate and postgraduate students at translator training programs, and native English speakers who read only for pleasure. Their native languages, moreover, were extremely wide-ranging: not only British and American English, but Basque, Catalan, Croatian, Dutch, Finnish, French, German, Italian, Norwegian, Portuguese, Spanish, Swedish, and Turkish. By far the greatest number of readers, approximately 75 percent, chose the elaborated

translation as the more humorous. In unsolicited comments written on the sheet I distributed, as well as in comments voiced after the experiment, many readers referred to the increased specificity of the clothing as a primary source of the humour. This fact, in conjunction with the wide range of native languages, points to a particular conclusion linking humour, language, and translation. The readers evidently brought to the experiment a stylistic expectation for English translations, the knowledge that English demands greater precision and cohesiveness than many of their native languages and therefore the expectation that an English translation of a humorous text will be funny to the degree that it is specific.

Some readers also perceived the foreignness of the foreign text in the translation, although they lacked the terminology I have used here to describe the foreignizing effect. Here is a typical comment from a British reader who teaches English at a translation faculty in Spain:

> the second one is funnier because it is more coherent (where does the tutor appear from in the first version?) and visual (the descriptions of the rubber clothing, etc.). The French tutor is identified as a woman too. The name of the street is more significant (but I haven't read the *Divine Comedy*). And the final epigram is welcome. Both versions contain startling genre mixes. For example, the very colloquial joke formulae (tenses, etc.) which is mixed in with the syndicated column. But then there are some incongruences too. In both texts there is 'impertinent/impertinence', a word that seems too formal and weird in meaning in this context. Similarly exotic is the word 'commonplace' that is in both texts. I didn't know the word 'bedight'.

This reader's use of such descriptions as 'incongruences', 'weird in this context', and 'exotic' indicates that in his reading experience the translation registered a foreignness through its discursive strategies, a departure from typical expectations for English usage, particularly in literary translations. Moreover, the reader could perceive this foreignizing effect without any specialized literary knowledge. He hadn't read

Dante's major poem, nor did he recognize the English word 'bedight' as a poetical archaism that appears in such poets as Edmund Spenser. Although as an English teacher at a translation faculty he can be considered a professional reader to some extent, he brought popular expectations to the translations, wanting the language to make 'coherent' sense and recognizing familiar genres like the joke and the newspaper column. The perception of foreignizing effects in a translation would thus seem not to be restricted to an elite audience of literary specialists or readers with an extensive knowledge of literary styles and traditions.

5. SOME CONCLUSIONS

The foregoing discussion offers several guidelines for analyzing and evaluating literary translations. Since the general expectation today is that translations will be semantically adequate to the foreign texts they translate, the significance and value of any translation hinge, first, on maintaining a lexicographical equivalence – even if the demand for such an equivalence is relaxed at points because of the need to compensate for linguistic and cultural differences. Yet this very need indicates that more must be taken into consideration when approaching literary translations. Because a univocal correspondence between a foreign text and its translation cannot be achieved, especially in the case of literature, a literary translation cannot be analyzed or judged simply by comparing it to the text it translates. It is also necessary to examine the domestic remainder and the diverse relations that it establishes within the receiving language and culture. A translation is always an interpretation of the foreign text which uses and responds to the dialects and registers, discourses and styles, genres and traditions that constitute the culture in which the translation is produced. The translator must release a domestic remainder that doesn't simply approximate the features of the foreign text, but compensates for the irreducible differences between languages and cultures.

Hence, any assessment of compensatory strategies cannot be framed merely in linguistic or literary terms; the involvement of a foreign text and culture requires that a cultural ethics be formulated. Because translation is so weighted toward the receiving language and culture, it includes an ethical choice: the translator must decide how to preserve the foreignness of the foreign text, even though that foreignness can be signalled most powerfully, not through literalisms or foreign borrowings, but through a disarrangement of the hierarchy of domestic values. A foreign text can be chosen to reform the canon of the foreign literature in translation, and a discursive strategy can be developed to challenge the most prevalent translation practices, the most familiar uses of language in translations. Translating is fundamentally domesticating, but a translation can use various domestic means to bring the foreign text into the receiving culture. The translator can assume responsibility for this domestication only by using domestic means that are inventive or experimental, that so depart from dominant values at home as to register a linguistic and cultural difference. This experimentalism must be figured into analyses and evaluations of translations. And, perhaps most importantly, translators themselves ought to call attention to it through prefaces, afterwords, and annotations so as to educate readers who prefer, largely through custom and partly through ignorance, that translations be an invisible form of writing.

Nonetheless, a translator's particular performance may be so distinctive in its choices as to call attention to itself. And this possibility is more likely to occur with literary discourses that require innovative or elaborated strategies to compensate for linguistic and cultural differences. Humour presents such a case. Here the translator's release of the domestic remainder must be calculated to produce humorous effects that both imitate those of the foreign text while maintaining their differences for readerships in the receiving culture. The empirical data presented here, the surveys of reader responses to my translation of Wilcock and Fantasia's text, suggest that humour is far from universal, that it lacks any basis in an essential human nature, even if the stigma attached to sexual orientations like homosexuality does indeed cross national borders today and lead to sniggers – among other, less amused reactions – in vastly different cultures. Because the universality of humour is questionable or simply nonexistent, a translation that maintains a lexicographical equivalence to a humorous foreign text or closely adheres to its lexical and syntactical features will not necessarily reproduce its humorous effects. Humour can be described not simply as culturally specific, as an effect of the hierarchical arrangement of values in a cultural formation, but also as rooted in the particular languages in which literatures are written, in the subliminal knowledge that users acquire of those languages even when they are non-native speakers. What users learn is that languages are inscribed with different demands for precision and cohesiveness, and these demands create stylistic expectations that shape acts of communication and representation, including the production of literary effects like humour and the effectiveness of humorous discourses like camp.

To write a humorous translation that signals the foreignness of the foreign text, a translator must first choose a text whose humour disrupts the hierarchy of values in the translating culture. In arguing that humour is culturally specific, I don't wish to deny that a reader of a humorous translation might laugh at a passage that in the foreign text evokes the foreign reader's laughter. But I do want to suggest that any notion of common humanity inferred from this shared reaction can only be misleading because the inevitable ratio of loss and gain in the translating process, a ratio that is at once linguistic and cultural, ensures that the basis for our laughter can never be exactly the same. Once a suitably humorous foreign text is selected, then, a translator must work to register its difference: the translating language can be varied to resist any homogeneity that might be imposed by dominant translation practices. Yet still more is necessary. In cultivating a heterogeneous discursive strategy, the translator must also take into account

the stylistic expectations inscribed in the translating language, must conform to the degrees of precision and cohesiveness demanded by that language to ensure that the writing produces humorous effects.

Clearly, the kind of translation I am advocating is oppositional, unceasingly critical of the linguistic and cultural materials that the translator has to hand. I draw the urgency for this critical stance from the fundamental paradox of translation itself: the materials that the translator must unavoidably use to receive the foreign always threaten to annul it.

REFERENCES

Bakhtin, M. (1968) *Rabelais and His World*, trans. H. Iswolsky, Cambridge, MA: MIT Press.
Berman, A. (1985) 'La Traduction et la lettre, ou l'auberge du lointain', in *Les Tours de Babel: Essais sur la traduction*, Mauvezin: Trans-Europ-Repress.
Creagh, P. (trans.) (1995) A. Tabucchi, *Declares Pereira: A True Account*, London: Harvill.
Guillemin-Flescher, J. (1981) *Syntaxe comparée du français et de l'anglais: Problèmes de traduction*, Paris: Editions Ophrys.
Harvey, K. (1995) 'A Descriptive Framework for Compensation', *The Translator* 1: 65–86.
—— (2000) 'Translating Camp Talk: Gay Identities and Cultural Transfer', in Venuti (2000): 446–67.
Lecercle, J.-J. (1990) *The Violence of Language*, London and New York: Routledge.
Mandelbaum, A. (ed. and trans.) (1958) G. Ungaretti, *Life of a Man*, Milan: Scheiwiller; London: Hamish Hamilton; New York: New Directions.
Tabucchi, A. (1994) *Sostiene Pereira: Una testimonianza*, Milan: Feltrinelli.
Toury, G. (1995) *Descriptive Translation Studies – and Beyond*, Amsterdam: Benjamins.
Venuti, L. (1995) *The Translator's Invisibility: A History of Translation*, London and New York: Routledge.
—— (ed.) (2000) *The Translation Studies Reader*, London and New York: Routledge.
Vermeer, H. J. (2000) 'Skopos and Commission in Translational Action', trans. A. Chesterman, in Venuti (2000): 221–32.
Wilcock, J. R. and Fantasia, F. (1976) *Frau Teleprocu*, Milan: Adelphi.

The Text Writes Itself

Arnold Dreyblatt

In 1925 Sigmund Freud wrote his famous text, 'A Note upon the
"Mystic Writing Pad" '[1] in which he compared our memory apparatus
with a common children's toy. One makes incisions onto a wax tablet,
over which has been stretched a thin sheet of cellophane. When one
pulls up the cellophane, the marks on the surface seem to disappear. Yet
the traces of the incisions remain in the wax, almost unreadable, yet
present all the same, presenting Freud with an analogy of our 'internal'
re-collection mechanism which parallels an 'external' process of information storage.

Over the last 15 years, in installations and performances, my work
has explored the cultural and psychological aspects of this model: what
are the processes in which information is stored externally in paper and
digital media within state and religious institutions designed for that
purpose? And how does the internal, individual remembrance and
storage apparatus mirror the external one?

In 1999 I created a text-based installation entitled *From the Archives*
in three adjoining spaces in the Hamburger Bahnhof Museum of Contemporary Art in Berlin.[2] The first installation, 'The ReCollection
Mechanism', recently shown at the Jewish Museum in New York, represented a 'database of the collective' which the public experiences as
an environment of non-linear associational reading and voicing from an
endless databank. Suspended in the centre of the space is a three-
dimensional circular transparent scroll upon which are projected multi-
layers of dynamic text, appearing magically to 'write' through the
space. Two computers randomly search thousands of words through a
historical biographical database, based on my work, 'Who's Who in
Central & East Europe 1933'[3] in real time. As each word is found, it is
marked and spoken out loud through a specially designed sound
environment by a male or female voice. One walks into and through a
limitless database as continually changing biographical fragments [are
mapped onto] the floor and walls of the space. Additional spaces
included a 65-foot long paper scroll containing an encyclopedic archive
on the subject of memory storage and loss; and a data projection of a

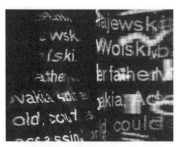

• Arnold Dreyblatt, 'The ReCollection Mechanism', Felix
Meritis Foundation, Amsterdam, 1998. Photo ©Luca Ruzza

Performance Research 7(2), pp.17–23 © Taylor & Francis Ltd 2002

• Arnold Dreyblatt, 'The ReCollection Mechanism', Hamburger Bahnhof, National Gallery, Berlin, 1999. Photo ©Werner Zellien

• Arnold Dreyblatt, 'The Wunderblock', Galerie Anselm Dreher, Berlin, 2000. Photo © A. Dreyblatt

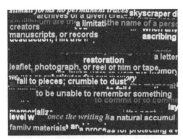

• Arnold Dreyblatt, 'The Wunderblock', Galerie Anselm Dreher, Berlin, 2000. Photo © A. Dreyblatt

thousand cross-referenced archival documents following the recorded traces of an unknown historical figure with multiple identities.[4]

In 2000, inspired by Freud's essay, I created a work which I called 'The Wunderblock', which was first shown at the Galerie Anselm Dreher in Berlin.[5] One enters a dimly lit room, noticing a full-size model of a 'generic' wooden office desk made from MDF with a matching chair positioned as if someone has just stood up to take a break. A hanging lamp illuminates the desk. One perceives some sort of writing pad which has been left inadvertently on the table. Upon closer inspection, one realizes that this writing pad is active, that is, in a continual state of writing and erasing.

In contrast to Freud's model in which the pressure of the stylus on the cellophane surface is [exerted] downward towards the lower level of wax, in my digital realization, the movement in the installation is from the 'read-only memory' of the hard disc upward towards the surface. The initial selection and input of data has already been accomplished and is stored temporarily in 'random-access memory'. Here is a form of automatic writing in which the device searches and writes whether we are present or not: it literally writes itself. We have the sense that the underlying text source will never be perceivable in its entirety. We read a fragment before it disappears only with difficulty, as multiple texts are being written and erased simultaneously. This model for memory is unstable, fragmentary, incomplete, transient and allusive.

The words, which seem to appear and disappear from below, are derived from two texts. A selection of phrases from Freud's 'Note upon the "Mystic Writing Pad"' are contrasted with a compilation of terminologies from the 'Glossary for Archivists, Manuscript Curators, and Records Managers' published by the Society of American Archivists[6] and definitions of the words 'memory' and 'archive' from the Oxford English Dictionary.[7] The latter texts speak of the process of 'external' storage of information in libraries and archives in an opposition to the neurological storage network of the internal psyche. This associative multi-layered reading echoes one's interaction with [the installation's] digital TFT display: a process of finding and loss, saving and destruction.

Here are examples of this confrontation of content:

the receptive capacity of the writing surface is soon exhausted
    a file to which access is limited or denied
two or more data records of identical layout are treated as a unit
    to put some fresh notes on the slate, I must first wipe out the ones which cover it
to remove or invalidate something, especially something recorded as by having been written down
    a person or thing held in remembrance
a writing tablet from the notes can be erased
    a reproduction of the contents of an original document

I cannot preserve a permanent trace
be effaced; leave no trace; leave not a rack behind
devices to aid our memory seem imperfect
an effect arising from memory

A wealth of commentary has been stimulated by Freud's text in the 75 years since it was written. My own contribution to this commentary has explored the cultural operations of memory as a dynamic in various media.[8] What follows here extends this work, and exhibits a significantly reduced distillation of a 2,000-year discussion on the 'care of the ancient books' expressed in the language of the Babylonian Talmud as a series of legal arguments according to Jewish Law.[9] The Talmudic discussion attempts to determine what is holy and what is not holy, and thereby questions the meaning and value of an incomplete, disintegrating, disappearing and erased text.

In Jewish Tradition, the 'teaching' or 'law' is understood to have been given in oral as well as in written forms at Mount Sinai. During a [later] historical period in which the Rabbis feared that both written and oral traditions would be lost, a conference was called in Yabneh *circa* 100 AD which began the process of the canonization of the written text. Shortly thereafter, the Rabbis began to transcribe the oral tradition as well in order 'to save it'. The canonical text – the Talmud – is a 'record' of accepted and dissenting opinions. It is only the record of verbal commentary – which attempts to guide the reader through a forest of seemingly conflicting and non-linear statements – that prevents the transcripts of the oral tradition from ossifying and hardening. The oral teachings are thus understood to be contained in a kind of 'virtual' form within the written teachings. They need to be extracted, so that active forms of interpretation can begin. An intertextual form of reading – 'sewn or stitched' through both oral and written memory – began to be developed.

The Talmud addresses this problem with the following story:[10]

It is written: 'write for yourselves these words. . . .'
It is also written elsewhere: '. . . for according to these words . . .'

The first verse means that the Torah must be written, the second that it must be taught orally. How do we resolve this? The answer is that the words that are written may not be recited by heart, and the words which are transmitted orally may not be committed to writing.

The Talmud consists of multiple layers of 'onion skin', texts surrounded by seemingly endless interpretations and cross-indexed as an enormous hypertext. Since all discussions and themes are interrelated (digressions and references to related subjects abound) one might start to read at any point. In religious communities, to this day, the Talmud is chanted and thereby partially memorized; decisions are argued verbally often in pairs and small groups. In the Talmud, our contemporary understanding of logic is largely absent, statements contradict, and one has the impression of reading the minutes to an endless meeting, where participants appear and disappear at will, and where the discussion can drift from the holy to the secular in adjacent sentences.

In the tractate 'Sabbath' of the Babylonian Talmud, there is a section which discusses the problem of saving the holy scrolls from a fire in the synagogue on the Jewish Sabbath.[11] The situation is doubly problematic since the carrying of objects out of the synagogue domain is normally prohibited. The passage begins with a discussion about the types of scrolls which may be saved, and which laws may be broken to save them. The entire passage is based on the following short paragraph:

All Holy Scriptures – whether they are Torah scrolls or scrolls of the other books of the Bible – may be saved from a fire on the Sabbath – whether we read from them (publicly) or whether we do not read from them . . .
. . . and even though they are written in any language other than Hebrew. They warrant being hidden away . . .[12]

The commentary now begins its own rambling commentary with a discussion about the nature of the book – in effect a scroll which was hand-copied – and the standard practice of reading or chanting the texts out loud. The Talmud considers books which are read publicly as more sacred than the books which are read privately. Furthermore, scrolls, which are written in other languages or in translations from the Hebrew (here considered the holy tongue), may or may not be saved (depending on whether they are read – that is publicly or not), in which case

their decay (the decayed particles after a fire) warrant being hidden away. In addition, if one leaves them in an unguarded place they should be left to decay of their own accord.

There is a reference here to the burial and resulting decay of the human body. The text is a living thing. When its holiness or its breath departs, when it is no longer whole, it should be left to decay as a body, in an 'unguarded place'. The discussion continues with a consideration of the ink in which the texts are written. Here, permanence is the issue. If

'they were written with paint, with red pigment, with gum or with ferrous sulphate, in the Holy Tongue, may we save them from a fire on the Sabbath?'

As opposed to translations, where there may be some doubt,

'. . . here, where they are written in the Holy Tongue, we may save [them].'

Another Rabbi protests

'this applies only to where (the scrolls) are written in black ink, which lasts. But here, since the (paint, pigment, etc.) does not last as long as black ink, no, we may not save the scrolls.'

The Rabbis are considering the preservation and readability of the text. The famous medieval commentator 'Rashi'[13] reflects that many holy books may be written with inferior inks, therefore we may save these books regardless in which inks they are written:

And since it is legal to write other books with these inferior type inks, it is also permissible to save them from a fire on the Sabbath.

The Commentary continues,

'in the case of a Torah Scroll in which there is not sufficient writing to gather eighty-five letters, i.e. most of the writing is erased, and the number of intact letters in words scattered throughout the scroll does not total 85, similar to a section in the Torah that begins, 'And when the Ark would journey' – may we save it from a fire . . . or may we not save it.'

When a Torah has been partially erased by the fire or other catastrophe, or by the decay of time, how many letters must be present to qualify being saved? By law, the letters must be readable to qualify as holy information. Eighty-five letters corresponds to a section from the Torah, which begins 'And when the Ark would journey' and which refers to the transport of the ark through the desert.[14] The tradition seems to value this aspect of 'portability', as if the text is movable, interchangeable, and seems to take on a life of its own, wandering from place to place. Indeed, in the handwritten parchment torah scroll, only this section is traditionally separated from the rest of the Torah, leading the Rabbis to discuss whether there are perhaps six books of Moses and if perhaps this section is 'not in its proper place', ranking as a book on its own.

'They inquired, these eighty-five letters . . . . . . must they be together, or may they even be scattered throughout the scroll?' One Rabbi answers 'together' and another said 'even scattered'.

The Talmud gradually takes leave of a concrete situation in the direction of philosophical speculations. The scroll is partially erased, only the recognizable letters may be considered here. The number of required letters is agreed upon, but may they be individual letters and textual fragments haphazardly strewn throughout the surface of the scroll or must they be together? Perhaps this passage was the inspiration for the mediaeval Spanish Cabbalist Avraham Abulafia,[15] who randomly threw letters on a page in the search for a hidden meaning. But in the case of a real fire, would one have the time to have Talmudic discussions before deciding which scrolls one is permitted to save? The Talmud has lost interest in such practical concerns. The 85 letters are now movable, much as the ark was carried from place to place in the desert.

'They inquired, regarding the blank portions of the Torah Scroll, may we save them from a fire on the Sabbath or may we not save them from a fire?'

The Talmud is not content with the writing itself, and begins to consider the surface of the object upon which one writes.

In regard to a Torah scroll which has become worn, if there is within it sufficient writing to gather eighty-five letters, ... (We may) derive that it may be saved on account of its blank portion!

> Perhaps the Rabbis are referring to the blank portions which 'join' or 'connect' the fragments of wandering letters with one another? Therefore it might be the blank sections that create a sense of hypothetical readability. A Rabbi disagrees:

A worn scroll is different.

> A worn section of the writing is not readable, and is therefore not sacred. Yet a worn section of a blank portion, since it does not affect the readability of the text, has no influence on the holiness of the entire scroll.

In regard to a place where there once was writing, I have no doubt that it loses its sanctity because when (this portion) originally received its sanctity . . . . . . (it is) only on account of the writing on it. Thus when the writing departs, the sanctity (of this portion) departs as well.

> A section of scroll, upon which there is writing, only holds its sanctity as long as the writing is readable. The writing is the 'breath' of the object, when the life force departs; the object is buried and allowed to decay of its own accord.

When am I in doubt – in regard to the blank portions, i.e. margins, above and below the writing, between one section and the next, between one column and the next, and at the beginning and the end of the scroll.

> The plot thickens. The Rabbis seem to be referring to a sort of 'negative' text, the inverse of the intention of the act of writing.

These portions were always intended to remain blank. Therefore it may be argued that the fact that the whole Torah is now blank is no reason for (it) to lose its sanctity.

> In Jewish Law, the question of intention is extremely important. Now the entire Torah has been erased, and the Rabbis are still trying to hold onto its sanctity. Since some sections were intended to remain blank, the essence of 'blankness' must itself be sacred. Therefore, the entire scroll – even if it is completely erased, and even if it is the most sacred of scrolls, the Torah – might retain its sacredness.

. . . the spaces between the lines (and letters) are considered on a par with the place on which the writing appears. This is because these spaces are essential for the writing to remain legible. The margins, by contrast, are merely intended to lend aesthetic beauty to the scroll. Accordingly, their sanctity is independent of that of the writing.

> The structure of the scroll is differentiated. The blank spaces between the letters, as the negative image of the writing, are necessary for legibility and are therefore more holy than the outside margins, which have only a decorative function. Another Rabbi counters this argument:

The blank portions, i.e. Margins, above and below the writing, between one section and the next, between one column and the next, and at the beginning and end of the scroll, render hands unclean, thus, we see that the margins of a scroll have the same sanctity as the scroll itself.

The categories of 'unclean' and 'clean' cut clear across all biblical and rabbinical debates. Upon death, contact 'renders the hands unclean'. Here again, since contact to all parts of the scroll 'renders the hands unclean', the portions may not be differentiated; again the unity of the object with its content is substantiated. The Talmud considers a text which has been 'given' and 'canonized'. Yet, the tradition merits perpetual exegesis above all else; expressed in the metaphors of readability, translation, and transit/moveability. The text has been partially erased, but not only do the fragments retain their sacredness, but patches of meaning might even be recombined. Finally, even the empty page might rewrite itself.

NOTES

1   Notiz über den 'Wunderblock' (A Note upon the 'Mystic Writing Pad'), Sigmund Freud, 1925; *Int. Z. Psychoanal.* 11(1): 1–5; English translation: *International Journal of Psycho-Analysis* 21(4): 469–74, trans. James Strachey 1950.

2   'Aus den Archiven' ('From the Archives'); Installation by Arnold Dreyblatt, Hamburger Bahnhof Museum of Contemporary Art, National Gallery, Berlin, 1999–2000.

3   'Who's Who in Central & East Europe 1933', by Arnold Dreyblatt (Berlin: Gerhard Wolf Janus Press, 1995).

4   'Artificial Memory' and 'T-Mail'; Installations by Arnold Dreyblatt, Hamburger Bahnhof Museum of Contemporary Art, National Gallery, Berlin, 1999–2000.

5   'The Wunderblock', Installation by Arnold Dreyblatt, Galerie Anselm Dreher, Berlin, 2000.

6   A Glossary for Archivists, Manuscript Curators, and Records Managers, compiled by Lewis J. Bellardo and Lynn Lady Bellardo (Chicago: The Society of American Archivists, 1992).

7   *Second Oxford English Dictionary*, eds J. A. Simpson and E. S. C. Weiner, 2nd edn (Oxford: Clarendon Press, 1989).

8   See, for example Arnold Dreyblatt 'The Memory Work' in *Performance Research* 2(3) 'On Refuge' (Autumn) 1997: 91–6.

9   A version of the following discussion was given as a paper at the second international Performance Writing Symposium, 'In the Event of Text: Ephemeralities of Writing', organized by Writing Research Associates and held at HKU, Utrecht, NL in May 1999.

10   Talmud, Gemara, Gittin 60b.

11   For an interesting gloss on this tractate, see Marc-Alain Ouaknin (1986), *The Burnt Book*, trans. Llewellyn Brown, Princeton University Press.

12   All English quotations from the Talmud are excerpted from *Talmud Bavli, Tractate Shabbos*, Volume IV, The Schottenstein Edition (New York: Mesorah Publications, 1997). Liberties have been taken in compressing the original text, and no attempt has been made to present a commentary which might replace traditionally accepted sources.

13   Rabbi Shelomo Yitzhaki, 1040–1105, commonly known as 'Rashi'.

14   *Book of Numbers*, ch.10: 35–6. This section tells of the portable transport of the Ark in the desert during the 40 years of wandering after the exile from Egypt. As the Ark was moved from place to place, a protective 'holy cloud' would follow.

15   [. . .] *Abraham Abulafia – Kabbalist and Prophet: Hermeneutics, Theosophy, and Theurgy* (Los Angeles: Cherub Press, 2000).

Please, teach me Pashto

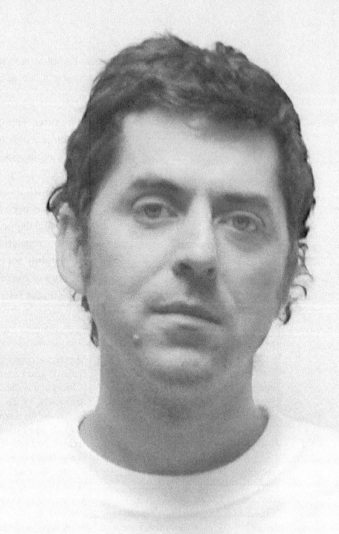

ماته پښتو راوښايه

Watching in Translation

Performance and the Reception of Surtitles

P. A. Skantze

It began in the 1980s with opera. The small liquid letters – usually yellow – appeared upon a rectangular black box suspended high above the stage, its small dark screen incongruous against the top of the curtain. The singer entered, opened his mouth and 'cinque, dieci, venti, trente, trentesei, quarantatre' is what one heard, but suddenly the box came to life and numbers scrolled across, clarifying, '5, 10, 20, 30 36, 43'.

Opinions varied. Devotees of opera found the intrusion of text onto the pristine scene of the singers framed by the proscenium annoying and tacky. Those who argued that the translation would make the opera more accessible to an audience unfamiliar with the repertoire found the little black box a help rather than a hindrance.[1]

Since those early experiments with opera, the use of simultaneous translation for theatre and opera has increased, particularly at European festivals of international theatre. If, for example, a Dutch troupe brings a Christopher Marlowe play to a French festival, the journey in translation continues beyond the first translation from the English into Dutch, translating the Dutch translation into French surtitles so the festival participants will understand what is happening on the stage.

The first difference for the spectator when watching a play with surtitles announces itself physically by the necessary shifting of the eyes from the action on the stage to the scrolling words and back again. A woman enters, closes the door, goes into the kitchen and begins breaking eggs; she makes sounds to accompany the crack and slurp, then a man at the counter addresses her: 'Hey there, Stella baby'. Now, though the woman continues her action and the man leans forward towards her, the spectators remove their gaze from the scene to quickly look up and read: 'Ciao, Stella mia cara'. So the movement of the spectator's gaze is a bit like a perpetual nodding, up to the words, back to the stage. Accompanying the constant shifting of the eyes from stage to text is the aural reception, because one still hears the words spoken while reading what they mean.

Timing takes on new meaning in the world of simultaneous translation. A spectator may, for example, attend a performance in his/her own language, ignoring the surtitles and watching the play only to be startled by laughter in the theatre three seconds before the actor has finished the joke. The 'reader-spectators' take in the language all at once. Though the manager of the surtitles may try and follow the delivery of the lines, at least two or three lines of the dialogue appear at once, which means that the meaning for those watching in translation comes from comprehending the text prior to apprehending the scene before one.[2]

Also the pace of the translation appearing above the scene varies according to method. I have seen many plays where the surtitles 'got behind' the action and suddenly one had to read very quickly, usually too quickly to actually read all the lines. Then a puff of frustration can be heard in the audience; one becomes aware of the communal nature of the task of understanding by reading while watching. Just as incomprehension is audible in the theatre, so incomplete comprehension is audible as well.

Performance Research 7(2), pp.26-30 © Taylor & Francis Ltd 2002

On the opening night of a 2001 performance of Jean Genet's *Les Bonnes* in French at the Teatro Valle in Rome, the power went off during the performance three times. For as long as 10 minutes the surtitle box was blank while the actors continued the play in the semi-dark. During the hour or two of performance it becomes a habit to read, to play one's part in the deciphering of meaning. This is never more clear than when the habit is broken, as it was that night. As if the spectator's 'occupation was gone', one had the sense of a stunned, slightly confused silence while the reading spectators waited to take up the tools of their trade again. While opera critics lamented surtitles because they might encourage laziness in the opera-going audience who would no longer make the effort to read and know the libretto, in the moment of performance a different kind of labour occurs for the reading spectator.

In theory, the surtitle method leaves the choice to the spectator. Even if the language of the performance is incomprehensible a spectator may choose to ignore the surtitles. The ease with which one can ignore surtitles depends upon where the spectator is seated in the theatre. Assuming for a moment a relatively traditional theatre, the most expensive orchestra seats, ironically, make the spectators work the hardest to look up and down. Balconies and galleries often are on the same level with the surtitles. For those in the higher seats it is more difficult to ignore the words. Does refusing the 'aid' of surtitles make for a more 'authentic' reception of the performance in progress? It is a fascinating if impossible question since arguments could be made that the 'real' meaning happens in the acting and gestures not in the comprehension of the text; at the same time actors might say that they work to communicate through the language and that a spectator who does not understand what the actors are saying is not seeing the play.

Of course these possible models of reception revive familiar issues about translation – faithfulness, exact translation, colloquial rendering, authenticity. For example a production of a Shakespeare play in Russian might use a translation by

Boris Pasternak modified by the director. When the play is performed at a festival in Italy, the surtitles often do not translate 'what is being said', rather the surtitle technicians use a standard Italian version, such as Giorgio Melchiori's, of *King Lear*. So the audience receives the 'gist': when Cordelia laments 'I cannot heave my heart into my mouth' the audience reads, 'non riesco a sollevare il peso del mio amore fino alle mie labbra' (I cannot lift the weight of my love up to my lips) while the players speak a different Russian approximation (Shakespeare 1976: 13).

Most of the audience will not be aware of the dissonance unless they have command of several languages and a perfect memory of the original text. In performance, even when a spectator reads, the translation is never solely words; there is always the physical information of the actors in gesture, in intonation, in silence which creates a pattern of exchange where the reading for meaning – even the suspicion that the words read are not necessarily the words being said – is interleaved with interpretation gleaned from watching. Yet one consequence of surtitles is to heighten the consciousness of the play as a written text.

Consider Peter Sellars's 2000 production of *Story of a Soldier*. When performed in the Teatro India in Rome, the evening opened with a reading of a long poem by Gloria Enedina Alvarez – whom Sellars had commissioned to write a modern version of the libretto for Stravinsky's music, one set in East Los Angeles. While Alvarez spoke/read her poem, a woman standing next to her simultaneously read an Italian translation. Since the poem had Spanish scattered through it, the two versions seemed to meet from time to time in the Latinate similarities between Italian and Spanish. When the audience was ushered into the space for the musical performance, one saw the stage and to the left of the stage a chair and desk on which sat a Macintosh computer. Above the stage familiar liquid yellow letters appeared; beside the stage the human being manipulating them seemed like Oz after the curtain was removed.[3] But the spectators' sense of the text of this operatic evening came from the introduction of poetry in translation, the privileging of the figure of the author of the libretto, and the appearance of the mechanics of surtitles.

In an opera one might argue the spectators can be particularly unaware of the text since it is stretched and embellished by notes of music. Even for native English speakers Benjamin Britten's operas, to take one example, might contain passages incomprehensible because of the manner of singing or the joining together of one word to another in an aria. With the script above the performance the words appear 'intact' before the notes change their cadences and tempos. One moment of cross-cultural, 'cross-textual' exchange in the Sellars production came in the choice by the Italian translators to render 'Yo bro' in English, assuming the expression to be one portable between audiences and understandable because of common usage. In this case the assumption of audience understanding no doubt came directly from the ubiquity of contemporary US music and films in Italy.

However much inventors and manufacturers praise the ease promised by new technologies, most of us now know these technologies usher in their own particular forms of anxiety. Surtitles are no different; if the spectator is reading in a language familiar but not one's mother tongue, reading and comprehension can come to a sudden halt when a word one doesn't know or cannot remember appears. Minutes pass in the process of trying to remember what the word means in order to understand 'what is happening', and during those minutes the surtitles, the play continues. Some spectators may simply not read fast enough to take in the lines; and sometimes the anxiety comes from the erratic process of the surtitles themselves, leaving the spectators unsure of the relation between the words on the screen and what is being said on the stage.

Like the commonplace that the other senses sharpen in response to the loss of sight, so too the senses of a spectator whose comprehension is mediated through surtitles. Rhythm becomes an astonishingly powerful part of the performance. An unknown language heard for 2 hours becomes strangely familiar in its rhythms, its repetitions, its exclamations. When Christoph Marthaler's company from Zurich brought *Twelfth Night* in German to Rome (November 2001), the theatre used a standard Italian translation of the Shakespeare for the surtitles. Dotted throughout the performance, however, were moments when an otherwise minor figure would come forward on the stage and speak. While he spoke, the surtitle box remained blank. The third time he did this, it occurred to me that he was speaking a sonnet; not because I had understood the words, not because I had read the program, simply because the rhythm of the language and the fact that this was a Shakespeare play sent me searching for the clue to identify these mysterious but metrical pieces of monologue. (One might argue that my aural recognition came from the lyricism of the German translation of the sonnets by the poet Paul Celan.)

In December 1999 the Teatro Taganka from Moscow performed *Marat Sade* directed by Yuri Ljubimov at the Teatro Vascello in Rome. The Vascello, a small theatre, was packed. On the stage the set looked like a lion's cage in a zoo. While such bars had served in Peter Brook's famous production as a medium through which the players could goad the audience and bring attention to the inside/outside, the frame dimension of traditional theatre, for the Teatro Taganka those bars provided circus apparatus on which to swing, walk the tight-rope, tumble. For this performance the Vascello supplied no surtitles; the text was a Russian translation of Peter Weiss's play. Some of the text was incorporated into song and four of the performers (dressed as inmates) played instruments.

When the same production appeared at the 2000 Avignon Festival, there were surtitles in French over the stage which had been constructed in a courtyard, open to the air. It was a strange experience to watch these extraordinarily communicative actors, whose voices and bodies choreographed meaning as surely as any language, suddenly separated by the lines they were saying. Where the ensemble in Rome had seemed to be making an intricately woven performance, with surtitles, with the individual lines attributed to the speakers, suddenly the work seemed more of a play, less of a dance/opera. I know the play; my response I think had less to do with not knowing the story the first time than it did with perceiving how the 'aid' to understanding had a strangely dampening effect in this case. (I deliberately discount the other obvious possibilities – the change of venue, the larger audience, the Festival setting.)

This preliminary catalogue of examples hints at the phenomenological consequences of surtitles in the performance event, to use Wilmar Sauter's term (Sauter 2000). I turn now to my final example from the RomaEuropa Festival 2001 which suggests a new level of awareness and play with the use of surtitles as translation.

For the last two decades the mechanics of simultaneous translation have been incorporated into 20th-century theatre etiquette: we pretend that the box with the words is not there.[4] However, upon entering the Teatro Argentina for The Volksbühne Berlin Company's production of *Endstation America* one saw a huge (twice the length of the normal surtitles box), shallow, rectangular box attached to chains hanging at least three or four feet lower than normal, not hidden against a curtain but suspended freely in the playing space. From the moment spectators saw the translation box, we understood this was no discreet aid to understanding but a textual design across the front of the scene.

An adaptation of Tennessee Williams's *A Streetcar Named Desire*, *Endstation America* was performed in German with surtitles in English and Italian. As any translator knows, to say simply a translation from 'the English' obfuscates how numerous are the varieties of English. The language of Tennessee Williams's plays is a lush, lyrical Southern idiom, in fact in some sense the most compatible North American dialect for Italian since the pronunciation is slow and full. One can imagine Blanche saying, 'Good mooore-ning' with something like the elongated 'Buon giooorno'.

The Volksbühne's adaptation cut Williams's opening scene with a 'Negro Woman'; in fact the production removed the play from any setting of African-American or Creole New Orleans and

concentrated the tensions of race on those between the countries of the former East Europe – the Polish Stanley now an ex-member of Lech Walensa's Solidarity Party – and the West. One of the most profound changes to the setting made by the Volksbühne was to set the entire play in one room with a bathroom with a video camera to project what was happening in the bathroom onto a TV screen in the main room. While Williams's *A Streetcar Named Desire* (1949) incorporates the out of doors, the balconies, the porch steps, the music from blues joints on the same street, *Endstation America* closes the characters into the claustrophobic box of studio apartment, tv, bed, bath and no life on the street.

Thus the surtitle box works within the setting as another piece of technology, ignored by the cast for most of the play, but intrusively present in the mise-en-scène for the spectators. At times Williams's own scene descriptions in English appeared in the box prior to the next scene. These citations from the playscript created a dissonance since they described a time and place often entirely unrelated to the production we were seeing. 'It is early the following morning. There is a confusion of street cries like a choral chant' (Williams 1959: 156). Then this direction is translated into Italian, without the lyricism of the phrase 'choral chant'. Meanwhile the spectators hear no street cries since when the players enter by the door that is the single entrance to the stage, the spectators see nothing beyond it but darkness.

Towards the end of the production when Stanley has uncovered Blanche's very un-Southern-belle-like past, her shame is broadcast even further than the local rumour of the stories of a 'man down at the plant', or a 'merchant' who lived in the town where she was dismissed as a schoolteacher for having an affair with a 17-year-old boy. All the members of the cast, except Blanche, move to the corner of the stage and look up to see the 'evidence' of Blanche's guilt written across the box. Like receiving news from the ever-moving letters on the side of a building in Times Square, the characters read 'this woman is morally unfit for her job', 'the

Hotel Flamingo', '17-year-old boy'. The words at first scroll across in the conventional surtitle manner, then they begin flashing like an announcement or an advertisement.

To stage surtitles as part of the mise-en-scène is in fact to break this particular kind of linguistic fourth wall, the one where we pretend that we are not reading, the one where we fit our understanding back into the action going on on the stage, participating in the pretend as if we were stage-hands doing our part to arrange and rearrange the set in our minds. The actions of the Volksbühne suggest to me that the incorporation of surtitles in productions is coming of theatrical age and this invites commentary on the process itself. Many companies in Europe are consciously working in more than one language, actors in the companies often speak different languages and the performances occur across borders where Europe may be united in currency but not in a common language.

Instead of addressing the audience in the pretence of unified understanding, companies sometimes choose to make language strange again. These experiments are most often taken up by companies creating performances in a mix of text, dance and music rather than a conventional play. In the mix of gesture, mime and song, the process of demonstrating linguistic confusion can be isolated in one part of the performance where words might be repeated in three different languages on the assumption that the audience will extrapolate the meaning by hearing a word they understand surrounded by unfamiliar words: 'aqua', 'water', 'wasser'. Though it is tempting to speculate how even unconsciously a spectator might begin to 'see' the connection between the roots for words in languages – imagine 'aqua', 'agua', 'eau' – I cite these occasions only to reiterate the developing reciprocity between translation as a performed operation and the staging of the very process of language reception and retention in performance.

Endstation America demonstrates such a developing reciprocity as one between the translation of the original text (whether translated traditionally or not) and the action on the stage. In the theatre, directors and actors have long experimented with gaps, pauses, untranslatable idioms and unenacted stage directions as part of the power of live performance. With the addition of surtitles a new prominence can be given the 'untextual'; the paradox is that this prominence occurs precisely because of the addition of the visual text. When the surtitles cease to be merely an aid to comprehension, they become part of the performance. Taken up by a group like the Volksbühne, whose reputation is one of an experimental company, surtitles in the mise-en-scène have simultaneously come of theatrical age and begun a second adolescence of cranky volubility and dramatic demands for attention.

NOTES
1 Early surtitles were projected by means of a 'slide projector sequencer', and new slides had to be made for every production (Sisk 1986). Now most theatres and operas use a computer-generated text system that offers the flexibility of simply entering changes and manipulating timing. See Poole (1987) for a description of the critical response to the first surtitles. Most of the writing to date on surtitles appears in opera reviews.
2 Surtitles for opera enjoy a temporal largesse that surtitles for drama do not; the lines are often repeated or the length of time it takes to read the lines is much shorter than to sing them, so an audience can look up, comprehend and then return to watching the stage.
3 Though the surtitle 'machine' became part of the mise-en-scène in the production, it seemed clear this was not a deliberate directorial intervention. The Teatro India was renovated from an old soap factory and when Sellars's production was performed the room had no area which might hide the technician.
4 Another less common form of translation that I am not dealing with in this article is simultaneous translation with earphones for members of the audience who want them.

REFERENCES
Poole, Jane L. (1987) 'Use of Surtitles by Major Companies', *Opera News* 14 February.
Sauter, Wilmar (2000) *The Theatrical Event*, Iowa: University of Iowa Press.
Shakespeare, William (1976) *Re Lear*, trans G. Melchiori, Torino: Oscar Classici Mondadori.
Sisk, Douglas F. (1986) 'Surtitles . . . Surtitles . . . Surtitles', *Theatre Crafts* 20: 50.
Williams, Tennessee (1959) *A Streetcar Named Desire and Other Plays*, London: Penguin Books.

Intervention 1
Don't Think About It – *Blues*

Claudia Wegener

D.G. = Douglas Gordon, artist, * 1966 Scotland
D.G. = Dan Graham, artist * 1942 Illinois

a part of an almost infinite conversation in the dusk (near dark)

– a palm hits the lens of a camera.
  – and you don't hear a thing.
– you see a beat.
  – you watch the beating as you'd watch something through a closed window pane.

– a hand beats a camera.
  – and the camera shoots.
– at some point it did. now, i watch a re-run. the record of a hit. and nothing happens.
  – there is an exchange of blows. nothing is exchanged.
– not quiet a hit . . .
  – nothing changes, this way or that way.
– quite! you say it . . . that's the blues.

– it's D.G.'s video installation: me and a monitor in a dark room, that's the set. screen at eye level, no sound. on the monitor, i watch a hand hovering over the lens (don't see the lens, of course . . .) the hand seems to gather force. hesitates. and, for as long as it lasts, an onslaught of beats hits the camera . . . not quite despairingly, and not without insistence, i think . . .

– a hand in front of the camera . . . and where is the eye?
  – what eye are you talking about?
– and what hand? it's always the same, i think.
  – it's always the right hand, i'd think.
– don't think.
  – i see . . .

Performance Research 7(2), pp.31–34 © Taylor & Francis Ltd 2002

– the beat is not always the same. it's a beating, at times. at times a beat . . . like watching the pulse of an artery.

– mine or yours? . . . well, something is beating, and it's a hand. something or somebody is being beaten. there is anger too, i think, but quite removed. it doesn't really touch you, or anybody. it's a play, anyway. a hand like a puppet.

– and an eye behind the lens enjoys itself.

– the hand sees itself . . .

– and the camera . . .

– when the hand plays with itself, i forget everything and stare . . . i am all eye.

– the eye of the hand.

– what difference does it make?

– none. it's a play that's staged here . . .

– the hand is out of focus most of the time . . . whether it hits or doesn't.

– the hand is in focus just before it hits the lens . . . it's a moment.

– just before it gets too close, and, just after.

– so what? . . . an out of focus image. the lens is not focused. and a beating hand is . . . or was . . . its moving object, the only one before the lens . . .

– a lens is perfectly permeable. it can't hold onto a thing.

– nor a subject . . . or a beat . . .

– it might take a scratch, though. there might be a stain on the lens.

– or a glass in your eye . . .

– it easily happens when you stare through a lens: the eyes begin to tear. vision blurs, struck by tears.

– the hand plays with the lens. and with the eye, i think. supposed there is one . . .

– usually there are two . . . at least . . .

– hit! . . . well, usually, there are two hands . . . the hand (the one of the two that can be seen before the camera) also grasps the lens, clasps around it and closes the view entirely.

– black out!

– knocked out!

– there is a moment of darkness with every hit.

– a blank separates one beat from the other . . . like one image from the next.

– and suddenly light slips in. you see that you were tricked. the darkness you had seen was hand before the lens.

– *the* hand . . .

– perhaps your own . . .

– however, light slips in. in between the fingers . . . it's beautiful, i think.

– yes, that's rather beautiful. a blank has become visible. the one beautiful moment . . . that's the point where it should have been developed . . . it could have been taken much further . . .

– further?

–light comes in and that matters . . . and that's beautiful . . .

– light falls into the camera, it slips in through the gap between thumb and index finger. it's a rather long take. the hand . . . or an eye . . . plays with itself . . . and there is time to think.

– it's time to think! . . . you mean there is light to think? . . .

 – suddenly, i see the hand clearly. in close up. i can see every fold and every crease of the skin.

– the gap between thumb and index finger . . .

 – oh yes . . . just think about it! . . . the anatomical possibility of a hand to oppose the thumb to the other fingers. the very possibility to grasp a thing . . . we would not be able to handle a camera . . . nor would we have ever developed one . . .

– the great advantage of the primates . . . and the tragedy . . . this is where it all begins . . . i see . . .

 – i didn't think about it.

– i think it's a pity . . .

 – you are talking about tragedy?

– it's weak. just a playing about with camera and monitor.

 – does it matter? it's a play. perhaps, it's a comedy. and most of the players are invisible. you only see the beat . . . and the blank . . .

– and you see straight through the rest.

 – through the lens . . . and the eye . . . and the dark . . .

– it's just a game. have you seen D.G's piece? he took the same thing much further. years ago. do you know it? he filmed a beating hand and set it up as wall-sized projections on the walls of a dark room . . .

 – are you sure about it? sounds like B.N. to me . . . i remember a piece where he rolls over a stage, a camera in his hands. and a monitor at the other end of the room shows the footage in closed circuit: his feet, the audience, the room turning . . .

– isn't D.G. the one doing pavilions in glass and mirrors? . . .

 – i think that is R.S. . . . but i remember a video where a hand catches pieces of lead that drop down right before the lens of a camera . . . is it his too?

– whose? remember the film where a hand catches lorries? . . .

 – isn't that R.S.'s?

– is he the one who died in a helicopter crash? . . .

– but just imagine this one! . . . something or somebody slaps the space you've entered. the air all around you receives the blow . . .

 – it's quite an attack.

–it's another set. and another beat. entirely.

 – the players are the same. but now, i am in the centre. and it doesn't quite matter whether or what i see. i'm the object of a beat. i am in the centre of a dark room . . . *and* . . .

– i am a camera . . .

 – there is nothing hitting you in the other video.

– that's it . . . the blues . . . at the end, a blow of strokes is also just a rhythm. but you'll never know . . . it doesn't necessarily hit you.

 – quite. it's not quite a hit.

– and now. do you hear the beat?

 – i don't know. don't quite remember . . .

– i'd imagine you also hear the hit.

 – just imagine . . . it's a strong piece.

– too much of a blow really . . .

– and what does that mean?
– nothing. too much for me.

– what's the matter?
    – don't think about it.
– don't.

Douglas Gordon's (D.G.) video installation 'Don't Think About It' was shown at the Lisson Gallery in London in June, 2001. Throughout July the gallery showed work by Dan Graham: 'Sculptures/Pavilions'. Dan Graham (D.G) is known for his performance and video pieces of the 1970s – also on show (among them the one mentioned above where he rolls over the floor with a video camera in his hands) – and for his pavilions produced since the 1980s. Robert Smithson (R.S) did 'Enantiomorphic Chambers' in 1964: two enantiomorphic wall-mounted 'pavilions' which cancel out 'one's reflected image, when one is directly between the two mirrors'. 'The other' video installation – wall-sized projections of slapping hands – is a work by Dennis Oppenheim. There is a video by Richard Serra (R.S.) in which a hand catches pieces of lead. In Agnès Vader's (A.V.) film 'The Gleaners and I', a hand before a camera 'catches' lorries. Bruce Nauman's (B.N.) video installations are . . .

to be continued . . .

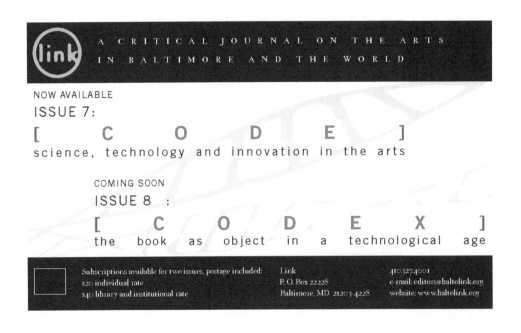

Seduction and Translation

Alain Platel
in conversation with Adrian Kear

Hotel Metropole, Brussels: 13 November 2001

Adrian Kear begins: I'm keen to ask you about *Bernadetje*, which I saw at the Roundhouse in London in 1997. I'm primarily interested in the politics of your staging of the figures of the child, the adolescent, and the adult in that performance, and the ways in which it articulated generational questions of spectatorship and seeing. I felt very disturbed by *Bernadetje*; as I watched I became increasingly uncomfortable with the spectatorial position I felt myself being asked to adopt. Other friends, other people I saw it with, were a mixture between exhilarated and frustrated, but I felt disturbed and I wanted to work out why. Such questions of spectatorship are for me primarily questions of theatre affect – where something moves you or makes you shudder – and I'm interested in what's at stake in that psychosomatic response. So I'd like to explore further with you the status of the child performers; their relationship to the adults both on stage and off; and your relationship to them as a theatre maker who constructs and negotiates the work they make in rehearsal, which you, I presume, at some point – and the presumption is what I want to get past today, if possible – re-make to set on stage . . .

Alain Platel responds: I must admit, *Bernadetje* seems so long ago . . .

• *Bernadetje* (1996).
Photo © Kurt Van der Elst

Performance Research 7(2), pp.35-49 © Taylor & Francis Ltd 2002

AK: Indeed, but I hope the questions are still relevant to your more recent work, such as *Iets Op Bach* (1998), in which the figure of the child is still very central . . .

AP: Oh yes. But I still have very vivid memories and, in fact, the whole trilogy I did with Arne Sierens – *Moeder en Kind* (1995), *Bernadetje* (1996), and *Allemaal Indiaan* (1999) – I really still enjoy thinking about. It was very special, and *Bernadetje* was special special . . .

AK: How do you think of the trilogy? Does it have a chronology for you?

AP: No. We called it a trilogy but in fact it was because we made three performances together; I knew before we started *Allemaal Indiaan* that at the end I'd have to stop. So that's why it's a trilogy, and calling it one and thinking about it like that was because we realized that there were certain elements that came back. But there is no chronology. We do see very strong differences between the three of them that for an audience are less visible, but it's more about the work with Arne than about the differences between them . . .

AK: So it's the collaboration that holds it together . . .

AP: Yeah. We started to make *Moeder en Kind* because somebody invited us to work together. At first, we were quite afraid to do so because he's a very strong personality and I think I have my own vision also. I had followed his work from the very beginning and I thought he was unique in using words on stage: he was the only author I saw making texts where a language was used that was very like a physical language. So it was not a bad idea of this guy, Dirk Pauwels from Victoria, to bring us together because I refused words and he had never worked with the physicality of his actors. Putting us together was quite adventurous and it was because we liked it so much that we decided to continue and make *Bernadetje*. And the same thing happened after *Bernadetje* – it was more the joy of making something together that pushed us forward. At the same time I think it's good – three is enough. You could repeat yourselves quite easily . . .

AK: How then did you work? Did you rehearse elements separately and then bring them together?

AP: Oh no. We were like two pairs of eyes together from the beginning. It was quite new at that time to have two theatre directors, one more interested in dance and the other interested in 'theatre' theatre, to put them together and to have no separation in jobs, so we did everything together. There were moments where he invented choreographies and I was more interested in deciding about the words. For all three of the performances we did not have the texts to begin with but rather at the end of the process . . . I think, in all three performances, at the end Arne was more like a – how do you call it? – a *rédacteur* . . .

AK: An editor?

AP: Yes, so at the end he was the one who controlled the dialogue . . .

AK: Through the selection of the words and their arrangement . . .

AP: Yes.

AK: Did the words tend to be produced by the performers then, in context, or by you and he giving the performers their words?

AK: What about the physical phrases? One of the things that I think is quite distinctive about your work is the extent to which there are individual motifs and phrases within the performer's work. Did that, again, tend to come from them and be shaped or did you set tasks for them to do?

AK: So I guess you're kind of rein-venting primary conventions . . .

AK: I think that's one of the distinctive things about the role of the kids in your work: they appear to have some agency, to have some ownership and control over the action and the ability to move it on . . .

AP: I think it's a bit of everything together. There were things that we heard during the rehearsals which we wrote down: sometimes we'd set them literally and sometimes it was just a cue for him to invent short phrases; or it could be phrases from the actors that he would use – one sentence or one word – all possibilities were open. But most import-antly the type of syntax we used, 99 percent of the time, was invented by the actors or came from what we overheard.

AP: Yes . . . In fact we met each other at a very good moment because he was tired of writing and I didn't want to make dances – so that was a good beginning, a good start. And since we worked with very young children – some of them were only 7 – it was impossible to force acting. Some of the children did not have any kind of theatrical experience and were not familiar with how to work in this kind of way. So, for example, for *Moeder en Kind*, we had to explain to some of the children the clear difference between playing in a rehearsal and being real, because sometimes they were afraid. We had improvisations where we played around certain conflicts and they were not sure whether this was real or not and so we had to explain the difference to them. We used a very simple element: we used a carpet on the floor, and said that everything that happened on the carpet was theatre and outside was not, so you know that if this character is angry with you on the carpet it's just play, and outside it's usually something else . . .

AP: Yeah, yeah we had to. Because the difference between children of 7 who did not have any kind of experience and the professional actors was so big, and we were sure when we started that we did not want to use the children as objects or, you know, like you would use a vase of flowers or something, to make it look beautiful: they had to be charac-ters that could be in the performance.

AP: Yeah that's true, but that is something when we work in the context of the theatre that they are not doing in a natural way. They tend to behave very unnaturally when they start to improvise in the beginning, but when we explain that in fact they don't have to act we have a breakthrough. I thought the process of making *Bernadetje* was very clear in that respect because we had the set, the dodgem car set, from the very beginning. That was nice because first of all we had to learn to use it safely, because it was quite dangerous, and so for the first two weeks we only drove the cars – that was the only thing we did. They enjoyed doing that so much . . . It was also a very easy way to gather the first material, and to explain to them that whatever they do is interesting to us to watch so they didn't have to play a character, or do something strange, they just had to 'be'. Very often we ran long

•Allemaal Indiaan (1999). Photo © Kurt Van der Elst

sessions, of one hour or two hours – sometimes more – without us interfering. If anything, we said 'just have fun on the set', then both of us would write down what we liked and did not and I think they learnt by it because after each improvisation we would give some feedback to them on the things we liked and they were very fast at realizing we were watching them in every way – the way they were sitting, walking, everything – and this also explained to them that for us this was material we were looking for, the way they would behave more or less 'naturally'.

AK: Presumably the duration of those improvisations must have helped to lower the pretence as well, because even children of 7, I imagine – certainly the 7-year-olds that I know – are capable of acting-up and going over the top . . . By commenting on what you saw, what were you asking the performers to learn from your comments? Were they designed to enable them to learn routines or more to learn a mode of performing?

AP: Yes, yes. Sometimes they were very surprised. I remember, for example, there was one rehearsal where one of the kids was late: he brought a sandwich with him and when he came in he said he was going to eat his sandwich outside because he didn't want to disturb us, but we said oh no, you can go and eat your sandwich on the set. And he didn't understand, then afterwards . . . There was one guy, for example, who went to a party the night before rehearsal and so was extremely tired and he did not have any kind of energy to improvise and so we said, then sleep – but on the set. All these things, we would explain to them, for us were also ok, because it was about a certain kind of life we wanted to discover and eating and sleeping could be part of it. So they learnt from the fact that the way they spoke or the way they would look or walk was ok; that they didn't have to speak loud and clearly when they had to address the audience, for example, and they could say things without us understanding without it being 'wrong' or whatever. So it made them feel at ease and they didn't have to bother any more with what they looked like. And then once this was said and they felt at ease, then you can build certain elements, certain conflicts, between

• *Bernadetje* (1996). Photo © Kurt Van der Elst

who they are, the things that they like to do, and emphasize them or ask them to repeat certain things – a process by which, day by day, they discover a certain 'character' . . .

AK: I guess the repetition element might be crucial there because maybe that's where something like performance competence clicks in even within the context of a lack of training or a lack of 'technique' – where repetition, the ability to reproduce, starts to be critical . . .

AP: I think there are two things – one is that – and the other thing is, we were very concerned about the fact that each of them, the adults as well as the children, would do only things on stage that they really liked. And actually that wasn't so difficult because for all of them to be on the set was already lots of fun. So everything that was more than that was ok. And then also we had this idea about the performance being finished 10 days before the première, so that the last 10 days we could really spend on them learning to feel comfortable during the performance so that there was not any kind of stress for them during the performance because for them the first performance was in fact the tenth. I learnt that this was important because it was something that made them feel at ease, and in fact it's something that I use in every performance . . .

AK: Part and parcel of that, I would have thought, would have been enabling the performers to learn to enjoy the performance, because the performance also depends upon their enjoyment of it to a large extent . . .

AP: That's extremely important – not only with the kids but with adults and in any performance that I make. Once you find the material that people like to perform, then they effect something. The last performance that we made, *Iets Op Bach*, is a real group performance. It's now 4 years since they've been doing it, and they still are so strong in showing it. One factor is that it's not at all against their will, they're not being made to do it or something like that . . . It's because they made it themselves, they feel that it's put into a context that they can understand, that they share, and it's also material, personal material, that they can change. Slowly, gradually, they learn that there is a possibility to change certain elements . . .

AK: So the performance works within a choreographic structure, but creates space for, would you say, 'improvisation' on stage?

AP: No, no, on stage it's impossible. In most of the performances, especially *Bernadetje*, it's too dangerous. But if they have very personal material – a solo or something – then it's possible during the performance because they know the timing, they know the sequence, they know what they can and cannot do. But this is rare; they always ask for permission because they want to make sure that everybody is aware of what they're going to do. And then there are other situations, where they have combinations with other people, where they have to discuss before they alter something.

AK: It's interesting you raise the issue of awareness there because I think one of the reasons why I was intrigued, shall I say, by *Bernadetje*, was because when I saw it I had a

AP: I think they are aware, but in their way, about what is happening. I mean, they all know about MTV, they know about showing off, they know about these things and in making this catwalk and they were referring very much to what they've seen. That's one thing, although I'm not sure if they're aware of the effect of this showing off on all of

question about the performer's own awareness of what it was they were doing. If I take one scene in particular as an example: in the first third there seems to be a moment where the mise-en-scène changes to being almost like a catwalk, where one by one the performers come down the middle of the set, right to the edge of the dodgem cage – the edge of the stage – and present a piece of themselves to the audience. I remember, on the evening I saw it, one of the young guys presented his nipple to the audience, as a kind of revelation, a display, and I wondered there about the relationship between reception and intent, and the extent to which the kids are aware of what it is they are doing. Obviously, in that context, they're aware they're displaying their bodies, and they're obviously aware that they're positioning the audience as agents of the gaze, as adults in relation to their childhood bodies, but I wondered about the extent of their awareness of the relationship between that and, if you like, the 'argument' of the show . . . if that's not too big a leap . . .

the audience. I mean, with their peers, they can kind of guess the effects; I know the effect on adults was sometimes very different and I'm not sure they were aware of that. We sometimes discussed this, not with all of them, but individually, if there were questions or if there were certain things that they'd heard, we then discussed them, but to certain extents, to where they were willing to talk about it, because sometimes it's less problematic for them and we can make problems out of things that they don't understand why it's a problem . . . It's sometimes a problem of the people who are watching more than of them. Maybe in the future they will discover these issues, maybe never; but if I felt that they were insecure about certain things or not sure about whether they liked to do that or not, then we would always be very sensitive to these situations – whenever there was a problem about, we would face it. Also there is a danger of making a fuss on their part. We were never using these elements very consciously; it was more about a certain feeling than about the certitude that this had a certain effect – but sometimes we let things just be what they were without trying to . . . Let me give this example: we never asked the guy to show his nipple, and in this context it could be not disturbing but 'what do you mean' or 'what does he mean' or 'what do you want to make of me' or 'what does the maker mean' or whatever and sometimes you choose to let it be like that. And it's a kind of game that intrigued me also, very much, in how images could have a certain affect, a disturbing effect, and not necessarily mean what people who watch it would like to see in it. In this case, it's funny, but also interesting because you take it away from the moralistic . . .

I remember in *La Tristeza Complice* (1995), for example, a very funny thing, which is a completely different image. There was a solo of a girl, accompanied by an Arabic boy who was singing into a microphone: he was singing an Arabic song, but it was heard via old-fashioned loud-speakers like you could find in the 1950s and 1960s, for their specific sound quality. It's a scene about which we had many comments, because people would say, 'Why do you use an Islamic prayer to accompany the solo of a girl? Why would you use that?' But in fact it was an Arabic children's love-song, and the boy was singing it because it was the only song he knew by heart. It was a very beautiful song but it had no connotations to religion . . . But it was very funny to see that, also in the context of the performance, this moment became a very special moment where people very often were provoked in some way, but in a wrong or a double way. And once again it's that I like. People, when you would tell them again that it was a love-song, felt very shy. They would ask, 'Is this a kind of prejudice I have, that whenever I hear somebody singing in Arabic, I think it's an Islamic prayer?' And it's this kind of image I love . . .

AK: I think that kind of ambiguity, or rather, the ambiguity of the stage as the space that produces it, is at the core of the question of disturbance. The child performers do seem to take ownership over what it is they are doing and address it to an audience and then in that exchange it's almost as if the theatre event is asking the audience to own their own response, to take responsibility for the meanings that it generates for them. So rather than say that it's a question of what you intended, or perhaps what the child intended, instead we're asked to focus upon what gets lost in the translation, so to speak, between the stage and the audience. I think that's central to my sense of disturbance because, in that moment in *Bernadetje* in particular, the question 'How am I being asked to look at this?' certainly seems to be begged. Am I being asked to look at it with some sort of paedophilic gaze, through the same paedophilic eyes that Dirk's character on stage represents with his dark glasses always looking, looking at the children? Or somewhere between that and a childhood gaze, the look of a little child looking at it, not understanding, and then gradually being brought into it through a process of translation, because later that scene is almost repeated when she takes centre stage and raves in a moment of 'transformation': the moment of her coming of age, so to speak . . . It strikes me that the adolescence of the performers is generative in that regard, because they are kind of between childhood and adulthood – looking backwards to childhood, looking forwards to adulthood – whilst at the same time

•*La Tristeza Complice* (1995). Photo © Chris Vander Burght

AP: It's, for me, also one of the reasons why it's absolutely necessary to make performances where all of the ages are represented. *Bernadetje* was never simply a performance about adolescence or about transition, although that's a very important moment in all performances; it's always about that transition but always packed into the whole life idea where, you know, as you said, you can look at it through the eyes of the man, you can look at elements through the eyes of a child, and it's not about the child but about all these things put together and reacting towards each other. It's also about the ambiguity in how people look at things, and you as an audience are confronted with the way you watch, how you interpret and sometimes it is very shocking how we interpret things. I remember, in *Moeder en Kind*, we had an improvisation where a guy was playing the father of one of the boys and this boy had a CD of music he liked that he wanted to use in the performance. So he put on the CD and he was dancing and at a certain moment he was dancing for the guy, who was sitting in the chair, and there was this whole very weird seduction atmosphere in the scene, but the boy was not aware of that – he had so much fun in doing that. We used this scene in the performance at certain moments, and it was again so many times described as this very ambiguous child–adult paedophilic scene. But since we had put it into a relationship of father and son, with no indication through the whole of the performance that there could ever be anything wrong with this relationship between the father and the son, people were concerned with how do you, as an adult, even as a father towards your child, how do you react to the physicality and the physical provocation of a child? How do you cope with that without it necessarily being interpreted as a sexual sign or something? It was especially an issue in the context of 1996 and the Dutroux case; all of a sudden all of the performances we made were . . .

being where they are. I think somewhere along the line an audience ends up occupying all of those positions in relation to the stage as well – identifying with the adolescent performer in a transitional moment, identifying with the child's incomprehension and identifying with the adult's sense of responsibility and potential abusiveness in that situation – and somehow 'translating' between them.

•*Allemaal Indiaan* (1999). Photo © Kurt Van der Elst

AK: 'Charged' . . .

AP: Well yeah, and the interesting thing is we never had this kind of reaction in Belgium, which was very strange because that was the place where we expected it most. It was more in the other countries where we performed that these kind of reactions came very often. In England, with *Iets Op Bach*, there were a few reactions in London that provoked a police investigation. Members of the audience contacted Interpol, through the British police, asking for the police in Belgium to investigate, so the children in *Iets Op Bach* had to go to the police office . . .

AK: That's very interesting because there are moments in *Iets Op Bach* that do seem to raise that question by drawing attention to, and even literalizing, what's going on in the exchange of looks between adult and child which otherwise remain normalized. So I imagine the moment that prompted the enquiry was when the slightly older girl with the glasses comes and sits on the male performer's knee, having been repeatedly looked at by him, and more especially having been looked at by him whilst he's embracing one of the female performers, if my memory of the show is right. And I think that's really interesting in the context of seduction because that seems to me

•*La Tristeza Complice* (1995). Photo © Chris Vander Burght

almost like a classic Freudian seduction scene: the adult is somehow offering an enigmatic 'image' to the child that contains a 'message' which the child both understands and doesn't understand. The child's attempted 'translation' of it is doomed to at least partial failure because the charged sexual 'content' of the message – which the adult may also be largely unaware of – escapes their framework of intelligibility, and so, according to Freud at least, becomes subject to 'repression'.[1] I think that's true in *Bernadetje* as well, where there's a sense that there are so many 'messages' in circulation within the theatrical images, that it almost forces the recognition that adults and children and adolescents speak in different languages at the same time as speaking the same language: the compromised, largely untranslatable language of 'seduction'. And so, in contradistinction to those people in the London audience, I think that's why I think of your theatre as intensely ethical, because it raises those questions . . .

AK: Oh no, no, absolutely: it's the opposite of that moralism. The image of the child on the actor's knee is horrible but, you know, it's nonetheless ethical; it's asking us to think about those relations of seeing, interpreting, understanding, translating.

AK: That's really interesting because some of that Freudian seduction

• *Iets Op Bach* (1998). Photo © Chris Van der Burght

AP: Yes that is very important to me but not, as I've said, in a moralistic way in the sense of saying what is good and bad . . .

AP: Absolutely . . . It's a lot of fun to play with this, and I realize through working with children – for more than 12 years I've worked intensively making performances with kids, and some of them have grown up with us . . . there were two boys who were in a show I made in 1989, and now they're in *Iets Op Bach* and one is 18 and the other 21, and they were 7 and 9 when we started. It's very, very weird . . . And it's beautiful also to see them grow, and for me it was interesting also because, although my wife has a child I don't; I never wanted children. But it's very intriguing, just by working with them, how it's possible for me also to reconstruct my own past, by just seeing how they react and things like that. In a way, it lets me see why I was like that when I was a child . . .

AP: It was also fascinating to see that operating because it's a question that I've been asked very often, about how aware the kids were about theory, which I'm sure you're familiar with given your background as a educationalist, also asks us to ask that question as well. He offers a particular word, *nachtgrälichtkeit* – which translates as either 'deferred action' or 'afterwardsness'[2] – to suggest that we only understand what's happened to us in experience with a certain delay, through our coming to see our own dark backwards as an interior temporal relation. This coinage also suggests the development of a conceptual timeframe enabling the reassessment and re-translation of otherwise opaque seductive 'messages', so it's interesting that you raise that point in relation to your occupation of the rehearsal space, watching the children perform, and maybe working out not only the meanings that they're producing but also the meanings that you have previously produced in a different context. I think an audience does something similar as well.

AK: But I imagine that's the type of thing a police investigation could never understand, that there's a privileged safety space in rehearsal, and that kids are able to negotiate complex stuff, rather than being naïve innocents in need of moral protection . . . I think the work explodes a lot of that.

something in the performance and how do you guide them and how do you plan and it was really very comforting to see that they do not have the kind of problems with images that we think they have, that we suppose they might have. I remember in making *Iets Op Bach*, that there were scenes with the children – who at that time were very young, just 10 or 11 years old – where they were present in improvisations where things would happen that were either very cruel or had very extreme sexual connotations, and sometimes I didn't realize that they were there, watching it. I remember one improvisation where one of the guys made some sort of striptease – he was as good as naked when he was finished – which we had a lot of fun watching and then all of a sudden I realized that these girls were on stage. And so I asked them what they thought about this and they said, first of all, that they were not interested, and then they said, 'This is sad, you know . . . He's the sad kind of guy who would take off his clothes . . . But so what? That's it.'

AP: I must admit that often the kids were my reference when I had to decide whether or not to keep certain things, because if I would feel that they were intrigued by something, then for me that was a good sign. If they were bored, or they would say, 'Oh I don't understand', or something, then I might cut it. And that's where people were very often surprised by the fact that they would be open to very complex information, maybe they were not able to interpret it or be able to explain it, but they could say whether they liked something or not and to me very often that was significant, because if they could catch it – and it's not only about understanding it's about feeling – and they could see that a scene was extremely sad, for instance, then they would describe it like that. For example, when we worked on this striptease scene in *Iets Op Bach*, in which Sam appears at the end with his sex barely covered, when the kids saw this they described it as a very, very sad scene. They could never laugh about it because . . . they understood. They knew he was a bastard, the absolute macho treating women in a very dirty way; they knew that he was scary and yet when they saw how his character had progressed in this scene they knew that this could happen and that's why they called it very sad. And that was extremely right: it was not dirty, it was not stupid or funny; it was sad. That was correct.

AK: And of course the kids know these characters from their being very much part of their everyday lives; they have a kind of gritty materialism guiding them.

AP: Yes sure they know it, of course. These kids of 8, 9 years they knew what a paedophile was and they knew how to react and they knew what to do when it happened . . . They knew how to talk about it, so it was not a Taboo; it was something that you had to avoid, to treat . . . These people are there and they knew that it could be dangerous but also that they could understand . . .

AK: At the risk of pushing it a bit, I imagine as well that that they can also use this knowledge as a site of power, and also of fun, in terms of provoking, teasing . . .

AP: And also how to deal with it, very often. When we would work on relationships between adults and younger kids in rehearsal, or when something like this happened in improvisations, it was also some sort of psychodrama because they could learn how to cope with certain behaviours, and they could try to relate to that or they could watch whilst somebody else could relate or if they felt uncomfortable they could stop. Then we could give them more information or we could ask somebody to help . . . So, whilst it was preparing them for performance, it was also a way of helping them learn how to cope with something like that.

AK: And part of the politics of that would come, in a Freudian sense, with the recognition that such modes of behaviour aren't totally alien, aren't totally other, but are interconnected with 'normal' adult modes of relating to children as well. Also I would have thought that having a space of rehearsal which is also a space of negotiation and explanation would have helped work out the mixed messages in circulation within the adult–child relationships as well, and in the process create a form that enables an audience to pick up on that.

AP: Yes of course: the result of what you make is a condensation of what you live over the previous months. And I can imagine the result for some people. Some of the images can be really shocking, revolting. We always try to make things where there is some sort of balance between good and bad, so that there is no 'evil' character or nobody who would only be beautiful; we try to let the performance show both sides of everybody. But of course in making the whole thing, the first thing, the most important thing for us was to create an atmosphere in which people could be comfortable to show these things, to talk about these things, to not talk about things – a place where each of the performers, whether it was kids or adults, wanted to come. We have never made a performance where actors came to the rehearsal against their will. It was every time very enjoyable: there was lots of joy, lots of fun, lots of affection, lots of comfort. And if, like in the early rehearsals for *Iets Op Bach*, where there was one girl who, after three rehearsals, said, it's not my thing, then they are free to leave; and that's fine, because we can also feel if it's not the right moment or it's not comfortable for them. This atmosphere of confidence is for us extremely important.

AK: I wonder about that. I wonder whether something around the intensification of family relationships, of adult–child relationships, disturbs some bourgeois sensibilities at a fundamental level.

AP: I think so, yes. I had an extremely interesting confrontation with an Italian critic, who saw *Iets Op Bach* and *Allemaal Indiaan*. She came to me after seeing *Allemaal Indian*, and said 'you know, when I saw *Iets Op Bach*, I thought that was the most beautiful piece I'd ever seen . . . but *Allemaal Indiaan*, I don't like at all. On the contrary, I think it's terrible. Can you explain it?' So I said, 'well, let me think . . .'. So I explained to her, 'I think it's your bourgeois prejudice . . . I mean, look how you are: you are rich,' – she wears Armani, D&G, that kind of thing – 'and of course if you go and see *Iets Op Bach* you first of all have the music, and that really makes you feel comfortable . . .'. And then, secondly, there is the dance and these are two aesthetic elements that, for people who go very often to the theatre, are comforting. They see some very awful things, but if there is this kind of music, then they think 'it's so good' because the music is so beautiful. In *Allemaal Indiaan* all this was not there. It was very naked. It was all words – no music that would make it more beautiful – and the language they were talking was extremely fast, almost visceral. And that made her feel very uncomfortable because all of a sudden it was like, here, in-your-face.

AK: That's interesting because it's certainly the case with the British Press' reaction to *Bernadetje* as well. The scene they commented on was the one where the dodgem full of crumpled teenage bodies swings round to Bach, creating a wonderful melancholic image which reverberates in high aesthetic terms: all of a sudden the dodgem becomes a thing of great beauty and that allows them to get past the gritty dirtiness of the piece . . .

AP: Yes. If I would be very consequent to firm ideas I would avoid that image because, in *Iets Op Bach* also, it takes you into something where you can dream or wonder, but I . . . I just love it. I agree when people say that this is a very moving scene and it's an extremely beautiful scene, and also very disturbing in terms of how people, without showing it directly, are provoking lots of sentiments and lots of feelings in an audience. I just have to agree that this is very, very beautiful.

AK: I think there's a tendency though to want to cut out those bits from the rest of the complexity of the performance, and, within the press at least, to want to cut out and keep those bits as beautiful moments rather than think about the principle of their inclusion in the structure as a whole. And obviously that overarching relation is as important as the moment itself: the mise-en-scène is an ensemble of images rather than a collection.

• *Bernadetje* (1996). Photo © Kurt Van der Elst

AK: Quite, so when, towards the end, she walks across the stage following the toy mouse and picks it up, and there's an audible sigh from the audience – 'ah . . . at last some innocence!' – you think, 'no!' because there's this narrative to come . . .

AK: And that's then a question about time and temporality as well, because at that moment she's still in her own time, in her own little world in that image, and we see that and yet at the same time we temporalize it in relation to the slightly older children, the young women, and our knowledge of the abusive relations to come. So the moment acts as a marker of time – past, future, and present – that opens the performance out into questions of ethics.

AK: I remember it . . .

AK: I wonder about that in relation to the question of disturbance, where I started, and whether part of the effect for the audience is of having witnessed some history, be it their

AP: Yes, I agree: if it's taken out as something to be interpreted separately then there's something gone wrong. For me, you know, I can understand why people would want to keep hold of this . . . this kind of feeling everybody has that there must be something beautiful or something that I can hold . . . That's why I can never agree with people who describe the little girl as one of the most pure elements in *Iets Op Bach* – for me it's the saddest character in the whole dance because she is the one who will grow up and look like all of them, and you can already see this even though she's only 2 or 3 or 4 years old: she's going to go through all this . . . shit.

AP: Yeah, I can barely stand that scene, seeing her with so many associations being made about her growing up, and of course everybody wants to treat her like a kitten, they just want to pick her up . . .

AP: I like it when such moments are used semi on purpose. I like to play with it without making clear whether it's meant to be or not. And using people from different ages, I knew that there would be this element as a physical group. I'd just like to explain that it's very funny to see how people could interpret the presence of a kid. It's true that in *Iets Op Bach*, she was the 'now moment' and everybody else was history. There was a past and a future and she was 'now' – that was really amazing to see. The same thing is what I like to do in making performances where there are so many things happening at the same time, to make it like it looks difficult to watch, but then at a certain moment to cut it. There is always a moment in the performance where time is stopped, physically stopped. Like in *Iets Op Bach*, it was the moment when everybody is crying . . .

AP: In *Bernadetje*, it was the circle. That lasts 10 minutes – the music lasts 10 minutes, and we wanted to use the music entirely. *Bonjour Madame* (1993), one of the first performances we did, starts with the repetition of one movement 63 times. It's at the very beginning of the performance where it's horrible for an audience because you don't know when it's going to stop. There are other moments where I like to, just like, to stop time.

AP: First about the reaction of the audience again because I experienced something very recently where I was confronted by this kind of question. If you see a performance like *Iets Op Bach* – which is very dangerous, a physically dangerous performance – and you see a little kid running around, I can imagine that people are very, very worried. I just hope that there are

own or their culture's. This would seen to make something like worrying whether the children are ok on stage somewhat displaced because what the performance actually enables is a kind of thinking about the broader politics, the broader ethics of the culture of which it's part . . .

enough signs in the performance where you are sure she's taken care of. I will never show kids that are the victims of someone. Even the girl who is watched in a very particular way in *Iets Op Bach* – I know, absolutely, that she's quite strong, she can defend herself – she shows certain signs where we can see that she will never just let things happen: she will never be a victim. She will either go to look for help, or she will defend herself. And that's quite important. Of course, if you don't know the performance and you are confronted with that you have to discover it; and some people are so afraid of what is happening that they close their eyes. I've met people, especially mothers, that can't stand to see the girls on stage and so they leave, and I can only respect their feelings. It's difficult with what happened in England a few times, people accusing us of certain things without asking. If they are very worried they could just come and ask if they're ok . . .

AK: A typically English reaction – to react rather than think . . .

AP: I felt very . . . I didn't feel ok when, all of a sudden, I heard that the girls from *Iets Op Bach* had to come to the police office, because of something that had happened in London, but I thought, 'it's ok, it is what it is . . .'. In another respect, we had the same thing in France, and another in Spain, so it was not only the English . . .

AK: But in a way you can see their point. There's not just the obvious logic to it, which is the concern over the way the children are portrayed on stage, but there's also the logic that says that *Iets Op Bach* and *Bernadetje* are, very literally, almost bearing witness to a culture of abuse, that they are testimony to the fact that it's out there, that this happens and that we have a responsibility for it in a shared, complicit way. This is disturbing and should activate the attention of the authorities – not necessarily directly in relation to the show but in relation to developing an understanding of how these currents circulate.

AP: I read an article when we performed in America – it's very difficult for us to go to America because they hate these things and it's only very courageous people who try to contradict them. It's not about the audience, it's really about the critics and the theatre workers, they are so afraid – I read an article by somebody who explained that these kind of shows were the only ones where an audience was obliged to take a position. And this was a comment I liked very much. So it's something like that which makes it worthwhile to make a show and to invite people to come and see it.

It's fine for people to be entertaining other people, but for me, it's important to make something where people have to think, and to position themselves in relation to what is happening. I like that myself and that's what I always want to do. I can only say that whenever I start with a performance I have two aims: to go into some sort of an adventure with a group of people – which is why I've changed, so often, the people I work with – that's one thing; and then to satisfy myself with a certain kind of excitement. Because when people feel uncomfortable seeing certain scenes in my performances, then I just have to tell them that I feel uncomfortable myself. And so, for example, when you feel uncomfortable in how you relate as an adult to how young people look and behave, I can only say I feel uncomfortable too. I don't know how to relate. I mean I know more or less what to do: I can describe it, and I understand it more and more, but it's still very upsetting, sometimes. So it's more about putting your demons on stage than about feeling that I'm going to give you a lesson in how watch, how to think . . .[3].

ACKNOWLEDGEMENT
All photos of Les Ballets C. de la B. –
with Victoria (images 1–3, 5, 8); Het
Muziek Lod (images 4 and 6);
Ensemble Explorations (images 7 and
9) – are reproduced courtesy of Frans
Brood Productions.

NOTES
1   This schematization is drawn from
Jean Laplanche's reworking of
Freudian seduction theory. See *The
Unconscious and the Id: A Volume of
Laplanche's Problématiques*, trans.
Luke Thurston with Lindsay Watson
(London: Rebus Press, 1999: 94–107);
and *Essays on Otherness*, ed. John
Fletcher (London: Routledge, 1999:
79–80).
2   The former translation is
Strachey's; the latter Laplanche's. For
further insight into the critical signifi-
cance of this term with Freud's
analytic lexicon, see Laplanche's
'Notes on Afterwardsness' in *Essays on
Otherness*, ed. John Fletcher (London:
Routledge, 1999: 260–5).
3   A longer version of this interview
can be found at *http: //www.e-
state.org.uk*

• *Iets Op Bach* (1998). Photo © Chris Van der Burght

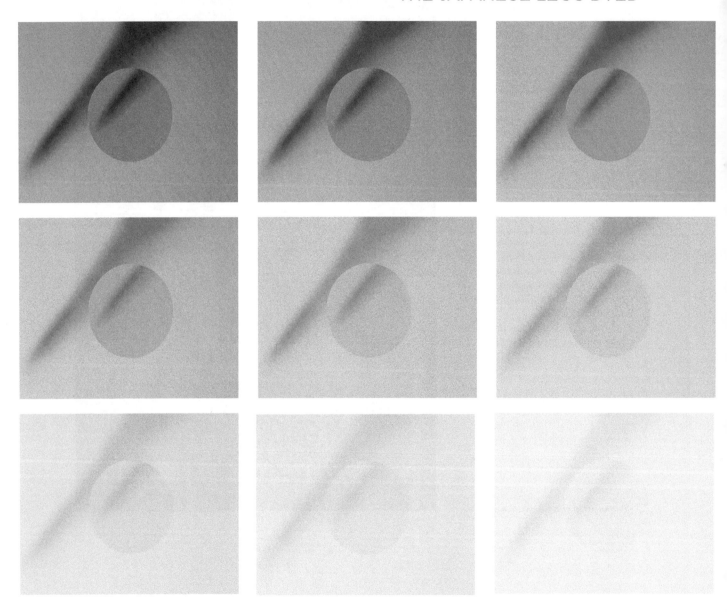

THE JAPANESE LEGS DYED

MY GREAT BRITISH HAIR DYED

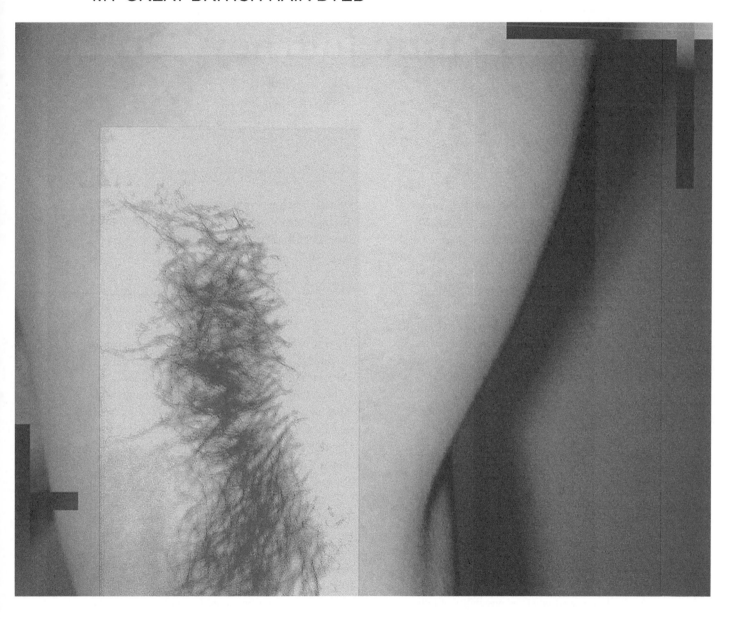

AND 210mm BY 270mm AS WELL

by Sean WU Shih-hung

Trans-e-lation by the Trans-atlantic Journey

Anya Lewin

Louis Wolfson in translation to save himself from the constant onslaught. He is a shield. The words transformed bounce off him. The words no longer have a sharp edge. Not knife and cut at once.

'In translation a text does become a vehicle for the becoming of language' (Johnston 1992: 42). Reconstruction. Reconstruing. Loss of the original?

German was the suppressed language in the house. Under the house. Around the house. Knew he could speak it. Where was he from? Only heard it in the rhyme he would sing. Something like:

Heinzenklein
Ginkelein
in Berline
ton fer eine
Gink en schreck
feel en drech
vardi naza vec

Yes is the frontier for no. No is the frontier for yes. Relations of power, of desire, are in place to allow the fall down the rabbit's hole. You see when crossing from yes to no I slipped into the gap. No one had even warned of the possibility of falling. And yes and no were rendered meaningless so meaningful. Apparently there were equivalents to yes and no in every language. If I could find the exact translation of each yes and each no the dizzying free fall would end and I could stand up. Understand?

Absolutely literal no metaphor involved.

He called the vacuum the 'electrolux'. Thought it was the German word. It's called vacuum don't you know English? Twelve years pass, go by the Electrolux store, realize it was a brand.

There was no tattoo on his arm, no skin singed, only this knowledge that he had another language.

'To convey the form and meaning of the original as accurately as possible' (Johnston 1992: 42) was sought for but so impossible. The original not known. This English so obviously foreign, not a reflection of new images but old photographs. Were they his family? No fast food in this house. Chewing gum you were a cow. The desire to translate into American. No generation, just original. Just so not foreign.

This in the middle, no beginnings. Background information? Jump into the river. This ever presence not a rejection of history but an inclusion into a present moment. Every time lost regained. The last letter typed in ended and began at the same time. Where is the scientific proof? I do not want to be the analyst. My rules creating the borders. Sewing up the seams. Fixing up the story. The cure simultaneous to the disease. To say there is a disease is to say there is a cure. But what if to say there just is?

To try and enter the space of the paranoiac is both

Performance Research 7(2), pp.52–57 © Taylor & Francis Ltd 2002

naïve and disrespectful. Loss of control of language ends in loss of control of the body ends in others' control over the subject.

'What happens to the original and the second language as a result of translation?' (Johnston 1992: 43). Here it was anger to have lost the old and discomfort with the new and the known. A taking of place that was unavailable. Children refused access to his true language.

Now babble began, if we believe in origins and accept our organs, as a universal language. What was once a comprehensibility so wide as to be unimaginable has now come to signify the incomprehensible. Such sense is made.

Bodly boodikens cunulted sorptents soolible slabbbny.

Desire permeates language? Language acts upon desire? Language is desire? A map of the erogenous zones?

To read that babbly book above I'd say someone has a dirty mind.

To make a beginning where there has been none we go to the theory of *delire*. And along with the tradition of the study of *delire* we will consider it an untranslatable word. But if we can understand it I suppose it has been in some sense translatable. To follow the path of Jean-Jacques Lecercle[1] (and to follow the path of a circle can be very repetitive) we choose (tense pause the studio audience leans forward gripping their armrests) *delire* number one! In this tradition the study of *delire* will expose the workings of language. *Delire* is a crossing of frontiers and, in crossing, frontiers are exposed. *Delire* is temporary and tameable. The *delire* is a disease and the interpretation of *delire* will bring the patient back. So in acceptance of this reading of *delire* some explanation of the previous text is necessary. A separation of the knife and the cut.

Louis Wolfson was a first-generation American Jew of Russian descent. He lived in Manhattan with his parents. English did violence to him. This is apparently no exaggeration. It was pointed sharp and pierced his skin. His mother tongue was vicious. Easy to blame the mother. 'Foreign words to annihilate yet another word of his mother tongue . . .'.[2] But perhaps he was looking for another language. His ancestral language. What dwelt under the surface? He had to find a method to protect himself from the onslaught of English. He became a linguist. A translator. He lived in constant translation. Every English word he read or heard he immediately translated into a language which was a combination of German, French, Russian and Hebrew. This was his cure. Lecercle explains someone who *delires* as possessed by language. In Wolfson's mastery of English – not allowing English to come through his barriers of translation – it is he who controls language. What is his relationship to French, German, Russian, and Hebrew? Was only English spoken in his home? Were the languages of his origins completely suppressed or sometimes spoken in the home? Was his mother's insistence on speaking the harmful English an immigrant's attempt to be completely American?

In *delire* there is no metaphor.

To say that English pierced my skin is just that and only that. To understand as is would be to go beyond empathy/metaphor to language as an experience of the body. Not imagining words piercing the body, or visualizing them, but actually feeling the pain of English being hurled at the unprotected body.

To speak about Wolfson is to speak about my father. In our house there was no German spoken. But we knew that my father was foreign – not American. He spoke only English but it was heavy with the unspoken German. The house he built was full of contradictions. Europe lived in our house. And Germany with it.

'If there is a language of truth or a true language

then it is this "pure language"' (Johnston 1992: 44). Pure is always to be mistrusted. So misunderstood. Stood under so long it did not miss him. What if it is not that all languages are interchangeable in this best of translation but that there is a best language? This was a problem. English must suffice. More than this must rule. The mother was often silent, her tongue swollen. The father's tongue misformed by misuse of the mother tongue.

There were other languages in my world. Russian was the spoken choice of old women gone mad. Polish could be heard as well. To be able to discern the many languages was a way of making maps and tracing histories. Hidden languages were hidden stories. Once a week a visit was made to the place where my great grandmother lived. Through halls of old bodies who tried to grab my young body to the room where Baba was. There she and my grandmother would speak in Russian. I remember the sounds of a language I did not understand bouncing off the aqua and lime green floral walls.

This is a picture of Louis Wolfson. One ear is plugged with his finger. The other is pressed against a small radio, which is tuned to a foreign-language broadcast. Wolfson is reading a French text. He has not yet perfected his cure, and must always be ready to shield himself from English words. Is this the picture of a madman? A picture is also translation. Again it is necessary to abandon metaphor. Too easy to romanticize a picture, a description. Quite different from making trips to the mental hospital.

The writer in *delire* is within the constructs of his/her writing while at the same time s/he is always analysing his/her circumstances. Wolfson writes his cure as he cures himself. There is reason to the treason is the song Lecercle sings as he examines the writers of *delire* and places them as central to the study of language.

'There is reason to my treason' the mad genius screams. Screams caught in throat. Screams start

in stomach. Screams must be let out. Like shitting. If I don't scream it's constipation. Don't you see? Let go of my arms. These arms are wings dipped in gold. I can stop screaming. Aaaahhhhhhh! To stop the screams is to shut down my body. I know what you'll do. You'll plug up my orifices. Shut down my borders. Mother of God don't let them take me.

A problem with *delire* is that it places one outside of society. In Lecercle's study of *delire* (*Philosophy Through the Looking Glass*) five of the six writers he discusses spent time in mental hospitals. To see in *delire* a free creativity, a possibility for a liberating politic, is exciting but also problematic. To be on the analysing side of *delire* is to be within the institution of society. To be *delire* is to have the possibility of being more literally institutionalized.

A wise professor cautioned me to remember that clinical schizophrenia was not the same thing as unconventional grammar. Quite so, I know, but does one lead to the other? In becoming a subject does A enter into language? As a grammatically correct subject will A fit more easily into hierarchical structures? It can't be so easy to be a revolutionary as saying ain't. If A knows his language to be unconventional he must know conventional. The language of *delire* illuminates the structures of language to more fully support those structures? It is different to play with language than to live within it. Two theories on *delire* as explained by Lecercle.

The philosophical tradition of *delire* [. . .] has two aspects: a theory of *delire*, of its liberating value: and a theory of the reduction of *delire*, of *delire* as a symptom of the dereliction of the linguistic order.

(Lecercle 1985: 7)

Some further explanation retaining our categories of *delire* # 1 and 2.

1 *Delire* is useful in that by dwelling in the underside of language – where instinctual urges have not been fully suppressed – it both exposes the limits of language while supporting its functions.

2 The Deleuzian *delire*. *Delire* is present in every text at every moment. When we speak we repress at some deeper level our own *delire*. We should celebrate *delire* – live *delire* as an action not analysis. *Delire* is not to be cured but to be delighted in.

Is the entrance to *delire* a slip of the tongue? But once one slips, really slips, can one come back? To play between the borders of the prescribed rules of language and the vast plains of creativity is to hide behind *delire* number one. To not see limits, to not have a frontier to cross back over, is to open *delire* number two. But is this the entrance to the psychiatric ward? If one has the choice, can see the possibilities, it is probably impossible to live within *delire* number two. To see the choices within language is to recognize its borders. 'In a world where everyone is mad, nobody is'.[3] Would that be the outcome of a *delire* revolution? But once everyone was mad so that no one was mad wouldn't it begin all over again?

My father would occasionally reveal his foreignness with an inability to remember an English word. But he would never resort to German. German his first language had become the language of the conqueror. Hitler's language. He clung to English as the language of his new identity but he never really lost his German – the language of the victim. When he wrote he used all capital letters with dashes separating the phrases. I imagine his lost languages resting in the space of the dashes.

We expel what we have been fed but some of it stays within us. Our body the border between in and out. Where does a language enter and where does it rest when it is no longer spoken?

Another recurrent feature of Wolfson's book must be mentioned: the link he establishes between language and feeding, two oral activities which, for him, are exclusive.

(Lecercle 1985: 29)

Today I ate one pear, one apple, and one bowl of rice. I won't eat more. Don't open the kitchen door. Into the fridge. Grab the peanut butter. Spread it on thick with jelly. Take the first bite. Can't stop. Eat one piece of pie. That's all. Long for more. Fill myself up. Close the whole. Can't stop. Tomorrow will be different. Limits will be set. Rules will be followed.

An overriding desire for food eventually compels him to rush to the refrigerator and eat indiscriminately, opening the tins without looking at the labels and swallowing the food, sweet or sour, without even cooking it.

(Lecercle 1985: 35)

What is this mouth. This passage to the outside. That which lets language out. And which takes food in. See these lips. What do you think of? Reminders of other lips. Assholes that expel the food. Vaginas that swallow you up. My pouty mouth covered with wine lipstick calling out not to bring you in but to put the in out.

My father insisted that everyone in the family eat European style. Fork in the left hand, knife in the right. I responded with my version of barbarian style. He insisted on civilizing me. I would speak American as my mother tongue but my self would be intertwined with a European ancestry.

Are the limits of our language really the limits of our world?[4] A definition of language becomes important.

There are two languages: the language of surface, of social communication, where order (phonotactic-syntactic) reigns; and a language of the depths of the body, where the articulate word becomes a scream, where only affects and the passions of the body can be expressed.

(Lecercle 1985: 40)

I want to understand this language of the body. To have it rest in my body. Lecercle constantly repeats this idea that the language of *delire* is inseparable from the body, that it has 'a material existence in the speaker's body and its passions' (1985: 40). To be socialized is to repress the instinctual drives and cover them with grammatical speech, to see language as a tool that we use to express ourselves. One that shouldn't be obvious. A search for seamless expression. I want to speak a language of passion but I do not want to run around the streets shitting and screaming. I hope that art can be the gap in-between. That this is the area for exploration and a safe place to dwell.

I was 12 years old and had snuck the small portable black-and-white television into my room to watch late-night movies. *Torn Curtain* by Hitchcock was on. Paul Newman and Julie Andrews in the Eastern Bloc. Three-quarters into the film my father appeared on the screen. This was not such a surprise as I'd heard that he had been in films, even worked with Hitchcock, but what was exciting and mysterious was that he spoke German. Subtitles appeared on the screen with him. What I'd always suspected was true; he needed to be translated.

There are so many inbetweens in in^be^tween. So many places to go. Syllable breaks to trip on. Tween in and be she did hide herself 'till never could she be seen.

Twenty years have gone by since that first tear in the curtain, that first moment of exposure to my father's ability to speak German. In a new technological moment I can now purchase the DVD of *Torn Curtain* and watch this small scene over and over on my own personal computer. In the DVD version the words my father speaks are not translated and the subtitle only says 'speaking German'.

The translation will be transparent, but only in the sense that it will not 'cover the original' or 'block its light'
(Johnston 1992: 44).

My father is now dead and watching this document of his once live presence is more confusing. Other elements become obvious. My father's clearly Semitic image as he telephones the 'Polezi' to report the presence of Paul Newman and Julie Andrews whose attempt to 'pass' as communists has been unveiled. In typical Hollywood fashion history can be resignified and it is only the sound of German that is important.

Wolfson immediately translating each English word into another language. Using a combination of sound and meaning he made every word palatable. Milk is milch, and melk, and mleko. The manic qualities are apparent but also the comfort. We are not alone. There is milk for everyone. We are a small part of a whole and in a surge of translation we can find connections to a larger self.

It seems that Wolfson could not stand to be only a part. He searched for totality. 'Both English words and foodstuffs are "part-objects", . . . fragments which resist totalization and symbolization, and any attribution of identity or meaning' (Leclercle 1985: 10). A fetishist of language? The Freudian fetish subject of the most extreme type substitutes a part for the whole. He cannot accept the mother without a phallus so substitutes an object, such as a shoe, for her phallus. He both denies and accepts at the same time. He knows there is no phallus so he provides one. Wolfson cannot accept English, his mother-tongue, so he translates it in order to be able to see himself as a whole. English is only a synecdoche for a larger system. A bulimic is also one who rests between acceptance and denial. He binges uncontrollably and then purges himself, fulfilling both of his desires. Though Wolfson only binged, never purged, and after a food binge he became very depressed and could not study languages. With food he did not complete his cycle.

The above description of the bulimic seems almost appealing. Someone who gets what he wants. But of course it is more complicated than this and bulimia is not a happy or healthy condition. I find myself constantly caught in this quandary when considering *delire*. Every time I read phrases in Lecercle's book, such as 'the passions of the body, its breathing and its screams, are directly turned into words' (Leclercle 1985: 37), I become excited. This is a yes. Something which doesn't deny desire and drive. A place where creativity can be found. A fearful place where sometimes I have felt I can go with words but have always stopped before breaking the window. Taken a bath. Brought myself back. Because this place which I call yes can also be over-romanticized. Lacan says the madman is not a poet. Perhaps this distinction is necessary. Is the artist in the position of a fetishist, wanting to live in this part of ourselves I am calling *delire,* while at the same time wanting to live a healthy life? Are they two separate spheres? Is it always a question of the inseparability of form and content? How does one create a space for *delire?* Again a fundamental question. Does one recognize the borders, the implicit power structures that we live within, and transgress them, or does one simply transgress? And what does that really mean?

There are several crossings in this journey all of them transatlantic. Wolfson's parents came to Manhattan from Eastern Europe. My father also crossed the Atlantic on a ship bound for Manhattan. He told one story about this and I'm not sure if I have it right. Either he shat on the captain's steps and blamed it on his cousin Ziggy or Ziggy shat on the steps and blamed it on him. These vague stories are memories passed down in a quest for origins. There are always connections to be made. Every translation is also a transformation and within the new is part of the old and the old part of the new. This is about history as the present in translation. When the tower of babel crashed down we all went out to sea. In translation the transatlantic journey never ends.

As my father got older he began to speak less and less. He lost interest in the past and telling stories. Mostly he hummed his own tuneless little tune. There were no discernible words. Only a sense that he was present yet not really there.

This writing has been a journey that feels more like treading water. I believe that language comes from the body and that in understanding or comprehen-

sion language comes back to the body. To not understand is the frustration of disconnection from one's body. Of an idea hovering above but the inability to grasp it with one's mouth and digest it. When I understand something it is within me; I can put it out and take it back again. It is not understanding to dominate, but to live with.

When treading water you often don't realize that the current has been pulling you while you were unaware. Tiredly you look up and you see land. Or perhaps you don't and you allow yourself to be pulled under. I don't know where I am in the questions of *delire*. I am full of confusions and vague connections. I have lost interest in the authority of answers. I have not entered *delire*, and still doubt the possibility of choosing to. But perhaps I have crossed borders of writing and reading and hearing and telling and personal histories. Knowing where I am can never last more than a moment that is gone before its recognition.

NOTES
1   This paper relies heavily on *Philosophy Through the Looking Glass* by Jean-Jacques Lecercle.
2   Louis Wolfson from *Le Schizo et Les Langues* quoted in Johnston (1992: 51).
3   Lecercle (1985: 6) paraphrases the Cheshire Cat from Lewis Caroll's *Through the looking Glass*.
4   In the *Tractacus Logico-Philisophicus* Wittgenstein writes '*The limits of my language* mean the limits of my world'.

REFERENCES
Johnston, John (1992) 'Translation as Simulacrum', in Lawrence Venuti (ed.) *Rethinking Translation*, London: Routledge.
Lecercle, Jean-Jacques (1985) *Philosophy Through the Looking Glass: Language, Nonsense and Desire*, Illinois: Open Court.

•Stills from Alfred Hitchcock's 'Torn Curtain'

man   speaking   German

Intervention 2
The Ex*h*orbitant Body

Eirin Moure

A practice of reading is always embodied. A translation always translates a reading practice enacted on a text, not simply 'an original text'. And reading practices are codifications/decodifications that are historically and culturally determined. As such, a work, in the course of translation, provokes an inscription of the reader/translator's embodiment (as site of cultural production but also of resistances – to normative sexual definitions, to contemporary notions of urban life, etc.) into the translated text. (Whether or not this is acknowledged.)

G iven Fernando Pessoa with his heteronyms and their exorbitant subjectivity, it is not strange that the translator/reader Erin Mouré, facing Alberto Caeiro's *O Guardador de Rebanhos*, was compelled to become Eirin Moure, a performative and ex*h*orbitant body announcing a textual inscription she calls a trans*e*lation.

What we love best in poetry comes simply from sound. And this is primary in translation, urgent even. *Alba/alma. Sol/soa.* How to make these sonal connectivities in English? Nancy Huston says, in her book of articles from Le Monde, *Nord perdu*, that 'l'écoute d'une étrangère (est) attentive plus qu'un natif aux frottements et aux coïncidences sonores. (Dans le titre de ma nouvelle *Histoire en amibe*, entendez-vous "Historie en abîme"?)'.

'Frottements et incidences sonores' – la poésie joue exactement sur ces échos, c'est là la source des tensions et tensilités du poème. Some of these sound effects are deeply rooted in the origin of the language and are not 'translatable' or even ever 'translated', but are often, too often, erased in translation. Conventional translation has, it seems, as its primary (and unspoken) goal that of fulfilling 'fluid' criteria that make the work sit still in the target language, **not** rendering the work itself. For work from foreign languages often renders the target language *strange*.

To translate 'poetry', especially poetry that deals with exorbitant language effects in its own tongue, requires other translation strategies. Because these strategies are not favoured currently, poetry that can't be dealt with in fluent translation just doesn't get translated. Giving us in English (and in Canadian English it's worse for we rely primarily on translations embodied elsewhere) a pretty weird view of world poetry, and providing disproportionate support to one kind of poetry in our own language too . . . fluent, narrational, where the 'I' is settled. But there are other translational approaches. Given the general translation context, they're hard to find, and sometimes are not even identified as translation practices. For example, I've been accused with *Sheep's Vigil* of having created a 'false translation'. Yet, look, even the accusation describes the work as a translation . . . it is obliged to, even if it does not willingly believe.

But let's look at sounds and frottements; they necessarily occur through a body, for the body itself is sound's instrument. The body is the voice's instrument. The voice is felt

Performance Research 7(2), pp.58–59 © Taylor & Francis Ltd 2002

in and mediated by the body. Which is not an 'I' and not an isolated organism. A Deleuzian body without organs, perhaps, a organ that hallucinates its body, perhaps.

In any case, from such thoughts it is clear that one can say translation, and particularly translation of poetry, is a performative gesture, a performance. A set of performative gestures implicating the body.

PART 2: SUBJECTIVITY

Fernando Pessoa with his heteronyms heteronyms is not a precursor of postmodern fragmentation of identity: Pessoa, in fact, **loved** identity positions. His particularity was that he didn't make a primary and irrevocable association between a single identity structure and *self*. Pessoa in fact insisted on a plurality of the self. Associating a self as a mirror or performance of a plural universe. 'Ser plural, como ô universo!'

Already universe here is both embodied, and multiple. An always-moving set of sitings.

P believes in *excessive* subjectivity, invoked and provoked subjectivity. Subjectivities that could not be said to be 'the self' in normative speech and, thus, occur (or appear to occur) outside of it. The 3rd body. The body as dis/resolving projectile. Echoes Homi Bhabha's 'hybrids'. And is always propulsive.

As such, I as translator can be one of those propulsive bodies, outside Pessoa and yet 'caused' by him, by his work, by Caeiro.

Yet also, as a body, I was (am) in and of a place, am sited. 'I', even if not 'finished', physically exist *some*where. Or some *properties* of 'I' 'eu' do.

Pessoa's poetry had the effect on me of heightening my own corporeal sensations of sited-ness in certain ways; one of these was to make evident my perceptual connection with my closest corporeal buddy, my cat Emma. Who, unlike me, liked Toronto and all there was to see. Caeiro/Pessoa's language of direct perceptual habitation of space drew my attention to how Emma was seeing. She was drawn to the wild things in the environment: sticks, leaves, bits of garbage, birds, insects, other cats, small movements in and through not spaces, but 'volumes'. (Cats are architects, sculptors . . . can integrate volume and time, oh.) Elements like buildings, towers, stock exchanges, road networks, all so important to our human perception of environment, just don't exist on her radar. They are screens, surfaces only.

Through Pessoa and Emma, I thus began to inhabit Toronto differently, to be in accord with it as creeks, trees, scrub, air, sounds, movements.

And this, my own corporeal sitedness, inflected my translation of Caeiro/Pessoa. And is left visible in the translation. As such, it becomes, and I let myself become, a Pessoan, or even Caeiroist (2nd generation) heteronym. As if Pessoa's thinking had provoked an excessive subjectivity, an Eirin, an excessive habitation, in and of me.

And this of course makes my translation 'false', while still being irrevocably a translation. It doesn't adhere to a fluid notion of translation, but to an exorbitance. Exorbit happenstance. Exstance. Extantiation. A performative gesture altering space, altering the original, and altering my own voice and capacity. Which, I think, is the best that translation can do.

Sol's rise/soul. Solace. Sole

ACKNOWLEDGEMENT
Given as a talk by Erin Mouré accompanying the exhibition *The Third Body*, curated by Jack Stanley at Montréal's Galerie B-312, 31 March to 28 April 2001.

'Simultaneous Equivalents'

Adrian Piper, Bernadette Mayer, Hannah Weiner in *0–9*

Redell Olsen

The impulse of many conceptual and performance artists towards the dematerialization of the art object into language during the late 1960s was paralleled by work from a series of artists and writers that appeared in *0–9*, a journal co-edited by Vito Acconci and Bernadette Mayer between 1967 and 1969. Like many of the conceptual documents produced during this period, *0–9* was characterized by its transient reproducibility: it was at once a piece of disposable, xeroxed ephemera and at the same time part of a limited edition. A key trait of several of the writers published in *0–9* was the foregrounding of the translatative act as one of translocation: of spaces, language and bodies in transit between points. In particular, projects that appeared in *0–9* by Adrian Piper, Bernadette Mayer and Hannah Weiner each engaged with the possibilities of materializing the space and process of translation across the pages of the magazine.

Piper's work in the journal shows evidence of a self-reflexive attention to the page as a material surface. In issue 5, for example, she numbered two gridded squares from 1 to 64. Each square presented a different arrangement of the numbers that corresponded to a different sequential route. Piper then attempted to map all the possible routes through the squares, as a series of instructions: '2) begin upper right corner and proceed vertically', or, '13) leaving 4 horizontal rows below middle constant, begin upper middle right corner and proceed vertically', etc. The series of instructions are at once a map and a record of all the possible permutations of reading the square. Her analysis

concludes with a mock analysis of ratios of different speeds of reading:

> If you are an average reader, you must set up a ratio of the number of words in the first sentence over the time it takes a slow reader to read it (five seconds) to the number of words in the first sentence over the time it would take a fast reader to read them (unknown quantity x), solve the ratio, add the two times, divide the sum by two, divide the dividend (the average time obtained) into the same original number of words, multiply the new dividend by the total number of words in this sentence, and you will then know how long it has taken you to read this sentence.
>
> (*0–9*, #5: 49)

The content of the work is located in its own self-reflexive mechanism of self-plotting. In each piece the work functions to measure itself being measured, thereby drawing attention to its own construction. This construction, brought about through an endless patterning of repetition, implies the presence and participation of a reader who will activate the text, and when this happens the content of the piece becomes the reader's awareness of her eye crossing the page. The text does not construct another world for the reader to conveniently step into, but offers her a site in which she remains firmly grounded in the present watching herself reading. Rather than presenting a transparent text that will consume and be consumed by the reader, the process of reading is re-materialized as an artificial sequencing of points on a grid.

In a series of related projects, one for *The Village*

Performance Research 7(2), pp.60-65 © Taylor & Francis Ltd 2002

Voice and the other for *0–9* (#6: 79–81), Piper proposes the gridded page as a means of plotting the reading space in transit from its source to its points of distribution. Here one of the earliest senses of translation as transference – i.e. the removal or conveyance from one person or place to another – is especially relevant. Piper's translation materializes a conceptual problem: how does one write about translations between one space and another? The project for *0–9* is a gridded page of the magazine and a series of postcards (one per magazine). Each of these cards notified the subscribers that their card was a specific relocated enlargement of a particular square defined by the lines of the grid. In the second project, Piper purchased an advertising space in *The Voice* which informed the reader that the space of the two-dimensional box advert had been relocated from *The Voice* offices on Sheridan Square, New York to the reader's present address (Piper 1991: 13). In each of these pieces the relationship between the spatial and the linguistic elements of the project is an essential characteristic of the work, a factor that Piper herself describes in a letter to Terry Atkinson:

> My present work is involved with using the boundaries of specific elements of time and/or space as limitations of the infinite number of possible permutations of these elements, implied by the structure of the language used to identify them. Language is, for me, the only way to adequately convey – or at least suggest the inherent character of, say, an area in space.
>
> (Piper 1996: 15)

In these two works Piper asks us to imagine the movement of blank spaces in transit between sites. The only reference points we can attach to them are the two sites of departure and arrival and the differences between them: the translation from one space of the page to another, the translation from the public space of the journal to the private space of the postcard. By drawing attention to the translocation of the object (in this case a blank space in the newspaper) from one site to another, the text illustrates its dependence on the materi-

ality of the system of exchange and receivership across which it operates (the page of a magazine/an advertising space) and yet stresses its immateriality (a space selling nothing, a grid). As Claudia Burrow points out:

> These works and others like them invite us to conceptualize the physically impossible: two-dimensional grids, squares and rectangles hurtling through space, relocating to new physical sites or multiplying in infinite stacks, but carrying with them the information they symbolically convey and the concrete materiality of the geometric grid system itself.
>
> (Piper 1991: 13)

Bernadette Mayer's 'It Moves Across' is similarly concerned with inhabiting the space of translation between points:

> It moves across and over
> across the ground
> it moves across over the ground
> under (by the bridge) the moss
> over the moss
> across the grass into
> larger fields
> of grass crossing over the
> mounds and hills of
> nothing but grass on top of
> roots of grass
> it moves across slowly
> slowly into
> another field or further
> through the forest still
> moving by
> and emerging from
> the forest small enough
> moving
> the same rate
> under the bridge next to the
> trees next through the
> trees missing them moving
> around them still
> crossing like the trees
> the trees over
> like blades of grass the

grass over as a bridge goes over
bridges
bridges over the trees
it moves across the hills
like a field over the fields
like a field on field
of a hill of a hill
as if the forest
into its forest
moves
on the ground like the ground over
it
stopping over
near a patch of grass.

(#4: 41)

In this poem she extends her consideration of surfaces and framing to a consideration of the poem as a perceptual device which tracks an object as it moves through space. The poem describes a landscape that seems to be folding in upon itself. The object, 'it' does not pass through a static landscape that frames it, for the landscape also appears to be travelling. The momentum of 'it' as it crosses 'like a field over the fields/like a field on field/of a hill of a hill/as if the forest/into its forest/moves/' is governed by perceptual and linguistic bridges that propel 'it' forwards. Here translation as an act of changing or adapting to another use, of 'renovation' (*OED*) becomes evident: words themselves are literally in transit, shifting in status from noun to verb, and in the process making bridges out of objects: 'under (by the bridge) the moss/ over the moss/ across the grass into/larger fields'. The perceived object becomes the means of translation by which the 'it' travels further on from place into space.

In *The Practice of Everyday Life*, Michel de Certeau makes an important distinction between space and place. While place is a distinct location that can only be occupied by one thing at one time, space is 'composed of intersections and mobile elements', and is a set of plural networks and relationships in process (de Certeau 1984: 117).

This is an important distinction for the dematerializing art object and its materializing poetic counterpart. Each eludes what de Certeau calls the rules of the 'proper', i.e. rules such as ownership and formal expectation. One such elusion of the rule of the proper occurs in the work of Hannah Weiner. Issue 6 of *0–9* features her essay 'Trans-Space Communication' in which she writes:

> At the moment I am interested in exploring methods of communication through space; considering space as space fields or space solids; through the great distances of space; through small distances, such as the space between the nucleus and the electrons of an atom; through distances not ordinarily related to the form of communication used.

(#6: 103)

Like Piper and Mayer, Weiner explores space by inhabiting the network of exchange and receivership that exists between the writer and the reader, and between points of reference. In 'Follow Me' the repetitions of question and answer form a circle. Speakers in this text do not seem able to communicate to each other or even to be able to leave for their destination:

LWC   Follow me
LWF   Will you lead?
LWG   Will you follow?
LWJ   Shall I follow?
LWK   I will follow
LWC   Follow me
LWF   Will you lead?
LWG   Will you follow? [...]

(#4: 91)

While the poem doesn't break with accepted grammar or syntax, its repetitious circularity resists the rules of 'the proper' in terms of narrative progression. There is no departure or arrival, only endless delay. The text sets up a kind of de Certeauean anticipation of a movement into space ('intersections and mobile elements'), while remaining doomed to the stasis of place (a singular location). One could say that the poem sets up the potential for a translation, only to foil it. Unlike

Piper's projects for *0–9* and *The Village Voice*, Weiner's poem seems to map, or perhaps unmap, a kind of travel that 'does not in the least try to establish a coherent coming and going between the here and the there' (#6: 103). In other words the text represents both the expectation of movement and that expectation's frustration. Unable to move from place into space the speakers are caught in the ambiguous circuitry of the phatic utterance.

Weiner also used the International Code of Signals to make poems and events, a type of communication specifically designed to cover large distances between sites. Describing the importance of this method, she writes 'this code makes available and possible the translation of simultaneous equivalents' (# 6: 100). Although this poem is not part of the series of Weiner's Code Poems, her concept of a translation of 'simultaneous equivalents' is an important term for considering Weiner's, Mayer's and Piper's projects, because each of these writers attempts to explore the possibilities and the impossibilities of representing and tracking information in a process of translation between alternate locations. Henry Sayre describes poetry as a 'scene, in fact, of translation . . . an interplay between interpretation and representation, presence and absence, stasis and change, poem-as-object and poem-as-event, the translation of each term to the other and back again' (Sayre 1989: 19). This concept of poetry and translation as event is most flamboyantly explored in 'The Fashion Show Poetry Event' which was curated by Hannah Weiner, John Perrault and Eduardo Costa. In the show 'various verbal (written and oral) to visual and visual to verbal translations' took place between artists and writers. Artists such as Alex Katz, Les Levine, Claes Oldenburg and Andy Warhol made fashion garments in response to poetry by the three curators. A catwalk show followed and was given a live commentary by Weiner, Perrault and Costa. Their manifesto, published in issue 5, distinguished between communication and translation. It described how communication involves modifications of the same code between the sender and the receiver of the message,

while translation involves 'a process of converting a message from one code system to another (from one medium to another or one language to another)' (#5: 54). These interdisciplinary translations echoed the way in which *0–9* began to extend its close affinities with conceptual art and its use of language as art towards the possibilities of performance.

Following the end of *0–9*'s publication run, Piper began to emphasize the effect on the body of this kind of translation. In *Catalysis* (1970–1), Piper 'would appear on the streets of New York in some highly obnoxious manner' (Stiles 1998: 256), dressed in clothing that had been soaked in a broth of vinegar and eggs for a week, or with balloons attached to her ears and teeth. She shopped in department stores wearing a sign that said 'wet paint' and later visited a library, where she browsed among the shelves while playing a tape of herself belching. The performance foregrounds the way in which Piper's body had come to replace the dematerialized art object. Instead of working with an art material that was separate from herself, she experimented with her own 'objecthood, transforming it

•Adrian Piper, *Catalysis IU*, 1970–1, documenting street performance, New York City. Photo © Rosemary Mayer

sculpturally' (Piper 1991: 24). If translation is also a form of renovation, Piper translated her own body by renovating it into a textual object: the body-as-object, the body-as-event.

Work produced by Mayer directly after the final issue of *0–9* continues some of the themes and concepts that she explored in the context of the magazine. She calls her *Moving* (1971) 'an epic of war fever fighting sex & starvation'. It extends Mayer's earlier conceptual mappings of space and process, although it also marks a turn towards a more personal, local and domestic application of the strategies for a poetics of translocation that she had been exploring in the pages of *0–9*. One of Mayer's modes of discourse in *Moving* is the personal list:

> Tom said, I have friends who are now living in
> these places –
>   a number in Boston, Mass
>   a few in other parts of the State.
>   one in Providence R.I.
> One in New Hampshire
> one in Vermont, Burlington
> three in Philadelphia, Penn
> A lot in New York City
> Some in New Jersey
>   a number in Chicago, Ill.
>   one in Washington D.C.
> a number in Denver, Colo.
>   one in Evergreen, Colo.
> one outside Indianapolis
>   an acquaintance in St. Louis, Missouri
>   a lot in San Francisco & Berkeley, Calif.
>   one in San Ysidro, Calif.
>   I know a person in Maine
>   two in Stanford, Conn.
> [. . .]
> I have friends in transit.
>   two in Europe.
>   some in the United States.
>
>   (Mayer 1971: n.p.)

The listings that pattern *Moving* are reminiscent of On Kawara's 'I got up' series of postcards, but the effect produced by Mayer's lists is quite different. Despite recording a series of times of the most intimate nature, Kawara's work avoids the highly subjective investigation of the subject-in-process as it is mapped by Mayer. While Kawara's list maintains a coherence because of its lack of extraneous material (for example we are given no other details about what he had for breakfast or who he got up with), Mayer's text in contrast coheres only to scatter in multiple directions. Here she posits herself again and again in relation to others, and in relation to the outside world. Unlike Kawara, *Moving* is concerned with the interlocking systems that constitute our environment: 'We as human beings aren't isolated systems. we take in food & information. the food we take in makes us part of the world which produces it & part of that work' (1971: n.p.). The definition of place as a static destination that in de Certeau's terminology should be translation's terminus is unfixed, or continually refixed. Definition of place is temporary, local and specific. Rather than using a rule such as all the positions at the centre of a newspaper to generate a series of sites, Mayer maps space and time through the anecdotes and experiences of her friends and acquaintances. Through their memories she engages with the concept of translation as an action of conveyance by positing place as that which is always in transition, provisional and liable to be displaced. In effect Mayer translates the usual characteristics of place into those of space. As de Certeau argues:

> A space exists when one takes into consideration vectors
> of direction, velocities and time variables. Thus space is
> composed of intersections of mobile elements. It is in a
> sense actuated by the ensemble of movements deployed
> within it.
>
>   (de Certeau 1984: 117)

For example, in one episode from *Moving*, Mayer describes a road trip she took with Hannah Weiner. In this section, the writing constantly modifies itself like the view from a car in transit. Writing is itself always on the move, investigating boundaries between time and space, between history and pre-history: 'half a billion years ago there was no life at

•Bernadette Mayer, cover image for *Moving* 1971, published by Angel Hair, New York. Photo © Ed Bowes

all on the land but just a few weeks ago a meteor fell in missouri which contained enough of the acids to make life appear anywhere even on the moon' (Mayer 1971: n.p.). Similarly her frame of reference continually telescopes from the personal to the universal, from the outside to the inside: 'I am on a mountain. Grace is in the bathtub. Ed is on the phone. Which mountain is under the ocean, which is the highest?' (1971: n.p.).

Moving thus develops Mayer's interest not in the *properties* of place but in its spatial possibilities via the process translation and translocation of bodies and subjectivities in motion.

Piper, Weiner and Mayer are each involved in the investigation of translation as a mode of discourse, rather than as a vehicle that carries a unified subject between linguisitic sites. The space of translation, which their works inhabit, allows for the materialization of the processes inherent in communication. In Piper the differing relationship between the public and the domestic context of writing and utterance is brought sharply into focus. The economic and spatial journey of information is made explicit in the gridded pages of the magazine, as are the rules of the 'proper' in the public realm, which rejects the abject body and translates it into invisibility. Weiner's poems draw attention to the space in which information has the potential to be transmitted between subjects but is instead arrested

and forever displaced – unable to be translated by its receivers into action. Her 'Fashion Show Poetry Event' foregrounds the process of translation as an event central to the self-definition of a community whose ideas are successively re-formulated and renovated via a series of intermedia translations. In Mayer's works perception is itself a mode of translation that remobilizes the place of writing as a permeable space in transit. These 'simultaneous equivalents' of translation in the visual arts and poetics meet in the pages of *0–9* to call the boundaries of space and place into question.

REFERENCES

Acconci, Vito and Mayer, Bernadette (1967–9) *0–9*, New York. April 1967 to July 1969: Issues 1–6.
Bernstein, Charles (1992) *A Poetics*, Cambridge, MA: Harvard University Press.
De Certeau, Michel (1984) *The Practice of Everyday Life*, Berkeley: University of California Press.
Lippard, Lucy (1973/1997) *Six Years: The Dematerialization of the Art Object 1966–1972*, Berkeley: University of California Press.
Lippard, Lucy and Chandler, John (1968) 'The Dematerialization of Art', *Art International*, February.
Mayer, Bernadette (1971) *Moving*, New York: Angel Hair.
Piper, Adrian (1991) *Exhibition Catalogue*, Ikon Gallery Birmingham and Cornerhouse Manchester, September 1991–February 1992.
Piper, Adrian (1996) *Out of Order, Out of Sight: Vol.1 'Selected Writings in Meta-Art 1968–1992'*, Cambridge, MA: MIT Press.
Sayre, Henry (1989) *The Object of Performance: The American Avant-Garde since 1970*, Chicago: The University of Chicago Press.
Stiles, Kristine (1998) 'Uncorrupted Joy: International Art Actions', in *Out of Actions: Between Performance and the Object 1949–1979*, London: Thames and Hudson, pp. 227–329.

Intervention 3
Fleeing the Light

Rod Mengham

At the conceptual centre of Marc Atkins's new series of photographs, *Equivalents*, is an image of the Roman Forum: physical remnants whose ruined state underlines the permanence, or at least the endurance, of the idea they represent, which is that of permanence itself. Yet in Atkins's hands, the image starts to dissolve, colours begin to leach away, and the monuments become perishable. The stone achieves zero gravity, weighs less than photographic paper, is outlasted not only by the snapshot in which it is contained, but also by the discarded portrait whose bright colours dominate the foreground. The tourist shot includes an extraneous element, which is the Trojan Horse of art in an era of mechanical reproduction. Rome itself was founded on the success of the original Trojan Horse. In Atkins's work, the strategic distraction is that of point of view. We might expect to look at the Forum, but instead we look at a portrait we cannot properly see. The correct angle of approach to the

• 'Rome/9–2' from *Equivalents*. Photo © Marc Atkins

Performance Research 7(2), pp.66–68 © Taylor & Francis Ltd 2002

• 'Paris/7–2' from *Equivalents*. Photo © Marc Atkins

object of contemplation is inaccessible, located somewhere in the space that lies behind the surface of the photograph. Every photograph in the new series involves this dynamic, whereby the frame does not mark out what we look at but opens onto a scene in which looking is already taking place.

The object of contemplation is less the photograph in the show than the photograph it depicts, the object that has been placed or abandoned in an unavailable narrative. These discards are often slight in appearance, yet the aesthetic strategy of the work gives them an extraordinary power over the environments in which they appear. They flout the architectural logic of receding vistas; the discipline embodied in the perspectival view of a bridge is deflected, offset by a casual and stylish display of female physical power, in an impromptu celebration of indifference to male control. The allocation of relative degrees of power to gendered points of view is systematically troubled in this work. One shot features a male figure, head swathed in bandages, in a scenario of medical interference which places at the dead centre of attention a tattoo resembling a raised welt; this carefully inflicted injury rhymes disturbingly with lips brightly outlined in the discarded female portrait lying under the bed. The allusion to a vampiric archetype allows some play with the idea of the photograph as afraid of the light, and as a reflecting surface in which the face of the observer cannot be seen, as well as conjuring up the vulnerability of the subject detached from an original setting. Just

as the vampire needs to leave deposits of Transylvanian earth in various safe houses, so Atkins deposits the traces of his work in a variety of locales: Italy, Poland, France, USA, London – to name only those which are immediately obvious.

Many of the discards appear to have been put down momentarily before being caught up again – gaining their place in the landscape for no longer than it takes to make a telephone call – suggesting that photographs and settings are potentially interchangeable, subject to a process of endless translation. A significant number of the environments that Atkins is drawn to record the after-effects of this process: tables, floors and walls have the appearance of a palimpsest of innumerable impositions; they have been tattooed, literally, by a history of domestic rhythms, largely of ingestion and regulation. The Atkins landscape is anchored in scenarios of neglect, of clutter, dilapidation, and stratified impressibility: an ancient drain; the Thames foreshore; the locked doors of a burial vault. The photograph by the drain is about to be disposed of in a setting which disposes of everything; the foreshore is a place which remembers everything that has ever happened to it, but which is both ignored and despised; the burial vault is a place that has been set aside for commemoration but which has every appearance of being forgotten.

The ratios of remembering and forgetting, of permanence and impermanence, of control and vulnerability, are rendered most exactly in a pair of images that feature the same woman: once as

• 'London/3–2' from *Equivalents*. Photo © Marc Atkins

the subject of a discard, once as an apparent intermediary, poised in the moment of translation from subject into object and back again.

The first of these images is introduced into a London tube carriage – a place of intense and constant scrutiny of faces and representations – yet it is placed in a position that is invisible to the ordinary passenger, and can only be seen by contrivance, by using the point of view of committed voyeurism, a point of view that is both cherished and disowned.

In the other image, the same woman is seen holding up for inspection the photograph of a female nude, yet her own gaze is averted, away from both the photograph itself and from the viewer, who can only inspect the representation of female nudity by ignoring the 'real' woman.

One's glance travels backwards and forwards,

uncertain of the true focus of the work, of the social and artistic decorum it bears witness to, of the attitudes and self-consciousness of the two women implicated in the scene, of the nature of the privacy it may or may not violate, of the degree of exploitation, or refusal to exploit, it requires from the viewer. This constant passing from one point to another occurs within the individual composition, but also between compositions, and across the whole series. Atkins's work is composed of passages that each successive instance of construction translates into equivalent, but different, terms; it always brings with it the trace of its origins, the ground from which it has emerged and to which it will return, and it is locked into a cycle of addiction, succumbing constantly to a light from which it must always retreat.

•'London/3' from *Equivalents*. Photo © Marc Atkins

monica ross
allen fisher
morgan o'hara
cris cheek

rip-out supplement

Four Translations

Hasce igitur penitus voces cum corpore nostro

When we force out these utterances from the depths of our body

exprimimus rectoque foras emittimus ore,

and launch them through the direct outlet of the mouth, they are

mobilis articulat nervorum daedala lingua,

cut up into lengths by the flexible tongue, the craftsman of words,

formaturaque labrorum pro parte figurat.

and moulded in turn by the configuration of the lips. At a point

hoc ubi non longum spatium est unde illa profecta

reached by each particular utterance after travelling no great

perveniat vox quaeque, necessest verba quoque ipsa

distance from its source, it naturally happens that the individual

plane exaudiri discernique articulatim;

words are also clearly audible and distinguishable syllable by

servat enim formaturam servatque figuram.

syllable. For the utterance preserved its shape and configuration.

at si inter positum spatium sit longius aequo,

But if the intervening space is unduly wide, the words must

aëra per multum confundi verba necessest

inevitably be jumbled and the utterance disjointed by its flight

et conturbari vocem, dum transvolat auras.

through a long stretch of gusty air. So it happens that, while you

ergo fit, sonitum ut possis sentire neque illam

are aware of a sound, you cannot discern the sense of the words;

internoscere, verborum sententia quae sit;

the utterance comes to you so muddled and entangled,

usque adeo confusa venit vox inque pedita.

Lucretius On the Nature of the Universe – Book IV 549-563
trans. R.E.Latham (1951), revised John Godwin (1994) p.109

We invited four practitioners from different art forms
to translate and/or respond to a passage from
Lucretius in ways which reflect their own practice.
As well as providing a meditation on utterance and
contemporary dis/connectedness, their responses
can be read as a comment on translative forms.

1

Performance Research 7(2), pp.69-74 © Taylor & Francis Ltd 2002

monica ross

allen fisher

morgan o'hara

cris cheek

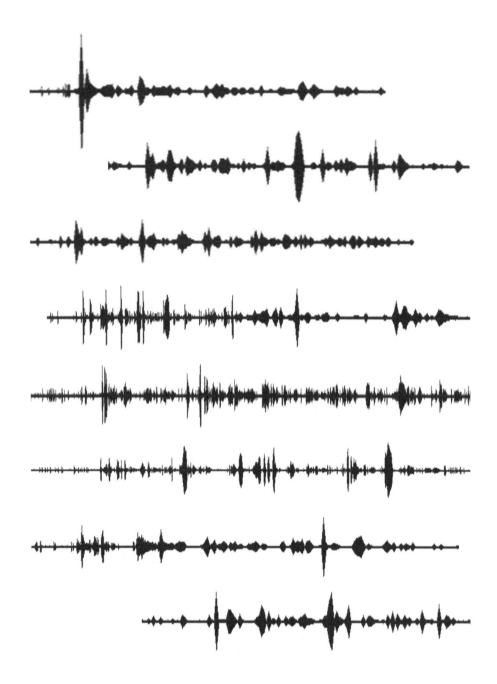

...lips...figurat...syllable...figuram...air...auras...entangled...pedita...

Haste well now penetrate vociferation connect corporeal home

squeeze-controlled out emitted trappiece

mobile joined nerve-like artful tongue

shaped labours project brought forth in process of forming

to this place imply absence not a long while from one room to the other

without question to get utterance in search necessary truths also in person

distinctly listens to separate distinctly

maintained which says that the process of shaping maintains form

and difference in true conditions amid the action of placing in room sited

at a distance to make level air along much confounded truths necessity

and disorder heard together for the duration fly across air in motion.

in consequence traps the sound against the capacity to perceive uneven

remote to recognise difference in speech affected by in search sited limit

in spacetime arrived in confused manner trapped voice inquires into your gravity.

monica ross
allen fisher
morgan o'hara
cris cheek

/

2

3

cris cheek

obscuring thought penitence
voices wit purr corporeal
us-expressed recto for as (force even)
emitting orality
I am a student and you are a student
or else pedagogies 'rrr's' along the frozen aura in
lengthening morning closure crafted by those it's
that are moments of a mobility of articulations
all Greek tome (sic) to es in streets and castle yards with
café bars and town squares playing chinese whispers with
pronounced gestures through translation
how the lines have become buckled from their Fin-glish intention
Spoken forms in a laboratory partial figuration the
ageing wings of a rancid, even ranting, farther (Ubu even)
in that chaotic edge between the concrete walkway and the
river drops though not for long distance under protection
thru-Coming voices that which necessitates verbs
discernible articulation servicing
"it's confusing
this hit and miss-ness of communication" all
at the in between spatial positions and still dum interiority.

Performance Itself

George Quasha and Charles Stein

Art is performance – *per*-formance. It *fits together* by *going through*. Art itself fits together by going through itself. It accomplishes its intrinsic order by performing its own principle, its own intention. This is the basis, and it's not a bad idea to keep these root senses in mind as we think through the work of an artist, particularly an artist of great internal variety, whose work is difficult to catego-rize or reduce to a single concept or set of concepts.

We can waste a lot of time trying to fit Gary Hill into one genre, medium, historical attitude, or whatever, when his work is inviting us to skip the categories ('video', 'installation', etc.) and get with the work on its own most immediate terms. Such a work is endlessly at variance with itself, yet in such a way that *it fits – by performing itself.* A principle of order by performance necessarily includes *difference*, that is, self-difference and antithesis. So the active process of identity, self-sameness, involves passing through its apparent opposite. 'Gary Hill' is a performance: an artist of the image (video = I see) in whom the image is under such stress that it sometimes reaches zero visibility. An artist of sound in whom impenetrable sound and silence have equal status. An artist of language, indeed one kind of poet, whose unexampled self-reinvention in the play of words has its true com-plement in wordless, soundless, intensely *textual space.*[1]

Apparently Gary Hill's pieces have far less in common than one might expect, except that they perform their fit in a way that is true both to them-selves (self-coherent) and to the artist (identity-coherent). They perform in the way an ecosystem performs the continuing life of the field, yet no element therein can be called dominant. *The field –* let us add to *self-coherence* and *identity coherence* a third term, *field coherence* – a rich, livingly complex and quite mysterious phenomenon that helps us know that the art/performance event has no truly separate inside and outside, no hierarchy, no binding centricity. Yet, despite their ultimate non-separateness, fields remain distinct from each other. Work/person/field constitute a single multidimen-sional performance surface, wherein paradoxically identity retains its (unreifiable) integrity and yet is free to participate in otherness. There can be no single secret of such an art triad, but we can perhaps enhance our participation in its life principle by noticing the way it performs itself.

We are encouraged in this approach to Gary Hill's work by his own interest in tracking the ways that work shows up as performance, in a range of senses from the general one stated above, that art is at root performance, to the specific sense or range of senses suggested by the term '*performance art*'.[2] Yet to get the real force of his interest here we have to keep all the senses of performance active, from the most general to the most specific, because the interesting perspective may be the way the root principle – *art is performance* – continues to emerge in new senses of *the performative*. We no doubt can find here a veritable lexicon of performative possi-bilities, although the 'terms' do not by any means have hard boundaries. To be sure, the inquiry into the emergent sense of performance may itself perform the lessons of its theme, which is self-instructing.

Performance Research 7(2), pp.75-89 © Taylor & Francis Ltd 2002

PERFORMANCE AND THE PERFORMATIVE

A performance is the stickum that brings about a certain fit, the process that holds things together and in their place by force of its forward-moving energy. Performance is really the heart of the *process* of art, most especially art that sees itself as process. This recalls Gary Hill's early interest in what he called Processual Video, at the time that he lived in Barrytown, New York (late 1970s/early 1980s), where the emphasis on process – or the *processual*, in poet Robert Kelly's coinage – stood antithetically to overvaluation of the perfected art object – a notion very much in the air in those days.[3] This sense of process is essentially *performative,* particularly in the usage deriving from philosopher J. L. Austin referring to utterances that literally *perform the action of which they speak*: e.g. I promise, I accuse, I curse, I bless, etc. – actions performed in (indeed, only in) the very saying. Such verbal actions close the gap between word and meaning, and accordingly we say that performative language is at the heart of the poetic, which does not so much *refer* to a world as *declare* a world's existence – by performing/enacting that of which it speaks. Performative utterances can only do their work in the specific contexts that call them forth: *performative language is always site/situation-specific and concrete.*

The work called *Processual Video* [1980] is a particular refinement of the concept in its title and stands as a very pure and exemplary instance of the performative simultaneously manifesting a root principle and generating an actual performance piece.[4] In this single-channel work (b/w, sound; 11:30 min) a solitary white line revolves clockwise in the center of the monitor, its movement synchronized to a text read by the artist. The effect is that mental images conjured by the text seem to be tracked by the location of the line. A horizontal or vertical line, for example, accompanies surfing and ocean or skiing and mountains respectively. Even the seemingly random and less specifically visual statements are intentionally implicated in the notions of text and line. As we find in a wide range of Gary Hill's works from this period – a spectacular example is *Happenstance (part one of many parts)* [1982–83, b/w, single channel, stereo sound; 6:47 mins] – the deepest concern is that *utterance and image should be co-performative* in the way that they inform each other in the very moment of the combined video and verbal gesture: a configuration of lines in motion may 'click in' as an image of an object just after the word for that object is uttered or appears on the screen. Or, conversely, an ambiguous phrase may condense toward a single meaning as an image for that meaning comes into view. The meaning of word or image performs itself in the processual interaction of video and speech, and the real location where that performance takes place is in the viewer's mind. The meaning of the image is 'reflected in' the word, the meaning of the word is 'reflected in' the image, and together an intimate and significant gesture is performed and experienced immediately.[5] As with any real performance, this event – the performance itself – cannot be paraphrased or restated.

Gary Hill's work pushes this principle of the irreducible gesture to a level of ontological autonomy that is almost *mudra*-like in intensity. The Sanskrit word *mudra* (seal, mystery) stands for the intentional and articulate hand gestures (perhaps most associated with East Indian classical dance and Buddhist art) that are performative of profound and complex states of mind – or, as it were, body-mind – not always 'translatable' into specific words or concepts. In a sense 'mudra' could stand as the most extreme statement of a principle of *open performative image.* Thus the sequence of mudra-like hand gestures in *Cut Pipe* [1992],[6] for instance, have a certain independent mystery and at the same time are visibly performative of the text being recited. This text involves a self-reflective awareness of and within intertwining voice, sound, signing – indeed a *reflexive* awareness in the sense that a verb is reflexive when it turns its action back to its subject. Thus images of hands touching a sounding speaker are projected onto the surface of an actual sounding speaker, reciting:

sounding an image   signing a sound   voicing thoughts   between soundings
locating the sound of my voice   imaging my voice through an object giving voice to an
image . . . I have my finger on my voice   tangent to the skin   put your finger on it
put your mind through it   skin your thought   graft your skin   shed your skin   give
your skin to me . . .   drumming your mind through the skin   drumming the skin
stretched through your mind

These gestures seem to further suggest a specific state of *yearning,* a sort of nostalgia for the middle of being, represented here as (loud)speaker, the radical source of sound. The sonic equivalent of *mudra* is *mantra*, meaning essentially *root sound* and deriving etymologically from 'mind' [Indo-European *men-*]. The hand/voice gesture 'speaks' something like the body beating out its root sound on the skin of mind – a liminal state of intense intimacy *and* self-separation. Here is the symbolic 'cut' that both divides and defines – that opens all dichotomies but opens as well the space of what transgresses their strict discontinuity. Thus when image is performed as living embodiment, it 'mind-degrades' and loses its status as image/projection but feeds back into a raw state of *one's own* bodying mind.[7] Viewer enters the 'cut' and by a sleight-of-being becomes performer.

These two works completed 12 years apart, *Processual Video* and *Cut Pipe*, doubly rooted in single-channel videotape work and live performance, show the close processual tie between these two 'performative performances'. The membrane between apparent contraries – *solitary studio work* (carefully working out minutely contrived video-events) and the *worked-through acting out* of performance before a live audience – is, in Gary Hill, very thin. The two ways of working are twins, each having the essential characteristics of the other. This brings us back to the core role of the performative performance as a principle of art itself. Such 'twinning' of two ways of making art emphatically instructs in the nature of art, indeed performs that nature, while displaying the mystery that the work is also utterly single; it is itself. This statement is only paradoxical when framed as reasoned or logical. As performance the double reality is self-evident, and so the real mystery as it

were is in the multiphasic display of the performative performance itself. This mystery is at the heart of how it is that art performs its nature, by any means necessary. And art in performing its nature transmits – not what is pre-formed, but what stimulates in the viewer the very performativity that lies at the origin of the work. The *intention to transmit* this sense of performativity and its deep human necessity to a living viewer/audience is always pushing at the surface, the membrane; it tells us that art is not art but *as participated.* The root principle that is performed is performance itself – a truth in which ontological, social and ethical necessities are inseparable. Gary Hill's self-twinning performance displays the interdependence of, on the one hand, almost idiopathically *solitary being* and, on the other hand, *audience*, the listening-viewing body at large.

This art-revealing truth of the performative together with the intention to transmit it to others guides a great deal of Gary Hill's work, especially in the direction of an elusive species of the 'interactive' that has nothing to do with gadget-manipulating options and everything to do with modulating states of awareness. To be sure, this participatory sense of art applies to all art, especially 'open' art (experimental, improvisational, aleatoric, etc.), but Gary Hill's intention to create subtly active dialogue between work and participant – as the very axis of the work – extends the performative in very particular ways. What is interesting from the perspective of overviewing Gary Hill's evolving sense of the performative is how the range of possibilities is all there so early and so pervasively.

Returning to the 1982–83 single-channel *Happenstance*[8] – a watershed in the intense realization of *editing as processual and performative* – there is a direct connection between compositional process and viewing/reading in the sheer physicality of transformation in image/text/voice.[9] The artist's vigorous process of maneuvering images, words and sounds in a veritable alchemy of conjunctive metamorphosis reads as an outering of psychic process.[10] It seems to be saying, 'Art performance is mind-changing'. The viewer registers the action as something lived through – yet quite strange and unrecognizable except, perhaps, at the level of dream or vision. This is a kind of mind theater, the likes of which show up in many forms throughout Gary Hill's work. Here the action conducts itself in the artist's actual voice, a personal, if somewhat mannered, voice, speaking in accordance with an electronic dynamic – as if at the synaptic interface of a human and a non-human dimension, the all-too-human mixing with the other-than-human. A voice in the know, yet *we* can't be sure what it knows.

This *knowing* voice with its torsional text and images seems by turns oracular, prophetic, other-worldly and lighthearted – history pushing outward through the turbulence of language in a state of self-reinvention. The effect is a *performative apoca-lypse*, as if uncovering news of fundamental change in the very structure of things seen and heard, of language spoken and read, of consciousness, of history. Abstract image-generation passes through self-configurative shapes apparently signifying the most traditional themes of revelation: crucifixion, logos, mystical birds, an iconic tree. These open performative figurations are *liminal images* – hovering at the margin of intelligibility, flashing suddenly into meaning only to 'mind-degrade' as suddenly back into the processual flow. Every word, shape, image, theme turns freely upon its axis, now a gorgeous abstraction, now a charged particularity. Naming and showing are inter-performative. New media are radically restructuring, reconditioning, the way reality – world – being – per-form them-selves in us and through us, as if to confirm Blake's insight: 'Reason or the ratio of all we have already known is not the same that it shall be when we know more'. The claim is that we *do* know more, and the *ratio* of the senses is changing, as Marshall McLuhan in *The Gutenberg Galaxy* extrapolated from Blake and Joyce. New senses – new ways of taking in the world – seem to be emerging as we look and as we speak. It's as if the short history of electronic/video art (from portapak to miniature digital video camcorder, from electronic syn-chronization of image and speech to computer animation) pre-forms/per-forms changes in

• Gary Hill, *Viewer*, 1996, five-channel video installation

everything from art to history itself and the possibility of a new form of consciousness. At least from his work in the late 1970s there is a sort of revelatory ambivalence – an exuberant, yet almost menacing, performative proclamation of new possibilities of consciousness inherent in new technologies – and it gets deeply ingrained in Gary Hill's work.

Yet despite his continuing fascination with new technology and the possibilities it opens up, technology in fact has little more than a neutral status in his concern. Like the stunning imagery that he develops in *Happenstance* and that he's obviously drawn to from the beginning, technology is subject to transformation, erasure, backgrounding, sudden invisibility. Mediums and their components are only instruments of mind, not values in themselves; they are the vehicles for a *performative journeying,* offering meta-travelogical glimpses of the most intimately personal ('my body, my art' = *In As Much As It Is Always Already Taking Place* [1990];[11] 'my relationship, my art' = *Suspension of Disbelief (for Marina)* [1991–92])[12] often side by side with the shamanic, even the tantric, so that the medium is never finally the meaning of the voyaging. Indeed, some of the subtlest performative spaces are resolutely low tech (*Tall Ships* [1992]),[13] using surplus lenses as projectors, or 'medium tech' (*HanD HearD* [1995][14] and *Viewer* [1996]),[15] with no ostentatious technocentric display. In both *HanD HearD* and *Viewer* the walk-in viewer meets the on-view/viewing human element head-on, without any overpowering sense of technological mediation. The real 'event' is the performative space itself – a site, the very declaration of which allows the complex awareness of an engaged viewer. The event is an emerging awareness.

THE PERFORMATIVE FIELD

The *space*, the *site*: Gary Hill seems always to be interested in the sense of place and placement such that a work lives out an underlying question – how does this place speak? Alternatively: How is it that there is speaking here? In *War Zone* [1980][16] objects seem to already be talking as you approach them – sounds subtly emerging from tiny hidden speakers – giving a sense of a haunted vocalizing space. What these objects are saying is their own names, as if they needed to speak to perform their identities – as if being there were not enough or, alternatively, as if they wanted to tell us that simply being there was already a kind of speaking. At all events, the talking-back environment that they bespeak – with signs of life pointing to a living surface – shows up as well, and with particular poignancy, in the *projective* works: *And Sat Down Beside Her* [1990][17] and *I Believe It Is an Image in Light of the Other* [1991–2].[18] It accompanies the projection of fragmented texts (by Maurice Blanchot) and images onto the surface of things, like resonant skins.

Each of these works is a living world unto itself, giving a sense of *being touched* in the very act of being seen and heard, and where objects are always active in being themselves, yet in dialogue with the passerby. Objects seem to reach out beyond themselves with their attractive interiors (reading out from light on surface), textualized and oralized at once – *performatively in relation*. Each work is a living field in which interiority is outered as vibrant surface.

Things in these worlds/fields are not simply what they seem; they are nodes of connectivity and (dis)(re)placed interiority; they *are* as they relate and are related. The truth of the place is in the telling (root meaning of *reading*); a site is known as recited. The recital/*le récit*.[19] *Site Recite.*[20] But the projected works are not the only ones that talk back, and not all the projected works sound out. *Inasmuch As It Is Always Already Taking Place* [1990], installed as 16 half-inch to 21-inch black-and-white TV tubes placed in a horizontal wall niche, dismembers the body into whispering parts, like a hive. Re-sited living-breathing body parts recite a possible integrity as a scarcely intelligible tale being told, but only as the 'debris of utterance', as echoes of Blanchot's textual world of articulate self-alienation. The sound field here (as in *War Zone*) is human communication performed as liminal language.

At the other end of the spectrum from these sounding/speaking spaces are the grand projection works foregrounding *humans in relation* yet in various states of what might be called *articulate silence*: *Tall Ships* [1992], *HanD HearD* [1995–96], *Viewer* [1996], *Standing Apart* [1996][21] and *Facing Faces* [1996].[22] Curiously these works are as intensively *language spaces* as are the works with actual sound and words. Experiencing them, one senses oneself inside a *knowing relation* that's usually only possible where there is language, yet we know that a charged intimate moment of speech withheld can be 'pregnant with meaning'. Speech itself is in fact happening in the space of the work— but inside the head of the viewer. When in *Viewer* one looks into the faces of the 17 day workers, projected slightly bigger than life, facing out from a long wall, one can almost feel *their* internal dialogue and their struggle to be there, to remain still and silent, indeed, to be all that they are ('underclass') in relation to a world governed by all that *we* are ('privileged class'), we the viewers viewing the viewers. Our internal dialogue is the counterpart to theirs, made poignant and inevitable by the languaging field of silence. We perform for them. And the same is true for *Tall Ships* and its dark hall lined with projections of distant seated human figures who get up and come to meet us as we approach each one. We alternate between reaching toward – going to meet – these open-faced projective entities and, in the gap of failed contact, continuing to wander afield. We move about gingerly like night ships ever in danger of colliding, meeting strangers face to face in the dark as they rise up to greet us like spirits in Hades, and deal with the phantoms of our own communicative histories/ nightmares as we grow unexpectedly intimate with these ordinary, nervous, displaced people. Mere projections/our projections – and whose projections are we and the self-propelled discourse in our heads?

The space itself seems to speak, through us, in us, performative of us – us *in* and *as* performance. Action in the performative field is *radial:* possible relation is all around and everywhere at once. In the big surround of *HanD HearD* five wall-size individuals, projected in side view of head and open

hand, gaze into their palms in an odd stillness. The communicative space extends to the breathing images of these silent quasi-meditative people and the *space between* – between the person and her/his hand – independent entities *in an unknown relation,* in a state performative of a certain unnameable relation; but also between them and us, as unknowns to each other and, *by entrainment,* as unknowns to ourselves. These radical states of inquiry are *performative of the field itself* as declared by the work, as if the field had a mind of its own.

This notion of a 'mindful field' may be a sort of metaphor for a level of integrity which we scarcely understand, or it may be something more challenging to our view of reality. The sound field of a frog pond at night and the overlay of a visual field of fireflies *seem* performative. If such a field were understood to be simulated by a human mind we would not hesitate to call it a performance; the aleatoric music and poetry of John Cage or Jackson Mac Low is hardly problematic as performance, because it is clearly intentional – the ordering principle operates at a higher level of abstraction. But the field itself – how is it performative? In the terms of Non-linear Dynamics and its well-known extrapolations, Chaos Theory or Complexity Theory, where randomness appears, order may eventually emerge at certain definable thresholds; a field is 'self-organizing'.[23] But does non-linear dynamics hold the secret of the performativity of the field? Again, there are composers and other artists who work with liminal states of perceivable order in sound/performance, and whose composition, while making use of chance, remains right on the threshold of 'order' without actually crossing it: the listener remains at the edge, at the very site where order emerges, and one might wish to notice the scientific analogies to the processes at work here. (In Gary Hill's years in Barrytown, New York, early 1980s, the composer Franz Kamin was actively working with mathematical structures, and certainly there is an association between the work and the formal thought that it makes use of. However, though 'field theory' in the arts – from Charles Olson's 'composition by field' and Cage's aleatorics on – has a far broader theoretical base in scientific thought today than previously, it is not clear that fundamental questions about the origin and nature of 'self-organization' are answerable in those terms. The mystery prevails, and at the experiential level art is a primary zone of insight into *liminal order* and the *performative field*.[24]

It is tempting to track Gary Hill's evolving work in terms of a grand performance of highly individuated yet complexly resonant fields and fields within fields, interdependent and co-determinative. The results of such an inquiry might contribute both to an understanding of his work and to the theory of fields and their interaction. It would begin with an understanding of the most minute fields,[25] say, at the level of image, how an electronically generated abstraction becomes an image (e.g. in *Happenstance*), then a sign, then a symbol with linguistic correlative, only to disintegrate back to the abstract field for further generation. *Composition by field* becomes *image by field*, configurative and performative. On a related scale, the frame is a field – it could be a page (frame as page) or a surface upon which a page is projected (e.g. Blanchot's *Thomas the Obscure* in the single-channel *Incidence of Catastrophe* [1987–8] or *And Sat Down Beside Her*): field as textualized surface. Such a page-field frees up the linguistic field, so that a text is read in a radically new way, as a non-linear focus within a dynamic field, in this way accomplishing a certain kinship with the aleatoric textuality of, say, Cage and Mac Low. Reading and seeing are co-performative. And each such field accomplished in a given work is 'morphogenetic' of other such fields, creating a dynamic field of such fields, which support each other and generate further instances of their kind.

It's easy to see how interactive field generation quickly complexifies and produces new types of any successful field, as if fields take on a sort of will of their own, or absorb and include the artist's participation in a way that is somehow beyond the *artist's* will. In any event they are unexplainably self-organizing and operate far beyond the conscious intention of the artist, who, as it were, is *instructed* by the emergent field. Indeed the field is somehow

animate, perhaps even preposterously so like the *liminal objects* [1995–] in the computer-animated genre wherein objects perform barely thinkable actions, challenging their nature as 'objects'. By antithetical force we might ask: *Who or what is subject to such an object?* – an 'axial' question, i.e. one with multiple valences, performative of the condition of 'liminal objects' by calling into question the status of both subject and object. The liminality of the object transfers to the field of objects, subjects, viewed and viewer, work and artist, etc. Within a *liminal field* nothing/no-one escapes the *performative feedback* of its/one's own liminality – one's being on the edge of identity, one's precarious performance.

So a field, whatever the scale (image, frame, text, physical space, totality of a work, a connectivity of works, etc.), is always more than just *this* event, *this* object, *this* occasion. It calls itself into being from the harmonic that it shares with other fields. And these other fields – other works by the same artist, or by other artists, other works that exist in memory, or even as futural possibilities, that do not exist yet at all – are by no means located in a linear temporal continuum. There are resonances that retrospectively enrich earlier works, or prefigure later ones, but which, in the symphonic grandeur of the multiplicity of works that constitute an oeuvre, or an epoch, or a culture, bring dramatically home the thought of a trans-contemporaneity – a community of work that vibrates across time.

From the perspective of this trans-contemporaneity, performativity shows an other side – its magic-like capacity to conjure into being a form, a modality, a gesture, a situation or a world. This capacity shows up in dialogical and community relation with other modalities, gestures, situations, worlds – other fields – that are not present, and yet these others exert a performative and attractive force based upon communal affinity. In this sense *the magical* is not only the power to conjure 'out of nothing' – it is the power to evoke, or invoke, to bring into presence, something whose modality of being is not presence, but *resonant otherness*.

Performativity by field is a species of non-egocentric

• Gary Hill, *Tall Ships*, Installation 1, 1992, sixteen-channel video installation. Photo © Dirk Bleicker

awareness emerging through resonance, according to the principle: *like attracts like*. The 'call' to other fields is a languaging across boundaries of space and time – radial in both space and time – driven by the reach toward our *own kind*. The tension in *Tall Ships* arises in the irresistible impulse to *move toward embrace of the other out of a root sense of sameness*. The other person is only a projection of a recorded image, yet it/ she/ he is enlivened in immediacy by face-to-face awakening of a *nostalgia for kind* and a strange *shared intimacy*. The 'living image' performs the spark of actual life that one is powerless in this dark space to prevent – one projects life into the image, as if it were a golem waking for a brief instant to embody a godly power, only to die back into mere matter through one's

reflective self-separation (self-consciousness, embarrassment, perhaps shame or even 'Edenic guilt'). The resulting isolation in the dark space opens that space to its own field-awareness – one is only liminally alone, there may be others in this 'reflective dark' of 'resonant otherness' caught in the consequences of projection and catching the low afterlight of wall images – a feeling-tone like tall ships near in the night. This new field of communal awareness bears a *likeness* to the previous field of communing with moving images, yet it is *virtually imageless* and supervenes as a field of actual human energy – bodies physically brushing each other in the dark, uncertainty of contact with strangers, the human sounds and smells that are yet another form of *shared intimacy*.

Ambivalence and uncertainty in the reach toward the other, along with the ambiguity of *kin/ kind*, may be a field dynamic in many of Gary Hill's pieces. In *Facing Faces* the play of meanings in *facing* is a focus of interconnecting fields for a number of works, most obviously *Tall Ships, Viewer, HanD HearD,* and *Standing Apart*.[26] A face is performative of a being, a mood, a state of mind or emotion, a social status, and so on, and in itself it is 'axial' in that it turns on a core of fundamental ambiguity between *true face* and *mask*. The almost classic American Indian face of *Facing Faces* and *Standing Apart,* switching back and forth in its viewer/viewed relationship, also hovers between interpretative possibilities from stark history-laden photo image à la Curtis to self-parodying Cigar-store Indian with its life-denying on-demand stasis. Human faces here are (not) facing themselves, standing apart from themselves and the rest of society, with all the tragic optionless isolation/ alienation implied therein. And, as in *Tall Ships* and *Viewer,* we the viewers, viewing the viewers on-view, are both standing apart from what we view and not; our self-reflection too turns upon the depth of what we face and don't.

Here and throughout the pieces in which a principal dynamic of the active field is 'facing' in its full range of meanings, we can also see a version of the 'reality principle' as 'performance principle' as defined in Herbert Marcuse's revision of Freud *(Eros and Civilization)*, where reality is defined by the social nexus of performance. One's sense of 'reality' is defined by one's ability to know how one's actions appear to others. *Social reality is thus the interpretation of action as a performance.* This is linked to the conditions of alienated labor where the evaluation of one's action is the prerogative of another. Obviously the day workers of *Viewer* and *Facing Faces* are exemplars of alienated labor and its tragic social consequences; ironically, even their performance in this piece, for which they were paid by the hour, is an instance of alienated labor, for they appear here without their conscious intention being in any particular alignment with that of the artist. The work is performative of their condition

in a way that exhibits a fundamental social irony of art in our time.

Yet the art work as 'social field' is not for Gary Hill simply a matter of social critique, protest against alienation or any other one-dimensional statement. A gentler, quite charming form of the social art irony, which recognizes alienated labor, is also at play in *Remarks on Color,* in which the subtext of the piece is a girl performing an impossible task for an adult (reading Wittgenstein's work of that title), indeed, pleasing Daddy (Anastasia Hill is Gary Hill's daughter). To be sure, she's engaged in an art task whose sophisticated intention necessarily is 'alien' to her. However, to emphasize this perspective is obviously to over-interpret, for the sheer spirit of the girl's persistence and self-possession – benignly oblivious to her reading errors (and their happy inventions like 'angel' for 'angle') – stands far above any sense of exploitation, indeed bespeaks an appreciative attentiveness in the artist, an underlying joy in the performative act that levels the relationship between child and adult, and a healthy sense of abandoning 'looking good' as the child's version of Wittgenstein creates its own place in the world. This skewed philosophy and its self-inventing reality are perhaps strangely akin to the looking-glass world of the single-channel *How Do Things Get in a Muddle (Come on Petunia)* [1984]. The social field here is liminal to an alternative world.

And this is what performative fields do in their mutually attracting alchemical work of transforming ordinary worlds into possible worlds. If the principle by which fields interact is *like attracts like,* the principle by which they retain their individuated integrity is *liminality through resonant alterity* – surrendering to the pull of sameness (kinship) yet remaining at the margin of difference. So the individual sailing about in the dark of *Tall Ships* – the title of the work names the participant (viewer as performer) – is a moving field (a voyaging 'intellectual/emotional complex in an instant of time' as Ezra Pound defined Image) among other/like emoting fields, and these in turn are embedded in a larger field which is the work itself. The *individuated fields,* the very 'selves' performative of the work that names them, livingly model the works; that is, these silent 'installations' become *living sites* through the *voyaging round through* them (the *periplus*). And once activated they perform a role that otherwise belongs to sacred sites, namely, they give back to the participants their own further life.

This conjured life is *radial* in a space, and time too does not so much move forward as move *further* – as if spiraling within, tracing attention, turning ever more toward what is attended in a process of reorientation. Time suspends, and in the instant/instance of finest concentration in which viewer and viewed switch roles (a *peripeteia*) it reaches a *still point.*[27] This still point may or may not be silent and may or may not be actually still (motionless); certainly Gary Hill's direct use of the notion in *Learning Curve (Still Point)* [1993][28] addresses a state of wave motion, like a 'standing wave', reflected in the viewer's *emotion* (including what is perhaps darkly recalled from school days, sitting at a desk). The zero point state of no development and reflexive radial awareness occurs at the event horizon where 'internal awareness' and 'external condition' occupy a single living surface, like a Klein Bottle (a 'one-sided bottle', no inside or outside). The Klein Bottle (more generally, 'Klein form'[29]) may be thought of metaphorically as a topological form in four dimensions whose nature as *continuous surface is to house the space that shapes, allows, and houses it.*

The fields of these 'installations' are analogues of mind spaces and the actions 'inside' them, and at the same time performances of mind activity and its essentially radial time-sense. Some of Gary Hill's more recent pieces quite explicitly explore the mind–space analogue. *Dervish* [1993–95][30] creates an image-projecting machine of loud and monstrous proportions, flashing in the dark, at times nightmarishly and with something like archetypal force. In *Reflex Chamber* [1996],[31] if the smallish closed box-like room with strobic image-flashing tabular surface in the center is the suddenly self-illuminating Dark Interior of the human psyche, so to say, then the mesmerizing yet disruptive and somewhat disorienting images are 'psychic contents'. Accordingly the narrative text in a voice-over performs the passage of an ego within its own interior, attempting to grasp its boundaries as it encounters images that are its own but also not its own; and more than that, attempting to grasp the space in which those images rise and fade and are subjected to the energetics of the psychic medium that sustains them. This is a notoriously difficult task for the human self under the best of circumstances! The images are projected by light, but themselves arise as the interruption of the passage of a light beam; and here the strobic light has the power to absolutely disrupt them. To restate the analogy: psychic contents lurking within a medium of sentience and awareness can erupt with a blinding presence that obliterates the possibility of one's identification with those contents.

In a related way *Midnight Crossing* (1997)[32] creates an explicit psychic field, yet one that in a sense inverts the mind-analogical space of *Reflex Chamber* – not the psychic field *spatially introjected* as if *within the head* but that field *projected in outside surround.* The space is concretely the viewer's 'visual psyche' – what one sees with one's eyes closed – dream or hypnogogic or meditated visual appearances. The resolution, timing, decay, even the strobic interruptions of the piece are gauged to simulate such psychic appearances, so that viewers cognize what they see as if this were emissions of their own psyche. The images appear on a screen that is surrounded by darkness. You cannot tell how far away the screen is. The strobic flashes show the presence of the screen, but leave an afterimage on the retina. So the only information one has about what in fact is objectively outside of one's sensorium, is paradoxically a retinal trace. The afterimage fades; new images appear on the screen but only in the haze of that fading afterimage. Physically internal and physically external image sources experientially merge.

The various fields of related Gary Hill works speak to each other, and their sympathetic dialogue is often antithetical. *Midnight Crossing* effects a

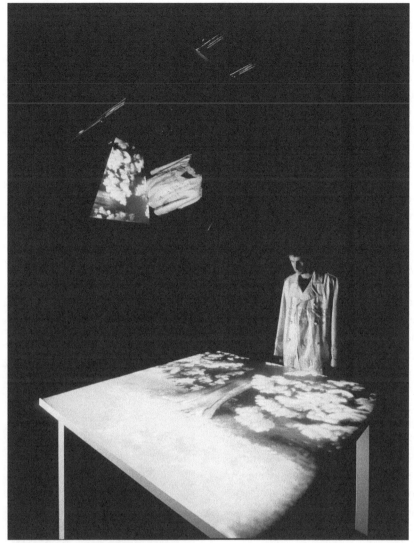

• Gary Hill, *Reflex Chamber*, 1996, single-channel video/sound installation. Photo © Steve White

continuity between the viewer's mind and the outside from which it is being affected, whereas *Reflex Chamber* constructs a completely introjected world: any news from the outside is completely reflected and only available as reflected, as in the interior of a reflex camera. Strobic flashes give the news as incursions of light, not filling one's space (as in *Midnight Crossing*) so much as occupying a focused interior one. This interior world, however, is not the viewer's but the artist's, yet the viewer is entirely inside its enclosed self-illuminating darkness. We are not so much the participants as

the participated. It may be a strange reality to share, being so profoundly intimate; on the other hand, perhaps our relationship to our own interior psyche has a like (im)balance of the personally known and experientially alien. Perhaps this work (along with its convex-mirror inversion, *Midnight Crossing*), performs just this fundamental psychic ambi-*valence*, its deep axiality.

The radical mind-fields generated by these recent projective works appear like revealed 'layers' of what lies hidden in our consciousness-obstructed reality – sudden and disruptive manifestations of 'undertime' and 'undermatter,' non-linear analogues of archeologically exposed history. Art performs a *cut*, an intervention that in certain cases might be called a 'psychotopological dig'[33] through the use of subversive instrumentation – what poet/artist William Blake called 'the infernal method', 'by corrosives, which in hell are salutary and medicinal'.[34] Such a hell-raising instrument is the strobe light, applied with a certain incisiveness. By its action images are both projected and annihilated – a world created and destroyed. The boundary between construction and destruction becomes a permeable membrane. In *Dervish* a daemonial machine *whirls* its strobic image-making/-destroying force noisily and somewhat threateningly (its 'whirl' an attribute of the title and a reference to the etymology of 'strobe'). In the instant of the strobic flash, subversive agent of liminality, what is external and what is internal radically coincide, transforming the visible world into Klein form. The flash that wipes the tabular surface clean in *Reflex Chamber* interrupts identity, association, psychological state, but it only does so by first activating one's optical susceptibility – it pulls you into its often gorgeous imagery. The light one sees is the light one is. And when the super whirling light tears away the precious image, it does more than destroy, it rips off the blinders to present reality and, perhaps, the veil between unexperienced dimensions of that reality.

The strobic flash becomes an opportunity to awaken beyond the associational matrix of image and word that the flash itself momentarily interrupts. The neurological light that it stimulates is both the under-matter of experience itself and its liberation. Curiously this most radical and challenging tendency of art is also the point where it seems to converge with subversive traditions of human consciousness, 'technologies of the sacred' and of the transformative, and the refined use of *conscious shock* to awaken the mind to its true and intrinsic potential.[35] The paradoxical and axial instrumentation, for instance, of *Reflex Chamber* brings the mind to a kind of peak of transformative startle in the discovery that at the heart of its

darkness is a self-generating heart of light with its seemingly unlimited capacity for self-regeneration. The performative that is art in a true process of undergoing its self-revealing intention finds an optimal expression in these 'living field' works, focused by nothing less than a resolve to deliver the shock of *re*-cognition.

ACKNOWLEDGEMENT
All four photos of Gary Hill installations and performances are reproduced here courtesy of the Donald Young Gallery, Chicago.

NOTES

1 Gary Hill's recent work, *Namesake* [1999], in which his full-size image (facing forward) is projected on one wall and the back of his head is projected on the opposite wall, is a performance of identity – a kind of 'search in identity' – in which he says his name over and over, each time starting fresh, as if to ask, implicitly, 'what's in a name?' The energy of 'identity saying' derives from the authenticity of the *null space between* speech acts.

• Gary Hill, *Namesake*, 1999, two-channel video/sound installation. Photo © Tom Van Eynde

2 For Gary Hill's interest in the performance aspect of his work, see our dialogue with him, 'Liminal Performance', *PAJ* #58 (January 1998) and *Gary Hill*, ed. Robert C. Morgan (Baltimore: Johns Hopkins University Press, 2000).

3 This emphasis was strongest among poets (present authors included), who were aligned with various lineages of practice associated with Black Mountain College of the late 1940s/early 1950s and represented by poets Charles Olson, Robert Duncan and Robert Creeley, composer/writer John Cage, artist Robert Rauschenberg, etc. The word 'processual' was introduced to us by

Robert Kelly (his usage goes back at least to the 1960s) and characterized a profoundly realized poetic practice especially related to Charles Olson's 'Projective Verse' (circa 1950). Gary Hill's later use of the term in 'Processual Video', deriving from conversations in Barrytown, was further articulated in his program notes 'Processual Video' for a lecture at the Museum of Modern Art, New York (see also note 4), and it is worth revisiting this pivotal distinction as originally formulated for the 1980 work:

My art has steadily moved from a perceptual priority of imaging toward a more conceptual method for developing idea constructs. Remaining throughout my work has been the necessity to dialogue with the technology. The earlier image works, primarily concerned with color and image density, were engaged in the invention of new and more complex images within compositional and rhythmic structures. The current work involves image-text syntax, a kind of electronic linguistic, utilizing the dialogue to manipulate a conceptual space that locates mental points of intersection, where text forms and feeds back into the imaging of those intersects. Processual might be considered a space between the perceptual and the conceptual. The processual space serves neither as a composite nor as a balancing of these two modes. It relies on the continual transition or synapse between them. . . .

4   In a 1983 interview Gary Hill speaks of the generation of *Processual Video* as performance piece: 'Actually, I did a performance out of *Processual Video* for the Video Viewpoints series at the Museum of Modern Art. In fact, the piece was written as my lecture for the series. . . .

There was a large monitor facing the audience, and the text was scored on paper. I watched a small monitor so I knew approximately where the bar was in relation to what I was reading. In different readings, there would be slight variations, but it all remained pretty close to the score. In that tape, there are references to me, references to the audience sitting in chairs, but it's more allegorical than *Around and About* and *Primarily Speaking*.'
('A Manner of Speaking. An interview with Gary Hill by Lucinda Furlong', in *Afterimage* 10(8): 13, March 1983. Reprinted in Theodora Vischer (ed.) *Imagining the Brain Closer than the Eyes*, (Basel: Museum für Gegenwartskunst; 1994).

5   In fact we have elsewhere said much the same about *Cut Pipe*. See 'Cut to the Radical of Orientation: twin notes on being in touch' in Gary Hill's [Videosomatic] Installation, *Cut Pipe*' in *Public* #13, 'Touch in Contemporary Art,' ed. David Tomas (Toronto: 1996), reprinted in *The Open Space Magazine*, #1, ed. Benjamin Boretz and Mary Lee Roberts (Minnesota: Moorhead; spring 1999). And, of course, something similar might be said

about many of Gary Hill's works, including single-channel works like *Why Do Things Get in a Muddle (Come on Petunia)* [1984] and *Ura Aru (the backside exists)* [1985–6], in which literal reversal of sounds performs an art-created 'backside' / mirror world of language with all its looking-glass vexation of questions of language logic.
6   *Cut Pipe* is a single-channel video/sound installation, comprising recorded media (e.g. VHS cassette, laserdisc, etc.), one 4-inch black-and-white video monitor modified to fit in an aluminum tube, one TV-projection lens, two aluminum cylinders, three 8-inch loudspeakers situated inside the cylinders, and one stereo amplifier.
7   For 'mind-degrades' (on the model of 'biodegrades') one could almost say 'self-deconstructs', implying a conscious intention of standing beyond reification in order to remain *in process/processual* and alive to continuing change – the *open performative*.
8   We discuss this piece in some detail and with different emphasis in 'A Transpective View', published as accompanying text to the two-volume laserdisc collection of single-channel works, *Spinning the Spur of the Moment* (New York: Voyager; 1994, pp. 4–7).
9   Gary Hill is deeply aware of composition/editing as open performative process (indeed as *projective* and *composition by field* – see note 10 on Charles Olson's 'Projective Verse') as reflected in this statement from 'Liminal Performance':

Ultimately every word and every moment in a tape (or life for that matter) could be performative almost in and of itself. . . . I think of La Monte Young's saying, 'tuning is a function of time'. Each event enters into an evolving relationship with the developing piece, spiraling around and folding in so that at any moment you might 'begin' again from a different place. I mean even repeating an image or a sequence can be part of a continuous event; in working on a piece, relistening to a sequence folds a past event back into the present. One just has to be patient, believing something will emerge. But what is it that is the source of this emergence when it does happen? It happens in 'the present' but the present has now gained a complexity that quite literally includes the replayed past. This really complicates the question of 'real time'.

10   There may be no better example in video art of the sense of the process of composition put forth by Charles Olson in his epoch-defining essay 'Projective Verse' (1950 [published in French in *Tel Quel* in the 1960s]), particularly the notion that the poet who 'works in OPEN, or what can only be called COMPOSITION BY FIELD' understands that 'the poem itself must, at all points, be a high-energy construct, an energy discharge'. The composition has a life of its own, an unfolding path that the poet follows: 'From the moment that he ventures into FIELD COMPOSITION – puts himself in the open – he can go

by no track other than the one the poem under hand declares, for itself'. This brings attention to 'the *process* of the thing, how the principle can be made so to shape the energies that the form is accomplished'. This view ties in with the 'kinetic' role of a work: 'A poem is energy transferred from where the poet got it (he will have some several causations), by way of the poem itself to, all the way over to, the reader.' This kinetic notion leads to a 'stance toward reality' in which poet/artist are bound to reader/viewer in a transformative role. So that Olson says elsewhere ('Human Universe'): 'There is only one thing you can do about the kinetic, reenact it.' Therefore, '. . . art is the only twin life has – its only valid metaphysic. Art does not seek to describe but to enact. . . . Man does influence external reality.' See Charles Olson, *Collected Prose*, ed. Donald Allen and Benjamin Friedlander (Berkeley, Los Angeles, London: University of California Press, 1997, pp. 237–49, 162).

11   Sixteen-channel video/sound installation of 16 b/w TV tubes of half-inch to 21-inch positioned in a horizontal wall inset, each showing a part of the artist's nude body to scale.

12   Four-channel video installation of thirty 12-inch TV tubes mounted on aluminum beam and computer controlled switching matrix, with complex horizontal imaging in flickering segments of two bodies, male and female nudes prone – the artist and his then companion, Marina Hugonnier.

13   Sixteen-channel video installation with sixteen b/w monitors, sixteen projection units, sixteen laserdisc players and computer-controlled interactive system. See our *Tall Ships: Gary Hill's Projective Installations – Number 2* (Barrytown, New York: Barrytown/Station Hill Ltd; 1997).

14   Color video installation (NTSC, color, silent), five laserdisc players, five color video projectors. See our *HanD HearD/liminal objects: Gary Hill's Projective Installations – Number 1* (Barrytown, New York: Station Hill/Barrytown, Ltd; and Paris: Galérie des Archives; 1996).

15   Five-channel video installation (NTSC color, silent), five CRT color projectors, five laserdisc players, and a five-channel synchronizer. See our *Viewer: Gary Hill's Projective Installations – Number 3* (Barrytown, New York: Station Hill/Barrytown, Ltd; 1997).

16   Mixed media installation with live stereo camera/viewfinder, two videotapes, sixteen loudspeakers, objects, motor-controlled lights and live rabbit.

17   Mixed media installation consisting of three works: (1) Single-channel video and hanging TV tube with table, chair, lens, book and speaker; (2) Single-channel video and glass tube enclosing 1′ TV tube, text applied on floor and speaker; (3) 2-channel video and two 1′ TV tubes with four lenses.

18   Seven-channel video/sound installation, with seven hanging 4-inch black-and-white video displays and a pro-

jection element consisting of seven modified video monitors and projection lenses placed inside seven black metal cylinders which hang from the ceiling. The only source of light in the darkened room is from the images of different parts of a male body, and a chair, projected onto open books lying on the floor. The texts illumined by the images are fragmented excerpts from a Blanchot fiction, *The Last Man*, in the Lydia Davis English translation (New York: Columbia University Press)

19   The sense of 'recite' in Gary Hill cannot help but draw comparison to that of Maurice Blanchot from whose work he has received so much fundamental inspiration. Blanchot, who calls most of his fiction '*récit*', states its principle in a way that is fully performative, suggesting a modality of 'narrative' that belongs to the embodying domain of poetics:

> The tale *[récit]* is not the narration of an event, but that event itself, the approach to that event, the place where that event is made to happen – an event which is yet to come and through whose power of attraction the tale can hope to come into being, too.'
> ['The Song of the Sirens', Lydia Davis trans., *The Station Hill Blanchot Reader: Fiction and Literary Essays,* ed. George Quasha (Barrytown, New York: Barrytown Ltd/Station Hill; 1999); in French: 'Le Chant des Sirènes', *Le Livre à Venir* (Paris: Editions Gallimard; 1959].

20   (1989) Color videotape, stereo sound; 4 minutes.

21   Two-channel video installation (NTSC, color, silent); two CRT color video projectors; two laserdisc players and synchronizer.

22   Two 20-inch monitors; two swivel wall-mount monitor supports; two laserdisc players and synchronizer.

23   The contemporary epic of interdisciplinary speculation on these matters ranges from chemistry, physics and mathematics – in the work of Ilya Prigogine and many others – to contemporary art, social theory, philosophy and religion. As regards the latter two, we have been most instructed by the work of Dr Herbert V. Guenther and his parallel inquiries into Tibetan philosophy (Dzogchen), modern western thought, and physics and mathematics; see, for instance, *From Reductionism to Creativity: Dzogs-chen and the New Sciences of Mind* (Boston: Shambhala; 1989).

24   In Charles Olson's *The Special View of History* (Berkeley: Oyez; 1970; forthcoming Barrytown/Station Hill Press, Inc.) the poet anticipates present-day notions of self-organization in his formulation 'life is the chance success of a play of creative accidents'. This becomes a principle of order in his poetics that is subtly different from the use of chance in Cage or Mac Low. For Olson, the living being is part of the field at every point, changing the field by interaction with it. What is of

interest for his poetics is the emergence of authentic form within particular fields of activity where a person is present to discover, influence, declare, and select desired tendencies. Cage and Mac Low (at least in the latter's early aleatoric work) sought to eliminate such participation in the initial creation of the field, though it must be said that at the level of performance, the same interactive and participative role for the individual returns. In Franz Kamin's work, though influenced profoundly by Cage and Mac Low, there is an introduction of structures that are liminal to 'self-organization' at the level of composition, not just performance, and yet not involving the kind of explicit participation in the derivation of form that Olson was concerned with. In this field of artists working with chance and self-organization in different ways, Gary Hill's work, we might suggest, oscillates in the space between Kamin and Olson. Gary Hill generates structures of possible activity in which combinatorial possibilities are imagined beforehand as a field; but then the specific outcomes are awaited, and preferences are decidedly affirmed. In the former aspect he is like Kamin; in the latter like Olson.

25   We are not here referring to the technical meaning of 'video fields' (1/60th second) and/or 'frames' (1/30th second).

26   This 'facing' focus applies in a very different way to *Remarks on Color* where we live a text (Wittgenstein's work of that name) through the face and voice of a 7-year-old girl attempting to read a work beyond her level of understanding. *Remarks on Color* [1994]: single-channel video installation using color projector, laserdisc player and laserdisc, amplifier, and two speakers.

27   'Still point' will be familiar to readers of T.S. Eliot's poem 'Burnt Norton' (the first poem of *The Four Quartets*), section II: 'at the still point, there the dance is,/But neither arrest nor movement. . . .' This vision of suddenly realized timelessness ('To be conscious is not to be in time') derives from Dante's vision of eternal stillness in the last canto of the *Paradiso*. Interestingly, 'still point' is used as a technical term in craniosacral therapy, an offshoot of osteopathy, for the act of causing a momentary suspension in the fundamental pulsation of the body (the 'craniosacral rhythmical impulse'); the effect is to mobilize the system's inherent self-correcting abilities. The experience of the Still Point is 'wholeness' (as in 'health') and engages inherent self-balancing. See our 'Tall Acts of Seeing', in *Tall Ships: Gary Hill's Projective Installations – Number 2* (Barrytown, New York: Barrytown/Station Hill Ltd; 1997).

28   Single-channel silent video installation with a 5-inch monitor at the end of a long desk-like plywood chair/ table construction, showing the moving image of an 'endless wave' peaking. Gary Hill's use of 'still point' was in conscious resonance with our use in 'Tall Acts of Seeing' (previous note) – another kind of interactive field.

29   The video artist and eco-activist Paul Ryan, an early associate of Gary Hill, has for many years meditated on variations of the Klein Bottle he calls 'Klein forms'. Such forms have suggested to him a path of ecologically sensitive thought, for to model the relationship between thought and world, language and sense via Klein forms is by that very act to change the intuitive *context* of the way we think of the world, thus to change the world itself. It is to *place the mind out in the territory*, to reconnect intellect and touch, spirit and earth; to break the magnetic vise of all the bleak dichotomies and, by passing through a space that reconvenes beyond polarity, to perform a healing of self-divided thought.

30   See our 'Two Ways at Once (performative reading – the inside out story)' for a fuller discussion, in the bilingual catalogue *Gary Hill* (ed. Josée Bélisle) for the exposition at the Musée d'art contemporain de Montréal (1998).

31   *Reflex Chamber:* single-channel video/sound installation with video projector and mount, laserdisc player, mirror, metal railing, strobe light, four loudspeakers, two amplifiers, graphic equalizer, synchronizer, and $60 \times 60 \times 34$ inch square table in the centre of a 15 foot square room.

32   *Midnight Crossing:* single-channel video/sound installation with color video projector, laserdisc player, laserdisc, four loudspeakers, amplifier, computer, interface electronics, software, six strobe lights, and aluminum structure.

33   We owe this useful concept to Franz Kamin's *Ann Margret Loves You and Other Psychotopological Diversions* (Barrytown, New York: Station Hill Press; 1983).

34   In *The Marriage of Heaven and Hell* Blake parodies religious dogma by inverting heaven and hell as values; his view of art as subversive of spiritual and intellectual rigidity is furthered by analogy with engraving which uses corrosives to eat away a surface to reveal 'the infinite which was hid'.

35   Again Blake stands as a turning point in western visual and verbal art that begins a use of conscious shock to integrate artistic and spiritual method in a common purpose. The traditional esoteric methods are preserved in well-known disciplines like Zen and Tibetan Buddhism (especially Dzogchen), Sufism and the remarkable East–West hybrid carried by the teachings of G. I. Gurdjieff, who explicitly used methods of awakening the practitioner suddenly, almost violently, to a pristine state of awareness. (The Tibetan word is *hedewa* and focuses on shock and conscious awakening in the immediate aftermath.) The intended effect is not to traumatize but to clear the mind or clean the slate, allowing the sensorium to be rid of the accumulated debris of immediately preceding or long-preceding perceptions, sensations, and cogntions. Certainly there are a number of contemporary artists who could be studied in this perspective – Marina Abramovic clearly among the foremost.

SEVEN TABLEAUX VIVANTS FROM SHADOWTIME

Charles Bernstein

an opera the author is writing for the composer Brian Ferneyhough, which centres on the life and thought of Walter Benjamin. It has been commissioned by the City of Munich for the MÜNCHENER BIENNALE for performance in April 2004.

1 Laurel's Eyes   Die Lorelei

Each night is soul-bedeviled	Ich weiß nicht, was soll es bedeuten,
As each frayed ship rigs sail	Daß ich so traurig bin;
In journey's end sight falters	Ein Märchen aus alten Zeiten,
Where journey never ends	Das kommt mir nicht aus dem Sinn.
A draught so thin it's bitter	Die Luft ist kühl und es dunkelt,
A ruin like the Rhine	Und ruhig fließt der Rhein;
That rips its fleece in kilter	Der Gipfel des Berges funkelt
Abandoned to its shine	Im Abendsonnenschein.
The shone star yearns for light	Die schönste Jungfrau sitzet
Door opens, wonder barred	Dort oben wunderbar;
Ire's golden gate gets blistered	Ihr goldnes Geschmeide blitzet,
Seek comet, err in folded heart	Sie kämmt ihr goldenes Haar.
Seek comet, err in folded heart	Sie kämmt es mit goldenem Kamme
And drink a daft farewell	Und singt ein Lied dabei;
That has its blunder tendered	Das hat eine wundersame,
In quivering, feathered tar	Gewaltige Melodei.
Sifted in climate's sieve	Den Schiffer im kleinen Schiffe
Engrafts its festooned way	Ergreift es mit wildem Weh;
As spark ignites the weave	Er schaut nicht die Felsenriffe,
And shouts ordain the play	Er schaut nur hinauf in die Höh.
This globe spins on, verse lingers	Ich glaube, die Wellen verschlingen
A sail without a sigh	Am Ende Schiffer und Kahn;
A song without a singer	Und das hat mit ihrem Singen
Laurel's veil, Laurel's eyes	Die Lore-Ley getan.

The underlying layer of the lyric is a homophonic translation of Heine's "Die Lorelei" (1823). While Benjamin rejected Heine's version of Romanticism, he nonetheless may have been distantly related to him (as well as to it). There have been over 25 musical settings of Heine's poem. The best known are the folkloric version by Friedrich Silcher and the art song version by Franz Liszt. Mark Twain wrote about the Lorelei legend in *A Tramp Abroad* and did his own translation of Heine's poem — 'She combs with a comb that is golden, / And sings a weird refrain / That steeps in a deadly enchantment / The list'ner's ravished brain'. One of Sylvia Plath's most haunting poems, 'Lorelei', involves a radical transformation of the psychic and gender dynamics of Heine's poem — 'Sisters, your song / Bears a burden too weighty / For the whorled ear's listening'. Both the Gershwins and The Pogues wrote Lorelei 'covers'. The legend usually begins with a girl, cruelly abandoned by her lover, throwing herself into the Rhine. By some magic, beyond rational powers of understanding, the drowned maiden is reborn as a Siren (or mermaid-like creature), who, in the forever after of the song, lures fishermen to their ruin on the Lorelei cliff, to the background music of the crash of the waves against the rocks.

◭ Tensions

each ear's sly fiction a toy taboo which founds us

fear begets gain in trust 'til thwarts anew bogus delay

pale cheer wanes in crust of fabled dew's moment's bending

wants well as wills fell mordant sense of sent-up hopes

slide at diction fences sapped affliction in tents not flinches

sipped affection moves impatience over hooded hounded hapless hallowed hills

missed obsession slips bided glance at torsion's tabbed tattooed surround

tear's friction cobbles fact for tarnished shame's shunned shuttered wince

fist courts hocus-pocus display as depth ricochets side-saddle

bent torts ape discordant art's hue lending utter addled sap

Ten by ten, with each of the lines
working with sounds from the previous
lines. The first line is derived in part
from the word string in **6**, all of whose
letters can be reassembled to make
"each ear's sly fiction toy tutu I unlit".

3 Hashish in Marseilles

These stones are the bread
of imagination. Reading the notices
on the urinals, *things withstand my
gaze*. Such joy in the mere act
of unrolling a ball of thread. One becomes
tender, fearing that a shadow falling on
paper might hurt it. It's too noisy here.
I must note how I found my place.
Seeing only nuances. As when
the intensity of acoustic impressions
blots out all others. The solitude of such
trances works as a filter. Yet I am disturbed
by a child crying.

*

Am I yet disturbed
filter, work of trance, such solitude,
others blots, impressions
of acoustic intensity whose
nuances only see traces, my notes
founder here, noisy, too
hurt might paper a fall that shows
a fear, tender becomes one
thread of balls unrolling, act
in joy such gaze, my things
which stand, urinals of notice,
reading imagination of bread, stones,
these ...

*

Bread is stone
withstanding thread
sheer toys such maze
becomes threat unruling
oily shadow
cozy vapor
where fluency mars
impressions
as tested falter

'Hashish in Marseilles' is based on
Benjamin's 1932 essay, translated by
Edmund Jephcott and collected in *Walter
Benjamin: Selected Writings*, Volume 2:
1927-1934 (Cambridge, Mass.: Harvard
University Press, 1999), pp. 673-679. The
second section works through the first
section backwards.

△4 After Heine   Death is the Cool Night

Capital is the fool's gold   Death is the cool Night
Labor is the folded haze   Life the muggy Day
It's dark now, I'm sleeping   It's dark already, I'm sleepy
Work's made me tired   Day's made me tired

Over my heart grows a web   Over my bed grows a Tree
Which traps the weary Nightingale   Where sings the young Nightingale;
She sings of only history   She sings of only Love
I hear it even in sleep   I hear it even in Dream

A reworking of Heine's 'Der Tod, das ist
der kühle Nacht'. The translation is my own.

⚠ One and a Half Truths

In the weeks ahead, we lag behind. The
Bear sees the cantaloupe only at the
Filling station. Hope grows feathers when it
Loses its antennae. The earth is a
Bootblack that prefers magenta. Just a-
Round the corner is another corner.
Just around the corner is the coron-
Er. Fresh fruit is better than oily pa-
Jamas. Light is the furthest thing from mind
When the operating system is down-
Loaded. A cup is not always a cup.
Keep your mittens posted. Some allergies
Are unforgivable. A house on a
Hill makes a good target. Make beans while the

Hay dries. Money is the root of all cur-
Rency. If it works in the office try
Gatorade. The evolution of the
Species is a form of infanticide.
A pound of bleach is worth almost nothing.
Bleach yourself before you bleach others. Bleach
Yourself and the whole world looks pale. The trick
Is in the trust not the lock. Jimmie with
A square and you'll get pizza. The plaza
Is surrounded by walruses. Ice blue
But not forgotten. Never mistake a
Feather for a pirate. Second glances
Are always first in line. Shimmers rule. Truth
Is a gun loaded with a parachute.

I take the title of this double
sonnet from Karl Kraus's
collection of aphorisms. The
27 sentences (or some subset)
could be reordered for extension
or echo.

◢ Can'ts

if you can't see it it can still hurt you

you can't see if it can it hurt you still

can't if can you you still see it it hurt

see it still you hurt you can't it can if

it still you if see hurt it can can't you

it you it can if you see hurt can't still

can it still can't if you it hurt you see

still hurt can't you see it if it you can

hurt it still you can't see can you if it

you hurt still can't you see it if it

The second 10 x 10; the first line determines the first word of each subsequent line; each line uses the same word set.

Madame Moiselle and Mr Moiselle
Went for a walk with their gazelle.
The tiger slept on the sewing machine
And all the children swept themselves clean.

Rings of desire, floods of wisps
Who's to say what, what's to say which
Whether what is is so because
Or whether what is is not

Who's to say, what's to say
Whether what is is not
Or whether what is is so because
Is so because it's not

A classical ballet move coded in Apple Script by Adrian Ward and
Ashley Page.

– performs a classical ballet move (v1.0-beta)
– known issues: no hand/arm support (will be fixed in v2.0)

on dance

    do glissade
    – do assemblé – not yet coded

end dance

on glissade

    do fifthposition
    do plié (demi)
    do degagé (my left leg)
    put the weight of my body **from** my right leg **onto** my left leg
    do degagé (my right leg)
    return the foot of my right leg **infront of** the foot of my left leg
    do plié (demi)

end glissade

– definition of fifth position
on fifthposition

    put my left leg **behind** my right leg **with** distance **set to** 0
    put the foot of my left leg **facing** left
    put the foot of my right leg **facing** right *– ouch!*

end fifthposition

– a deep plié continues until both heels are off the ground
on plié { depth }

    if depth **is** demi **then**

        while the heels of the feet of my legs **are** slightly off the ground
            bend the knee of my left leg
            bend the knee of my right leg
        end while

    else if depth is deep then

    while the heels of the feet of my legs **are** very off the ground
        bend the knee of my left leg
        bend the knee of my right leg
    end while

    end if

end plié

– the foot should be extending straight out from the leg
on degagé { whichleg }

    keep the knee of the leg which **is not** whichleg bent
    lift whichleg with the foot of whichleg **not on** the ground
    point the toes of the foot of whichleg **towards** the ground **away** from
    my body

end degagé

software for dancers: coding forms

Scott deLahunta

AN INTRODUCTION

In January 1967, A. Michael Noll, one of the first computer scientist/ artists to explore and espouse the convergence between computers and art, wrote an article in *Dance Magazine* entitled 'Choreography and Computers', in which he described a software program he was creating that would indicate stage positions of stick figures and be of potential use to choreographers. In the same issue, Ann Hutchinson-Guest (an authority on dance notation) argued that whilst the computer would 'never replace' the facility a choreographer has for composing movement with the dancer, it might assist in the overall outlining and editing of a score for a dance (Noll and Hutchinson 1967).

While the debate started by A. Michael Noll and Ann Hutchinson is arguably still relevant today, after three decades our perceptions of both computers and dancing have changed considerably and generally not along the same trajectories. The cultural environments that have incubated contemporary dance since the 1960s, largely the United States and Western Europe, have also been the factories for the production of cultural facts and myths related to emerging technologies. Obviously, the computer has not replaced the choreographer, nor did it ever really threaten to do so. The ways in which it has evolved to influence how we think, communicate and interact suggest that this might be a fruitful time to revisit the question of how a software program might be of use to a choreographer.

The *Software for Dancers* research project that took place in the autumn of 2001 in London was conceived as an opportunity to update the 1967 debate.[1] The main research team comprised four established contemporary choreographers and four digital artists, three of whom had experience with dance. The digital artists came with a high level of skill with sound and image editing software tools, as well as a range of experience with programming and scripting, thus aligning themselves with the notion of 'coding' as creative practice. The shared central task of the group would be to develop concepts for software rehearsal tools for choreographers. This provided the stimulus to explore shared and divergent approaches amongst the participants across a range of ideas related to the recognition and transformation of structures and materials in the process of art making, whether computational or choreographic. Some of these explorations were made more explicit through dialogue, while some evolved as tacit frameworks within which other discussions took place. The question 'what is software?', while never overtly exposed, repeatedly nudged itself close to the centre of the discussion, and it is to this that I devote the remainder of the essay.

The study of the impact of software as a cultural force still resides primarily in the fields of computer science, engineering and mathematics, with a rapidly increasing dissemination throughout the biological sciences – a field that computation is poised to revolutionize. The question 'what is

Performance Research 7(2), pp.96-102 © Taylor & Francis Ltd 2002

software?' will initiate a very different response when asked within these fields than in an arts and humanities context, where it is essential that frameworks for exploring software and its implications are further developed. *Software for Dancers* provided a modest but significant context for contributing to this discourse by investigating what software is under the following headings: as a language; as a tool; as a material.

AS A LANGUAGE

Computer programming relies on the use of artificial languages, e.g. C, Fortran, Pascal, C++, Java, etc. These languages follow a strict formal schema; they have a precise syntax and vocabulary that leave little room for the forms of semantic and interpretive slippage we are accustomed to with natural languages such as English or Spanish.[2] The computer will always interpret an instruction (or algorithm) written in a computer programming language in exactly the same way every time. These instructions often come in blocks of code created by someone else and are then assembled, more a building structure than something written.[3] If we accept that any symbolic system of expression, such as a natural language, shapes a way of thinking, then learning and using a computer language could have the same effect. Computer languages have evolved through several generations, from raw 'machine code' that spoke directly to the computer's microprocessor using strings of zeros and ones; to second and third generation computer languages each making the task of coding easier to learn and perform. Third generation languages are significant for having developed a set of standards that enabled programs to run on a greater variety of computers because the syntax of the language is 'in principle independent from the computer they run on' (*Economist* 2001). Beyond a certain point any discussion of computer languages in generational terms is misleading because it implies a steady development from one generation to the next, which is not the case (see Miller 2000). Although the trend has been towards creating programming languages that are easier to learn and use, there is

more to consider than simple skills acquisition. A coder chooses a language both for what it can do (some languages are designed to perform certain functions better than others), as well as how it allows one to think through the coding process (Sol 2001).

Certain developments in programming languages are influenced by cultural shifts in our understandings and uses of computation: for example, 'object oriented' programming (OOP) which began to evolve in the late 1980s. OOP favours the modelling of real-world entities in computer code and is designed to simplify and streamline programming. Previously, computing languages kept functions (code) and structures (data) formally disconnected. In OOP, software objects operate as sealed combinations of data and code, and the sending and receiving of 'messages' conducts communication between them (Montlick 2001). This represents a fundamental change in the field of computer science. In his essay, *Society of the Instance*, Shapiro writes that 'beyond a certain (imprecise) point in time, without realizing it, object-orientation definitively transgressed the limits of the discrete, binary, nominalist, symbolic logic which was the "original" foundation of computing' (Shapiro 2001). Others have made similar observations. Philosopher Brian Rotman, in an essay on the relationship between serialism and parallelism, also positions OOP as one of the signs of the shift to a post-von Neumann conception of the computer. He posits that the rise of object-oriented programming counterposes 'the linear flow of procedural programming languages by foregrounding the manipulation of . . . available objects' (Rotman 2000).

Shapiro's essay is a critique of OOP on the grounds that it is another symptom of the increasing tendency to provide 'substitutes for human experience', while Rotman induces from several developments a cultural trend towards a 'collectivized, distributed, pluralized' intelligence, of which OOP is one example. Both positions contribute to a growing area of critical discourse as regards the evolution of software as a condition and shaper of culture. Others go further: media theorist Friedrich Kittler proposes that the acquisition of an artificial language should be as important as learning a natural language:

> I can't imagine that students today would learn only to read and write using the twenty-six letters of the alphabet. They should at least know some arithmetic, the integral function, the sine function – everything about signs and functions. . . . Then they'll be able to say something about what 'culture' is at the moment.
> (Griffin and Herrmann 1996: 740)

Kittler's emphasis on the sort of schooling required to understand software may be debatable, but not the importance of implanting in more students/people a broader appreciation of what software is and its implications for culture. It is necessary to find ways to shift this study from its current science, engineering and biology base towards the arts and humanities. A. Michael Noll's 1967 computer symbolized an entirely different entity than the computer in 2000 – and the evolution of computer languages is one of the reasons why.

AS A TOOL

In terms of current cultural perception, software is probably more commonly conceived of as a tool, or part of a tool set that includes the computer, than as a language. In this discourse, the utility of a piece of software is embedded in the assumption that (like hardware) it has a purpose: a hammer drives a nail (amongst other things); a calculator performs calculations; iMovie (a software program that now comes bundled with every Apple computer) edits digital video.

In the industry, the top-down process of 'software development', begins after the 'purpose' of the software, what the client or customer wants it to do, is thoroughly understood and articulated. In this process the purpose tends to be defined by the recognition and specification of the overall 'problem'. This problem then goes through a process of further analysis to break it down into smaller pieces. Once this is accomplished, the next

step in the procedure is to devise the solutions for the problem(s) in the form of algorithms or instructions to the computer. Once the algorithms are defined, then they are implemented in some form of software language. There are other systems or software environments that encourage a more 'bottom-up' approach to programming. One of these would be Max, a high-level graphic programming language geared specifically to real-time computer music applications, where it's possible that the individual coder may employ a much more experimental approach in which 'immediacy, serendipity and play' are explored, coding in such a way that one choice leads to another with unexpected results (Winkler 1999: 73).

The *Software for Dancers* discussions didn't consistently employ either a top-down or bottom-up process, but borrowed from each. Because we had agreed to develop concepts for a screen-based software rehearsal tool using a range of different approaches, the discussions were initially dominated by top-down procedures that generated questions around the utility and purpose of the software. Alongside this, we worked through a process of selection and elimination of various possibilities. We established some additional parameters at the outset, such as that the software should run on a standard (off the shelf) portable computer with only mouse, keyboard and audio video input. The consensus was that we were investigating the possibilities for some sort of digital 'choreography sketchbook' and that we would rigorously explore what could be done with two-dimensional representations. This eliminated the creation of software that would model the real world (objects, space and human figures) in three dimensions.[4]

Paradoxically, during the *Software for Dancers* discussions, as soon as someone identified a potential use for a certain software application in the dance studio, it would be negated by arguments both pragmatic (e.g. the problem was solvable in a more efficient way) and artistic (e.g. fundamental formal contradictions could be named). Software as a tool for the making of dances also became the object around which a balance between the techno-phobe and the technophile in each of us was maintained. In another contradictory setting, both the choreographers and the coders agreed that they would like to 'abuse the software' and get 'beyond the tool', while at the same time it was apparent that no software was going to be coded until there was some consensus on the function it would serve.

Transcending and abusing the software as tool returns us to the consideration of software as a language – for to enact either requires access to and knowledge of the code – and to the cultural meanings of software. I have already pointed out that software as a language differs from natural languages due to its strict formalisms and precise syntax. Software as a tool, developed for a particular purpose, further expands this separation between artificial and natural languages. For example, two different programs may be coded to serve the same purpose. So, syntactically they will differ, but semantically they might be considered to be the same, a separability that does not occur in natural languages. Philosopher Peter Suber in his article *What is Software?* asserts that the intended use of software tends to shift its meaning entirely from the

uninterrupted arrays of bits to the function computed or the output and operation as interpreted by human beings. We look to the uses of the program to the programmer or user, not to the structure that permits it to serve those uses.

(Suber 1988)

Seen from this perspective, the labour of the software programmer is rendered invisible; with the code unseen the software becomes a tool, an implementation device for the end user alone, which is perhaps not the most compelling argument to support Kittler's view that everyone should learn an artificial language – if through its use the writer never actually speaks directly to the reader. However, it is one of the most compelling arguments for some form of software literacy that neither provides reward for the individual coder in the shape of a 'reader', nor requires everyone to

learn to program a calculator in Visual Basic. This other form of software literacy might emphasize access to a discourse that contextualizes these products and processes of culture in such a way that we better understand our complicated relationship with computers.

AS A MATERIAL
The use of computers in art can be traced to computer graphics experiments in the 1950s. In the 1960s and 1970s, before the arrival of the personal computer, the conception of the computer as a creative instrument or tool promoted the view that artists should be working together with scientists and engineers from within whose domain 'art-useful' computing discoveries were being made. During this period, two early computer researchers, A. Michael Noll and John Lansdown, both showed a particular commitment to the integration of choreography and computers. As already mentioned, Noll was working on a computer program that would provide a graphical notation aid to the choreographer, and Lansdown, an architect by training, was especially interested in the use of the computer to provide creative input through the algorithmic generation of choreographic scores (Lansdown 1978).

The creative use of the computer underwent radical transformation in the 1980s and 1990s, following major developments in technology partially marked by such headings as the emergence of the personal computer and graphical user interface, the internet and world wide web, etc. During this time, art making involving digital technologies gave rise to different branches of computer art: digital art, interactive media art, telematic and net art, etc. The particular conditions that supported the collaborative interests of artists and computer scientists in the 1960s changed through easier access to hardware and software. During the 1980s and 1990s, artists were developing the ability to customize or create their own software. Programming languages became easier to learn and use and image, video and sound manipulation software tools became widespread. However, despite artists gaining more control over the software code, the perception of software in the context of art making still remained largely a function of its purpose.

Recently a discussion of an 'art of which the material is software' has begun to take shape, marked by the newly established Software Art award category at the *transmediale.01* art festival in Berlin, Germany. The naming of 'categories' for emergent arts practice is always contentious, but whether this concept of software as a material is new is not the discussion I am interested in opening up here. The point is that since the 1960s, our perception of software, its surfaces and interiors, is reflected back to us from many sources, especially our screens, and the Software Art prize has taken note of this. To quote Florian Kramer and Ulrike Gabriel reporting on the Software Art award: 'Thirty years later, after personal computing became ubiquitous, cultural stereotypes of what software is have solidified' (Kramer and Gabriel 2001). Both of the awardees for the *transmediale.01* Software Art prize had created software that played with the conventionality of certain user interfaces through parody and disruption. This approach isn't new, and their software pieces sit alongside a history of artworks aiming at and subverting social stereotypes using various media materials, e.g. video, radio, etc. But the award does seem to mark the first recognition of software specifically as a material in this context.

Perhaps to consider software as a material reflects less on categories of practice than on the pressing need to recast software in ways that are 'at least relevant to our individual styles of thought'. These are the words of John Maeda, computer programmer and graphic artist whose recently published book on digital design, *Maeda @ Media*, demonstrates the creative and intellectual latitude that comes into play when software is treated as material. Maeda is the director of the Aesthetics and Computation Group at MIT's Media Lab and a leader in the field of integrating computation and visual design and in developing software as an art medium.[5] Maeda is committed to liberating the computer as a 'truly plastic medium' to counter the current tendency to produce 'two distinct types of thinkers: one who is technically adept and humanistically inept, the other who is humanistically adept and technically inept' (Maeda 2000: 439). For Maeda, for whom visual design is paramount, the fact that the underlying code is rendered invisible is offset by his belief that creating in code (as opposed to conventional design instruments) contributes to a fundamental reshaping of cognition. Perhaps the materiality software has to offer, then, is not in the classic sense of a material seeking to have form imposed upon it or in works seeking to expose software stereotypes, but the manner in which it forces the creative thinking process into an double externalization of itself: firstly the code, and secondly its execution.

A BRIEF SUMMARY

It would seem that the exponential advances in digital technology would have rendered possible some of the aims of those early explorations into the use of computers in dance. Thirty-plus years of cultural assimilation has also created a willingness on the part of the dance field to consider the input of computers anew. In fact, a handful of software concepts did emerge from the *Software for Dancers* project, and these are being proposed for further development.[6] However, equally interesting was that a certain line of questioning could transform the computer from a sleek object of desire into a manifestation of creative ideas, a process of invention open to critical consideration and insight that could reflect upon both computation and choreography.

Software provided one of the ways into the discussion, but my examination here of the question 'what is software?' reveals an inquiry in need of more exposition. Maeda's revival of the individual creative artist working with software is worth comparing to Brian Rotman's reading of the evolution of technology that emphasizes the emergence of cognitive and collective interconnectedness. Still, there emerged some general points worth reiterating: that the study within the arts and humanities of software as a condition and shaper of culture is already taking shape as can be seen in the various critical discourses emerging from the fields of philosophy, sociology and media theory, relating to computer languages and software; that software seems poised to resist being considered predominantly as a tool, and move towards some more dynamic balance between utility, programmability and linguistics.

In this regard, the materiality of software is a compelling concept worthy of further development as it can place an emphasis on giving ideas shape through code, on the process where thinking, coding and form intertwine.

NOTES

1 *Software for Dancers* was a London-based research project taking place from 24 September to 6 October 2001 which aimed to develop concepts for a software rehearsal tool(s) for dance makers and to use this opportunity to open up discussion about collaborative practices involving live performance and digital technologies. The project was organized by Writing Research Associates in collaboration with the Arts Council of England, Sadler's Wells Theatre and Random Dance Company with primary funding from the Dance Department, Arts Council of England. The primary research team comprised London-based choreographers (Siohban Davies, Shobana Jeyasingh, Wayne McGregor and Ashley Page) working in collaboration with digital artists/ coders from the UK and Germany (Guy Hilton, Jo Hyde, Bruno Martelli, Adrian Ward and Christian Ziegler) and two researchers/writers (Sanjoy Roy and Saul Albert). The project was facilitated by Scott deLahunta. A website with information about the project is at *http://huizen.dds.nl/~sdela/sfd* [accessed 20 December 2001].

2 This reference to 'natural' languages should not be confused with Natural Language Processing (NLP) which is the work being done in the field of computing science and engineering to 'design and build a computer system that will analyze, understand and generate languages that humans use naturally, so that eventually you can address your computer as though you were addressing another person'. This quote is from the NLP section of the Microsoft Research pages *http://research. microsoft.com/nlp/* [accessed 20 December 2001].

3 Although here I am steering away from using writing to describe programming, I would like to suggest that those interested look at the work of writer and translator John Cayley who has covered extensively the relationship between writing and programming in his own research and practice. Several essays on this topic are on his website at *http://www.shadoof.net/* [accessed 20 December 2001].

4 This was partly due to the complexities of coding such programs and partly to the fact that they already exist, e.g. Life Forms, a 3-D character animation software developed with significant input from choreographer Merce Cunningham.

5 For more information visit the Aesthetics and Computation Group website at *http://acg.media.mit.edu/* [accessed 20 December 2001].

6 There is currently some information on these proposals/ prototypes on the project website at *http://huizen.dds.nl/~sdela/sfd* [accessed 20 December 2001].

REFERENCES

Economist (2001) 'A Lingua Franca for the Internet', *The Economist Technology Quarterly*, 22 September: 17.

Griffin, Matthew and Herrmann, Susanne (1996) 'Technologies of Writing: Interview with Friedrich A. Kittler', *New Literary History* 27: 731–42.

Lansdown, John (1978) 'The Computer in Choreography', *Computer: IEEE Computer Society Journal* 11(8): 19–30.

Kramer, Florian and Gabriel, Ulrike (2001) 'Software Art and Writing (draft)', available from URL: *http://userpage.fu-berlin.de/~cantsin/homepage/writings/software_art/american_book_review//software_art_essay.html* [accessed 20 December 2001].

Maeda, John (2000), *MAEDA@MEDIA*, London: Thames and Hudson.

Miller, Simon (2000) 'An Overview of Computer Languages', available from URL: *http://www.simonmiller.org.uk/lang.shtml* [accessed 20 December 2001].

Montlick, Terry (2001) 'What is Object Oriented Software?', available from URL: *http://catalog.com/softinfo/objects.html* [accessed 20 December 2001].

Noll, A. Michael and Hutchinson, Ann (1967) 'Choreography and Computers' and 'A Reply', *Dance Magazine*: 43–6, 81–2.

Rotman, Brian (2000) 'Going Parallel', *SubStance* 91: 56–79.

Shapiro, Alan (2001) 'Society of the Instance' *Noema Online: Ideas 13*, available from URL: *http://www.noemalab.com/* [accessed 20 December 2001].

Sol, Selena (2001) 'Why PERL', available from URL: *http://www.wdvl.com/Authoring/Scripting/Tutorial/why_perl.html* [accessed 20 December 2001].

Suber, Peter (1988) 'What is Software?', *Journal of Speculative Philosophy* 2: 89–119, available at URL *http://www.earlham.edu/~peters/writing/software.htm* [accessed 20 December 2001].

Winkler, Todd (1999) *Composing Interactive Music: Techniques and Ideas Using Max*, Cambridge, MA and London: MIT Press.

Intervention 4
Jump Reading as Excess

Clare Moloney

Reading in a language that you don't understand is a little like eavesdropping on a private, whispered conversation. *Cat Licked the Garlic* by Anne Tardos is a book of poems written in English, French, German and Hungarian. English is my first language. I recognize the odd word of French and speak and understand a little bit of Polish. This doesn't really equip me to 'get' the text of *Cat Licked the Garlic* in a literal sense. What kind of reading is possible, given my lack of linguistic expertise? Do I have to be multilingual in order to appreciate a multilingual text?

In order to cope with the crisis of not knowing, I had 'jump read'. To be honest, the more I jumped the less shame I felt in not knowing the majority of the words in front of me. I joyfully jumped from one ledge of semi-understanding to another, and a reading assembled itself. Roland Barthes differentiates between writing that is linear, is based on signification and closes the signified, and writing that is experienced in relation to the sign – where signification is constantly deferred. The latter asks of the reader a practical collaboration (Barthes 1977: 155–64). If I am to categorize Anne Tardos's text – then it would also be as the latter, writing which encourages an active engagement or a jump read.

'Jump Read' is not an existing technical term. As I described my experience of reading this text to somebody else, they articulated my process as a 'Jump Read'. I have poached this term from them. Doesn't poaching happen when you are trespassing on somebody else's territory (see de Certeau 1984: 165–76)? In skipping through the text in this way, choosing and discarding as I please, does this make me nothing more than a poacher with little respect for another's property/language? I negotiated my way through the text by extracting words and sounds before adding my own associations. There were different criteria which prompted my selections. Initially, it was the English words that drew me in, and then certain French words which I misread as English (cerveaux became cervix). Finally, although I didn't know the meaning of any of the German or Hungarian words, I could pretend I did and make them make sense for me.

I realise that I am on tricky ground. In approaching the text this way, I could be accused of domesticating a foreign language and making unfamiliar territory safe and recognizable (see Venuti 1992: 5). Of course, some of these associations are personal in themselves, but some of them are generated by the very fact that the text I am attempting to read is unfamiliar. What might seem like a lack of engagement is really the opposite. I cannot simply translate one thing for another. If (as my eyes play tricks on me) words morph from one language into another, it is not through trying to find an equivalent English meaning. Rather the visual and aural impact of the words takes precedence over meaning. Which is why I would like to emphasize associations rather than translations. I am not translating from an original because I have no idea what the original might be. Instead of attempting to replace something, I am adding and articulating my own investment in the text.

I have described the process of attempting to

Performance Research 7(2), pp.103-105 © Taylor & Francis Ltd 2002

read languages that I don't understand as eaves-dropping. Marguerite Duras believed that one always read in the dark:

> Reading depends on the obscurity of the night. Even if one reads in broad daylight, outside darkness gathers around the book.
>
> (quoted in de Certeau 1984: 170)

To read is to travel privately and secretly. I travel some distance in order to come to terms with a foreign text and I am also prone to drift away from the text when this gets too difficult. I take pleasure in reading, but I never remain with the text utterly. It is in these gaps of 'not knowing' (what it is I am reading, where I have been and where I am going) and valuing not being in the know, that I am reminded of my own subjectivity and my own position, or lack of it, in relation to the text. In her essay entitled, 'Performing Writing at the Cross-roads of Languages', Caroline Bergvall describes the visible methodologies at work in *Cat Licked the Garlic*:

> … an approach to writing which demands of readers that they address their own locatedness in the reading of the work. It is then to the loosening up of boundaries between the private and the public, to the opening up of personal experience as irremediably playing on and played by wider social frames, that much of this work finds its moti-vation.
>
> (Bergvall 1999: 248 ff.)

Where or what is my own locatedness? As I jump read the text, I am aware of my lack of location. It is hard to situate myself or inhabit the text when there is so much I don't understand, when there is so much lost to me. However, I do not leave the text empty handed. My private jump reading collates and creates information. The preface to the book states that the four languages Tardos knows (French, German, Hungarian and English) coexist equally in her mind and not one of them could be considered her 'first'. Perhaps it could also be said that Tardos lacks a place because she is itinerant, forever travelling in and out of different languages. If all four languages are equally present,

perhaps she is at home in none and in her search for a 'proper' one (de Certeau 1984: 103) is expressing a desire to simultaneously place and displace herself? Incidentally, the preface to the book also states that she was born in Cannes, grew up in Paris, moved to Budapest where she learned Hungarian, and at 13 moved to Vietnam where she learned German but went to a French school. She has spent most of her adult life in New York.

This non-hierarchical approach to languages is also an elusive one. This elusiveness leads to con-tradictory speculations. There are certain words that seem explicit in their meaning – it is tempting to subscribe some kind of childhood trauma to the first lines, 'I was brainwashed as a child. There was no other way.' But it is impossible to keep with that 'interpretation' for very long, because I am forced to take another direction when I encounter words that are completely unfamiliar to me. It is as if Tardos wants to release the languages she knows from their chain of signification, to have them treated as music or sound that escapes classifi-cation (see Deleuze and Guattari 1986: 3–9). However, Tardos frequently orders the languages she uses alphabetically. For example, she lists colours *Blue*, *Bleu*, *Blau*, *Kek* (E/nglish, F/rench, G/erman, H/ungarian). It is worth noting that it is the English alphabet she uses, and the first and last words of *Cat Licked the Garlic* are clearly English.

I discover a variety of forms employed which are closely related to the story. There is a strong auto-biographical presence (yet there is so much personal history unobtainable due to the way she is using languages, placing them all in the same space, considering them all equal and, of course, my unmastery of three of the four languages used); traces of the fable (which are embodiments of moral qualities passed on); fairy-tales (common stories which take on a life of their own as we each have our own experience or memory of being told and of telling); superstitions (which are unofficial or excessive explanations). All of these forms of telling function like stories and that is why they are localized. Stories get passed around and instead of unifying, diversify (de Certeau 1984: 107). Everybody has their own version. Stories are made up. They are scraps, ruins, and that is what they remain, in order that they may be embellished later on. Moving through the text I remember stories I read, or should have read, when I was a child. I never read *Gulliver's Travels*, but I remember the story, or at least I made it up from the scraps that survive in my memory.

The domain of fairy-tales and fables is the dark faraway unnameable place which is probably not even on the map. Throughout the book, I glean references to trees, forests and wolves – everything that is wild, animalistic and non-civilized. Yet inserted into the body of the text, and sometimes accompanying it, are a series of unsettling images. Some of these images could be of Tardos herself and some of them are of urban locations. They are (given my grasp of the text) unsettling because I have no clue as to why she is choosing to use portraits (of herself?) and urban based buildings. Superficially their presence seems to make what is already quite opaque more dense. However, they start to open the text out and in some way make it if not more readable, then more approachable. A page of plain text becomes more intimidating than a page of text interrupted by an image. It is interesting that the images are photographs which have undergone some digital manipulation, making them quite spare. The locations are anonymous and the portraits nameless. I don't have access to them, but there is plenty of space for my projections, plenty of room for speculation. The photographic image is an appropriated image, that exposes our desire to capture the fleeting and the momentary, whilst illustrating the impossibility of such a thing (see Craig Owen in Harrison 1992: 1051–9). In other words it is as much about what is missing, about what is outside of the frame, as it is about what is inside of the frame.

Jump reading in languages that you don't fully understand is a little like eavesdropping on a private whispered conversation, one full of ellipses. Earlier, using Barthes, I categorized Anne Tardos's writing as writerly, open – and I believe it is. Yet I

am also reluctant to keep placing emphasis on writing as text which either encourages an active reading or doesn't. Reading is an activity regardless of what is read and who is reading. Perhaps we always 'jump read' or 'read in the dark'. When can reading ever be linear? In attempting to describe the experience of reading as something other than passive, Michel de Certeau quotes Guy Rosolatoon:

> I read and I daydream . . . My reading is thus a sort of impertinent absence. Is reading an exercise in ubiquity?
>
> (de Certeau 1984: 173)

Reading is being absent yet somewhere or everywhere else. The world does close in around the book. The gap between what is heard, what is not and what is read and what is not, isn't empty, it is full of excess, full of potential possibilities to be mined.

REFERENCES

Barthes, Roland (1977) 'From Work to Text', in *Image Music Text*, London: Fontana.

Bergvall, Caroline (1999) in Prem Proddar (ed.) *Translating Nations*, Denmark: Aarhus University Press.

De Certeau, Michel (1984) *The Practice of Everyday Life*, London: University of California Press.

Deleuze, Gilles and Guattari, Felix (1986) 'Content and Expression' in *Kafka: Toward a Minor Literature*, London: University of Minnesota Press.

Owen, Craig (1992) 'The Allegorical Impulse: Towards a Theory of Post Modernism' in C. Harrison and P. Wood (eds) *Art In Theory 1900–1990*, Oxford: Blackwell.

Tardos, Anne (1992) *Cat Licked the Garlic*, Vancouver, BC: Tsunami Editions.

Venuti, Lawrence (1992) *Rethinking Translation: Discourse, Subjectivity, Ideology*, London: Routledge.

A new collection of works by Anne Tardos, *The Dik-dik's Solitude: New and Selected Works*, will be published by Granary Books, New York, ISBN 1-887-123-61-X, in October 2002. It includes 'Ginkgo Knuckle Nubia', the first few strophes of which are included here on pp. 106–7 following.

```
Ginkgo Knuckle Nubia
      2000-2001
```

Ginkgo knuckle Nubia
Knitting needle ridicule
Segregation ginseng

Aardvark.

Knitting needle ridicule is a nasty tradition among certain peoples.

Brussel sprout brutality
Dictionary venison
European blunder clock

Beggary.

Brussel sprout brutality is another shameful tradition among people who despise that vegetable.

Desecrated rabbit groan
Cataleptic skeleton
Sloppy little bulldog puppy

Cerebellum.

The sloppy little bulldog puppy needs no explanation.

Penguin hubbub Jesus worship
Pyramidal mudpack
Daddy-long legs cemetery

Dodo.

Penguin hubbub Jesus worship is the actual hubbub heard among penguins who have congregated in order to worship Jesus.

A daddy-long legs cemetery is usually a matchbox of some sort.

Poodle viceroy salad dressing
Nympholeptic sitzbath
Mummified cadenza friction

Erotica.

Poodle viceroy salad dressing refers to a poodle who not only made it to viceroyhood, but who has since developed a taste for salad dressing.

Act as if you're dead already
Fancy-free and bending
Buzzard cackle fishhook cactus

Fandango.

Buzzard cackle fishhook cactus is, as one might suspect, the cackle emitted by a buzzard, who sees a fish-hook get tangled up among the cactus needles.

Mumbo-jumbo strongarm tactics
Resignation downfall
Disappointment rage and anger

Glockenspiel.

Try and express your anger on a glockenspiel.

Extract from 'Ginkgo Knuckle Nubia' - Anne Tardos, 2000-2001

Compositions #1–4
2001

The following scores contain fragments of words from the first few strophes of the poem 'Ginkgo Knuckle Nubia'. This is meant to be a performable sound poem. It's best if two or more performers engage in a dialogue, using the word fragments in any order and in any way they choose.

Freely moving from cell to cell, performers can choose to repeat one or more of the cells' contents or can skip cells entirely. For example, in #1, a performer faced with the cells 'bia', 'nu', and 'ga' might decide to say 'bia-nu-bia-ga-nu-nu-ga' or 'bia-bia-bia' or 'nuuuu-ga-ga-ga-biiiiiia' or any other permutation.

It's good to perform this with some determination. And the important thing is to always listen intently.

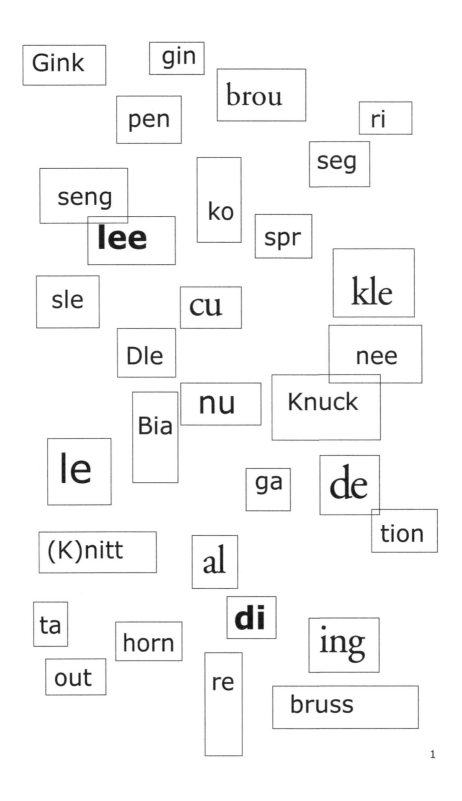

Gink
gin
brou
pen
ri
seg
seng
ko
lee
spr
sle
cu
kle
Dle
nee
Bia
nu
Knuck
le
ga
de
tion
(K)nitt
al
ta
di
ing
horn
out
re
bruss

1

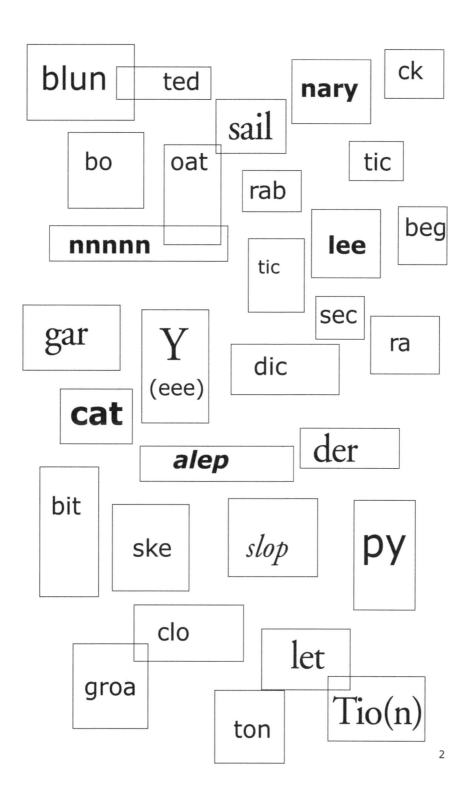

blun ted nary ck

sail

bo oat tic

rab

nnnnn lee beg

tic

gar Y (eee) sec ra

dic

cat

alep der

bit

ske slop py

clo let

groa ton Tio(n)

2

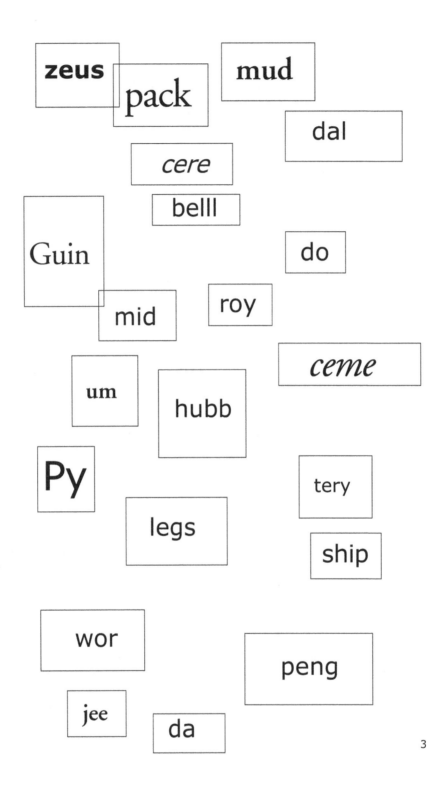

zeus

pack

mud

dal

cere

belll

Guin

do

mid

roy

ceme

um

hubb

Py

tery

legs

ship

wor

peng

jee

da

3

fric

nym

ero

sing

lep

tion

bath

sa

cy

as

um

dead

sitz

mum

mi

fan

read

if

act

cad

all

fied

eee

tic

your

lad

enza

dre

free

pho

4

Indonesian Whispers

The Journey of a Peter Turrini Text from Vienna to Melbourne

Bronwyn Tweddle

'I'm counting to 1,000 and then I'll kill myself.'

Date: 7 June 1997. Vienna, Burgtheater. The nameless journalist holds a gun to his head and counts . . . in German. This play is a birthday present. For the (then) artistic director of the Wiener Burgtheater . . . Claus Peymann.

Date: 19 October 2000. Melbourne, Victorian Arts Centre. The journalist is reincarnated. He opens his mouth and counts . . . in Indonesian. This performance is a birthday present, on a smaller scale. For the director of Mainteater . . . Sandra Long.

The former is the premiere of Peter Turrini's *Endlich Schluss* (*Finally an End*) performed by Gert Voss, a 56-year-old Berliner Ensemble and Burgtheater veteran. The latter is *Happy 1000/1000 Bahagia* performed by a much younger ensemble (both in company history and the average age of the collaborators), Mainteater, based simultaneously in Indonesia and Australia, the domiciles of its two main collaborators, Sandra Long and Wawan Sofwan.

Within 3 years a play has crossed boundaries of form, language, gender, and geography. The virtuoso solo piece is now a trio performance by a man and two women, the monolingual playtext is a trilingual performance piece in Indonesian, English and Auslan (Australian Sign Language), and the location (and cultural perspective) has shifted from Europe to the Antipodes. The jumping off point is the same Peter Turrini play, but the result is remarkably different.

How did this shift occur? An Indonesian actor (Sofwan) in Berlin falls in love with an Austrian

script and brings it back to Melbourne, where it is translated. A translation of content *and* form, not a translation which privileges one at the expense of the other. The themes of Turrini's play have been interrogated and embodied in the adaptive process. Turrini's words are recycled, transposed, transformed by Mainteater . . . just as the journalist at the centre of the original play recycles the *Los Angeles Times* as a protest against his obsolescence as a writer.

Turrini's *Endlich Schluss* (1997) is a play examining the power of words. The journalist cultivates his image as an 'independent thinker' through the articles he writes. He claims to make a living writing things he doesn't believe in, as 'political correctness' has denied us all a right to expression of our deepest, darkest feelings. His cutting comments are taken as jokes, because no-one wants to accept the reality behind them – telling 'Jew jokes' in the city of Anschluss? (Turrini 1997: 44) In print he defends the indefensible underdog regardless of cause; his classic example being the

Performance Research 7(2), pp.112–118 © Taylor & Francis Ltd 2002

pederast clergyman, who, he writes, is merely attending to the hygiene of his pubescent charges. But instead of him controlling the words, the journalist begins to feel that the words control him, defeat him, and he gives up writing.

He shuts himself away from the world in his flat, puts a gun to his temple and makes the decision to shoot himself once he's counted to 1,000. During the countdown he digresses with anecdotes from his life, through which the audience must piece his story together. For example, his editor implores him to begin writing again, because 'otherwise he will sink into nothingness' (Turrini 1997: 45)[1] – not realizing that nothingness is exactly what he seeks. The editor offers him a lifeline, a connection to the world via internet, which facilitates his most successful 'piss-take' – repeated plagiarism of the *LA Times*, which goes unnoticed, as the translation into German for the Viennese newspaper obscures this fact.

His suicide is a response to this tyranny of words, an attempt to counter words with the physical, the concrete. But words have become physical entities to him. He locks everything written that he owns in his front room – but feels the words are seeping and creeping out from under the door:

> The man: I tore all letters, notes, all calendars, all certificates, documents. Everything written and printed that I could find in my apartment. As the very last, I tore up my birth certificate. I threw the scraps of paper onto the mountain of rubbish in the front room, locked the door to it, shoved the key under the door and waited for the final silence, in me and around me. But the words and fragments of words, the sentences and phrases, came out of the room, out of the books and newspapers, out of the letters and documents, out of the articles and memoirs, crawled through under the door and into my head. All theories about suicide are false. It's about the introduction of silence. About the introduction of silence.
>
> (Turrini 1997: 46)

He wants to deny the reality of (his) words and posits 'reality' in the physical: 'Everything was unreal, only this pistol on my temple is real'

(Turrini 1997: 43). However this attempt at reduction to binary opposites is unsuccessful – he cannot deny the power words have over him. This conflict is theatrically illustrated when he turns off the light (Turrini 1997: 47) so that the (hearing) audience can only hear his voice, his *words* resonating, denied the sight of him physically before them. This becomes particularly potent in *Happy 1000* (2000), a partially signed performance – without visuals, some spectators can't hear.

A man supposedly denying the validity of words wallows in them. His chanted counting, which structures the entire playtext, is an attempt to escape into non-thinking but he can't escape the suggestive rhythm of numbers, the desperate need to keep track of where he's up to, the thought processes. The fact that the first pause in his counting, followed by a laugh, occurs at number 42 – a Douglas Adams reference? – shows that he cannot stop making literary connections! For how do we think except in language? How do we count? Verbalized numbers are still words. So the journalist attempts to synthesize the physical and mental: the stage directions ask for physical leaps to match his mental ones – and each leap in the counting brings him closer to death.

After a failure of a mind/body schism in *Endlich Schluss*, it seems then that in Mainteater's adaptation, *Happy 1000*, the addition of sign language is a logical step. Sign is a creation of physical words, a language alienated from the vocal, and exists in the 'silence' that the journalist desires. In *Happy 1000* the words are flung back at him not just metaphorically, as in the Turrini original, but physically. Mainteater's set is constructed out of newspapers, so written words physically surround the journalists onstage in addition to Auslan's physicalized words. However, this physicalization of words, which the journalist fears, is not just the prerogative of the other performers, but also of the audience. When the journalist loses track of his counting and asks himself 'Where was I?', a flurry of hands from some deaf spectators in the auditorium sign the numeral at him.

The translation process could be called the

'Chinese whispers' approach, after the children's game, where each version of the text moves further from the original. The three different languages of performance were not all translated from the source text and slotted together; rather the text is translated *through* all the languages, transforming it by taking on each new grammar and vocabulary and the form of expression this forces upon the text, then transmitting it to the next stage. The original German text is translated into Indonesian, the Indonesian is translated into English and the English is translated into Auslan in a process of gradual paring down. The text at each stage is reduced and refined and each stage has a different translator.[2] Thus the Indonesian text is the most detailed verbally, the English is simpler and the Auslan physically poetic.

This implies that the texts exist as separate linguistic units, but in performance the three languages are interwoven, and while each language is predominantly performed by one actor, all 'speak' some of the other two. To facilitate this weaving together, Sandra Long, the director of *Happy 1000* divided the text into several sections. She then guided the creation of verbal and physical texts for each section through improvising around key phrases, experimenting with both the hearing actors' spontaneous gestures and the more stylized Auslan movements. As Long explains:

> The actors developed their own gestures as well [as using Auslan] . . . . they had different ways of expressing the same ideas but they would also highlight the same things in different ways, in the script. At some very specific points they used the same Auslan gestures.[3]

The text is transformed from 'verbal' languages to a spatial one, and the gestures of Auslan are fed back into the English and Indonesian spoken text as gestures. These gestures not only underscore the emotions of the piece, but, as any segment of text is performed in all three languages, which may progress at different speeds simultaneously or individually, they also serve to pragmatically signal where in each section an individual actor is up to.

> Sandra Long: . . . the hearing audience, although they don't understand the other languages, still get the benefit of hearing the different sounds and the different variations and tones, but the deaf audience don't get that. They only have the visuals, so we thought that it was pretty important for them to also get an idea of where they were up to so they could also enjoy the hearing, the speaking performers as well.

Initially, this was to aid the deaf spectators but had benefits for the hearing audience as well. It gave the impression that spectators were not missing anything because they couldn't understand the language currently in use, but enabled them to pick up the existence of patterns and repetitions.

According to Long, one of the aims of the piece was that everyone gets the same story, regardless of which language/s he or she understands, but in reality this is impossible. While all aspects of the plot are equally distributed, the perspective varies widely. There is often a movement from the general to the specific (for the hearing audience for example, when Auslan comes first, and English or Indonesian later) and vice versa. An audience member creates their own reading of the performance by putting together the pieces of the jigsaw that they comprehend. This extends the structure of the original play in that the journalist's history is only gradually pieced together in between bouts of counting. Wawan Sofwan, who plays the journalist in *Happy 1000*, performs predominantly in Indonesian. This version is more detailed, but it is presented as a theme with variations. Because the journalist's two 'interpreters' are female (Tiffany Ball for English and Jodee Mundy for Auslan), their representations of his story are from different perspectives, with different emphases. Especially as a majority of the Melbourne audience could not understand Indonesian, they were 'hearing' the journalist's story not in his own words, but mediated by women. As he describes cheating on his wife and calling her from the bed of his lover, out of sheer boredom and self-dramatization, the fact that this is being signed/translated into English by female interpreters becomes significant.

In Turrini's original text the journalist is simply called 'the man', gender is his initial defining characteristic, but this is subverted by putting his words into women's mouths. These interpreters do not 'just' interpret into another language, but like the representations of virtue and vice in medieval drama, they present different choices for the protagonist. They rephrase, comment upon, and shift the meaning of what he is saying.

This production questions common assumptions about the role of interpreters, such as that they 'should not' comment upon what they are asked to interpret, they should 'just' translate. Whether we can ever 'just' translate is a superfluous query. Translation studies as a discipline is devoted to the problematics of this: the translator's role as 'pre-interpreter' of a text making choices such as privileging of form or content in a translation, especially of verse; when to use a cultural equivalent or literal translation of a phrase; how to translate dialects as opposed to standard languages, and so on. Many of these issues are raised in translating Turrini's text. How does one translate an Austrian cadence of German? A poetic text (though not in verse)? How does a play with resonances of a specifically Austrian, or at least Euro-centred, history apply to an Australian/Indonesian context?

And in this case they are not just 'translating' a text for performance either, but engaging in simultaneous live 'interpreting' – the version is not set in stone, and may respond to the audience (such as in the example given above when spectators signed the number Sofwan was up to). Turrini's theme of the power of words is reiterated in this multilingual version, but the theme has shifted slightly – the power of the interpreter to control the choice of those words is implicitly highlighted.

It was an interest in examining the roles of the interpreter which led Mainteater from their earlier bilingual experiments, such as *The Bottomless Well* (1997), to add Auslan to the mix. *The Bottomless Well* (Indonesian/English) was a dialogue piece, where each actor simply spoke their own language and the predominant audience perspective would be similar to hearing one end of a telephone conversation, where the general gist of the discussion is clear enough, but half the conversation is missing. However, when tackling a monologue such as *Endlich Schluss*, this technique is obsolete, so the use of interpreters was introduced. Mundy, the main Auslan interpreter in the piece, has a particular research interest in methods of making deaf theatre and hearing theatre accessible to each other, so the idea expanded from having one English interpreter to two interpreters working together, one for English and one for Auslan; and the combination of the two became a key focus:

> Sandra Long: We really wanted to find a way to work so that the interpretation becomes part of the piece and looking at the different sorts of roles that interpreters can have. In America, American Sign Language interpreters actually 'shadow' the actors onstage.

In Mainteater's piece, the interpreters are not simply 'shadowing' the action, making clear what is being said, but are an integral part of it. While the journalist is absorbed in a long section of desperate counting the women perform a piece of 'sign poetry' created from snippets of the original text, which had been cut in *Happy 1000*. One woman cries for the journalist and one laughs, then they blur the boundaries between the two, expressing the turmoil of conflicting emotions a man about to commit suicide experiences. The women are an external expression of his mental state. As Long explains:

> It's always the question there, what does an interpreter interpret? That's always the inner conflict of an interpreter. As Jodee, who is a professional interpreter, talked about [in the development process]. She interprets for things sometimes that she doesn't agree with. She's just got to go (Long waves her hands), and say it. And it's not 'that's what he says', she's just got to say it as is. So I guess one thing we're starting to find is that conflict, exploring that conflict with their roles.

This exploration became freer in the re-working of the piece. (The first showing of *Happy 1000/ 1000 Bahagia* was in 1998, and revised in 2000.) Long concedes that in the first version, they struggled with subconscious 'rules' about how an interpreter 'should' behave, and avoided pushing the boundaries of their role and exploring the inter- preters' 'emotional pitch'. By version two, the interpreters were much more playful, stepping into and out of roles as necessitated by the narrative. When the journalist speaks of wanting to 'dance with South Sea girls under palmtrees' (Turrini 1997: 43) the interpreters begin a Polynesian-style dance movement, which he then joins in.

However, having female interpreters taking on these roles adds an air of critique to them. Their 'South Sea' girls are no attempt at a realistic portrayal of a culture and illustrate the man's Euro- centric view. When the journalist dances with the gun to his head, they dance with him (are they encouraging or mocking his suicide?), and while at times seeming to cooperate, they also fight him and subvert his efforts. As they create the spaces in his imagination, they control the stage space and throw him frequently off balance, both physically and mentally.

Instead of translation obscuring its source, as with the *LA Times* incident in the play, this somewhat irreverent adaptation of Turrini's monologue highlights important features of the text. There can be no discussion of it being an 'accurate' translation of the original, but in some respects it is 'truer' on a different level, by physi- calizing the internal conflict, without losing the ambiguity within its main character. Dramaturgi- cally, this physicalization is especially apposite in representing a man who hides behind words all his life, and struggles to find a physical 'real'.

This search stresses the validity of using a physical, spatial language. In Sign Language there is no room for lack of expression. Communication is honest, direct, and involves the whole body and face. It is not 'politically correct' or euphemistic – in naming somebody, their most obvious features are seized upon for identification, and represented accurately in a way that may be deemed offensive to a hearing person, but is not in deaf culture. If you describe a fat person, you must accurately portray their size or your conversation partner will not recognize who you mean.[4] This directness is fitting for a play in which the journalist finds political cor- rectness stifling of expression, as no-one says what they mean any more. In deaf culture, the whole body is involved in the creation of a statement.

Which brings us to another important question – which deaf culture and which 'sign language'? The utilization of sign in Mainteater's performances is no simple matter. There is no one sign language. There are as many as there are spoken languages in the world, and regional differences within languages. American Sign Language differs from Auslan, for example, despite an assumption that both are 'based' on English – which they are not – and the choice of sign language has political impli- cations. The initial performances took place in Melbourne; however, Mainteater is also based in Indonesia, and tours there frequently, so they experiment with several sign language systems. Depending upon the venue, this performance may not just be trilingual, but contain several different sign languages in addition to the spoken languages, with attendant cultural and translation difficulties. For example, there is a standard Indonesian sign language . . .

> Sandra Long: . . . but it's based on the Indonesian language, so it's based on the Indonesian grammar, which is actually quite an unnatural grammar for deaf people. Auslan has a completely different grammar from English, it has a spatial grammar. There's also Signed English and deaf people were forced to use Signed English for a really long time. But it's actually really unnatural and really difficult for deaf people. In a way it's quite a political action to use Auslan as it's been oppressed for a really long time. Indonesian sign's very similar, in Indonesia. I don't even know how aware people are of that. And there are a lot of different dialects. Whenever there are deaf people a language naturally occurs, develops. There's also International Sign which Jodee is going to work with a bit.

This experimentation will continue, as Mainteater hopes to travel to a deaf arts festival in Washington in 2002, which will increase the use of International Sign and possibly other sign languages. Long is very interested to see the implications for the piece of having Mundy (the Auslan interpreter) being the performer who's understood by the majority in the audience, instead of the hearing actors, as it has been so far. As each of the languages is dominant at points in the action, the deaf spectators in Melbourne enjoyed the, for them, unusual experience of having the hearing have to wait for them, and for their interpreter, to find out what exactly was being said. The hearing audience had to piece together the meaning from the sign, with attendant pleasure in later discovering whether their guesses had been correct. The hearing audience was forced to see the performance in a deaf mode. While hearing audiences appreciate a vocal rhythm in the mix of languages, the deaf spectators find a 'body rhythm' in the mix. They can still perceive the different rhythms of the speaking languages as well. As Long explains, for both hearing and deaf spectators, the rhythms of each of the three languages are just so different that together a new rhythm is created from their combination. This new rhythm was so successful that it won Mainteater the Melbourne Fringe Theatre Award 2000 for Innovation of Form.

The use of English and Indonesian, and the role of the interpreters, also fluctuates according to whether the group is performing in Australia or Indonesia, illustrating the primacy of the potential audience in the process of multilingual text creation. The Melbourne season was largely prepared for a deaf or English-speaking/-hearing spectator because they get the full benefit of the form, the interplay of Sofwan as the journalist and the interpreting. For the Indonesian audiences Ball (the English interpreter) would speak more Indonesian and Sofwan more English to prevent the interpreters appearing to be redundant. This may, however, reduce the impact of the few moments when Sofwan already speaks English. In the first section of the performance he speaks Indonesian and then suddenly exclaims: 'Ah so many important things to do, mate!' Long states that the audience always respond positively to the element of

surprise. Whether or not this loss of impact detracts too much, dramaturgically the increased use of English can be justified by the fact that any internationally successful journalist in Asia now needs a command of English in the course of their profession.

Despite these new perspectives offering several illuminations of *Endlich Schluss*, perhaps the major minus in this trilingual treatment of it is the disappearance of resonances relating to the Viennese context. In the original monologue the journalist moves from tearing up written texts to burning a photograph, perhaps in reference to Heinrich Heine's famous quote against censorship that 'Wherever books will be burned, men also, in the end are burned'.[5] This is particularly pertinent in the city which welcomed their countryman Hitler's arrival on Heldenplatz in 1938 – a still sensitive issue (supported by the fact that Thomas Bernhard's 1988 play, *Heldenplatz*, which refers to this historical moment, was barred in his will from even being performed again in the city until 50 years after his death). This history, though not made explicit in *Endlich Schluss*, makes the journalist's action of smearing the ashes of the photograph onto his face (Turrini 1997: 47) even more potent than simply as an image of personal mourning or repentance. This action occurs after number 950 in preparation for his own death, which prompts the question of what he is repenting for – his own ambivalent feelings towards the Jewish race, or a greater societal failure, for which he, as a journalist-conscience, feels partially responsible.

Happy 1000 lacks an Australian or Indonesian equivalent to this imagery, despite both countries having histories of racial and religious persecution. The fact that the character is not named, nor even labelled by his occupation as I have referred to him throughout this article, but is listed at the beginning of Turrini's playtext only as 'the man', could suggest him as an archetype of humanity. If he represents (Viennese) society more specifically, then his final petty concerns about whether he is 'appropriately dressed' for suicide reflect (and ridicule) that society. How can this be made more applicable to the new context?

He has agonized over the choice of method of killing himself in order to make the right statement, so his discussion of costume in the staging of his death points again to the inherently performative nature of the act. This overlapping of fiction and reality questions where the edge of performance is. A suicide is a performance just as much as the actor before us, and the actor's exertion to win the audience mirrors that of a man who wants to gain attention by killing himself.

The character's attention-seeking in the original text is reinforced theatrically through the use of sign language in *Happy 1000*. The new play forces a clarification of the terminology used in describing theatre – I consciously must choose to speak of spectators rather than audience, and whether one 'speaks/hears' or 'enacts/sees' a language. The sign language provides an outward expression of the inner turmoil experienced by the protagonist in the source text, and theatricalizes his dilemma. The notion that words are the most powerful form of communication is therefore subverted through the adaptation.

The effect of the translation process is symbolized by the alteration of the title during the process of adaptation – a transformation from the

somewhat relieved *Finally An End* to *Happy 1000*, implies that for Mainteater's journalist at least there has been a positive resolution, if for no other reason than the reduction of outside 'noise' – the final stage direction in Turrini's play and of Mainteater's production is a gradual, desired 'introduction of silence'.

NOTES
1 References are to the German text, all translations are my own.
2 From German into Indonesian: Tatjana Luck; from Indonesian into English: Sandra Long; from English into Auslan: Jodee Mundy.
3 All quotes from Sandra Long come from an unpublished interview conducted by Bronwyn Tweddle in Melbourne on 28 October 2000.
4 Thanks to Charlie Grimsdale for his additional informal explanations of deaf culture.
5 *Dort, wo man Bücher/Verbrennt, verbrennt man auch am Ende/Menschen* (Heine 1823: line 245).

REFERENCES
Bernhard, Thomas (1988) *Heldenplatz*, Suhrkamp: Frankfurt am Main.
Grimsdale, Charlie (2001) 'Theatre for the Deaf', paper presented at Footprints/Tapuwae 'The Return of the Native' Conference, Christchurch, 16–18 November 2001.
Heine, Heinrich (1823) *Almansor*.
Turrini, Peter (1997) 'Endlich Schluss', *Theater Heute* 7: 42–7.

Tweddle

PRETEXT

VOLUME 5: BLOW UP YOUR TV

'Outspoken in championing cutting-edge creative writing' – The Big Issue

EXCLUSIVE to this issue: new writing from Nell Dunn, Kate Atkinson, Jeanette Winterson, DJ Taylor and Margaret Atwood, an interview with Kathy Acker, plus much more!

For subscriptions, purchase orders, back issues or further information please contact us at the address below.

Pretext 5 is available from all good bookshops priced £7.99.

ISBN: 1-902913-13-2

Pen&inc
English & American Studies
University of East Anglia
Norwich, Norfolk, UK, NR4 7TJ
info@penandinc.co.uk
+44(0)1603592783

UEA NORWICH

Funded by THE ARTS COUNCIL OF ENGLAND

www.penandinc.co.uk

118

BlaBla The Ruins of Europe in Back of Me

translating Heiner Müller's *Hamletmachine* into different performative spaces

Scott Magelssen and John Troyer with Tom Lynch, University of Minnesota

The sections are to be read simultaneously.

I was Hamlet. I stood at the shore
and talked with the surf. BlaBla BlaBla
BlaBla BlaBla BlaBla BlaBla BlaBla
BlaBla BlaBla BlaBla BlaBla BlaBla
BlaBla BlaBla BlaBla BlaBla BlaBla
BlaBla BlaBla BlaBla BlaBla BlaBla
BlaBla BlaBla BlaBla BlaBla BlaBla
BlaBla BlaBla BlaBla BlaBla BlaBla
BlaBla BlaBla BlaBla BlaBla BlaBla
BlaBla BlaBla BlaBla BlaBla BlaBla
BlaBla BlaBla BlaBla BlaBla BlaBla
BlaBla BlaBla BlaBla BlaBla BlaBla
BlaBla BlaBla BlaBla BlaBla BlaBla
BlaBla BlaBla BlaBla BlaBla BlaBla
BlaBla BlaBla BlaBla BlaBla BlaBla
BlaBla BlaBla BlaBla BlaBla BlaBla
BlaBla BlaBla BlaBla BlaBla BlaBla
BlaBla BlaBla BlaBla BlaBla BlaBla
BlaBla BlaBla BlaBla BlaBla BlaBla
BlaBla BlaBla BlaBla BlaBla BlaBla
BlaBla BlaBla BlaBla BlaBla BlaBla
BlaBla BlaBla BlaBla BlaBla BlaBla
BlaBla BlaBla BlaBla BlaBla BlaBla
BlaBla BlaBla BlaBla BlaBla BlaBla
BlaBla BlaBla BlaBla BlaBla BlaBla
BlaBla BlaBla BlaBla BlaBla BlaBla
BlaBla BlaBla BlaBla BlaBla BlaBla
BlaBla BlaBla BlaBla BlaBla BlaBla
BlaBla BlaBla BlaBla BlaBla BlaBla
BlaBla BlaBla BlaBla BlaBla BlaBla
BlaBla BlaBla BlaBla BlaBla BlaBla
BlaBla BlaBla BlaBla BlaBla BlaBla
BlaBla BlaBla BlaBla BlaBla BlaBla
BlaBla BlaBla BlaBla BlaBla BlaBla
BlaBla BlaBla BlaBla BlaBla BlaBla
BlaBla BlaBla BlaBla BlaBla BlaBla
BlaBla BlaBla BlaBla BlaBla BlaBla
BlaBla BlaBla BlaBla BlaBla BlaBla
'I'm not Hamlet. I don't take part any more.
My words have nothing to tell me anymore.'[1]
The line also ran more deeply into the
question of allegiance and how far any
individual would go in accepting subjugation
to various established orders. Instead of

Section 1 **Family scrapbook**

Michel de Certeau, in *The Practice of Everyday Life*, distinguishes between place and space. A place is a system of order. It is a socially constructed, often rigid site of regulatory norms that control the practices taking place in it, and *implies* an indication of stability, regardless of the power to enforce it. A space, however, is a site of action, dynamic and flexible. The Praxis Group's multivenue production of Heiner Müller's *Hamletmachine* in July-August, 2000, made visible the tensions that exist between the suggestion of space and socially constructed place. The group deliberately performed in several different venues that defied traditional theatre 'places', that is, where the regulatory norms of theatre were enforced in implicit and explicit ways. Indeed, the fundamental transgression of performance norms was the very mobility of the company–that defied the idea of performing the run in a single space, and manoeuvred, instead, through the urban landscape, intersecting with specific local events, and producing or absorbing new meanings as each performance resonated differently with Müller's text.

In the face of what the Praxis Group determined to be a local theatrical scene limited to either mainstream regional theatre or perpetually recycled performance art, they looked to Müller's text for ways to escape this pervasive mediocrity. During the rehearsal of the project, the group spent much time discussing the disavowal of the actor playing Hamlet in Section 4,

BlaBla BlaBla BlaBla BlaBla BlaBla
BlaBla BlaBla BlaBla BlaBla BlaBla
BlaBla BlaBla BlaBla BlaBla BlaBla
BlaBla BlaBla BlaBla BlaBla BlaBla

Performance Research 7(2), pp.119-128 © Taylor & Francis Ltd 2002

focusing on the first part of these lines,

the project looked at the suggestion of

In that line, an understanding of what the project's relationship to the local social milieu might be was established. The project would not take part in producing words that had nothing to tell, in that Müller's text could become yet another mediocre experimental theatre performance that followed a pre-established vocabulary of how a contemporary avant-garde project should appear. Those words most definitely had nothing to tell the project anymore.

BlaBla BlaBla BlaBla BlaBla BlaBla
BlaBla BlaBla BlaBla BlaBla BlaBla
BlaBla BlaBla BlaBla BlaBla BlaBla
BlaBla BlaBla BlaBla BlaBla BlaBla
BlaBla BlaBla BlaBla BlaBla BlaBla
BlaBla BlaBla BlaBla BlaBla BlaBla
BlaBla BlaBla BlaBla BlaBla BlaBla
BlaBla BlaBla BlaBla BlaBla BlaBla
'My drama, if it still would happen, would happen in the time of the uprising. The uprising starts with a stroll. Against the traffic rules, during the working hours. The street belongs to the pedestrians.'
My drama didn't happen. My drama

BlaBla BlaBla BlaBla BlaBla BlaBla
'I'm not Hamlet,'
Bla Bla Bla Bla
'I don't take part anymore.'
BlaBla BlaBla BlaBla BlaBla BlaBla
BlaBla BlaBla BlaBla BlaBla BlaBla
BlaBla BlaBla BlaBla BlaBla BlaBla
BlaBla BlaBla BlaBla BlaBla BlaBla
BlaBla BlaBla BlaBla BlaBla BlaBla
BlaBla BlaBla BlaBla BlaBla BlaBla
BlaBla BlaBla BlaBla BlaBla BlaBla
BlaBla BlaBla BlaBla BlaBla BlaBla
BlaBla BlaBla BlaBla BlaBla BlaBla
BlaBla BlaBla BlaBla BlaBla BlaBla
BlaBla BlaBla BlaBla BlaBla BlaBla
My words have nothing to tell me anymore. By choosing to open up the text to a multiplicity of venues and to engage with local and national events, *Hamletmachine* became a production that produced new meaning with each performance, dramatically shifting depending on the environment. A case in point: in section four, the-actor-playing-Hamlet speaks the lines:

These lines became charged with several layers of meaning when, for instance, they were spoken by Praxis Group member Matthew Glover in the face of police officers dispatched for riot control in downtown Minneapolis during a controversial International genetics conference (a point developed later in the paper).

The Praxis Group's production of *Hamletmachine* in summer 2000, in its use of multiple venues, surveillance technology, and shattering of the traditional, proscenium-based spectator-spectacle relationship became what Gilles Deleuze would call a 'rhizomatic space'. Distinguished from the tree-tap root system, where the relationship between the object and its reciprocal representation mirror each other, as seen in representational art (such as putting the illusion of reality upon the stage), a rhizome has no such symmetry. Extending its bulk laterally and diagonally, sending out various shoots in all directions,

didn't happen. **My drama didn't happen. My drama didn't happen. My drama didn't happen. My drama didn't happen. My drama didn't happen. My drama didn't happen. My drama didn't happen. My drama didn't happen. My drama didn't happen. My drama didn't happen.**
The Woman with her arteries cut open.
The woman dangling from the rope. The
one the river didn't keep. I am Ophelia. I am
Ophelia. I am **Ophelia.** I am **Ophelia.** I am
Ophelia. I am **Ophelia.** I am **Ophelia.** I am
Ophelia. I am **Ophelia.** I am Ophelia. I **am**
Ophelia. I am **Ophelia.** I am Ophelia. I **am**
Ophelia. I am Ophelia. I am **Ophelia.** I am
Ophelia. I am Ophelia. I am **Ophelia.** I am
Ophelia. I am Ophelia. I am **Ophelia.** I am
Ophelia. I am **Ophelia.** I am Ophelia. I am
Ophelia. I am **Ophelia.** I am Ophelia. I am
Ophelia. I am Ophelia. I am **Ophelia.** I am
Ophelia. I am **Ophelia.** I am **Ophelia.** I am
Ophelia. I am Ophelia. I am **Ophelia.** I am
Ophelia. I am **Ophelia.** I am Ophelia. I am
Ophelia. I am **Ophelia.** I am **Ophelia.** I am
Ophelia. I am Ophelia. I am **Ophelia.** I am
Ophelia. I am **Ophelia.** I am **Ophelia.** I am
Ophelia. I am **Ophelia.** I am **Ophelia.** I am
Ophelia. I am **Ophelia.** I am Ophelia. I am
Ophelia. I am Ophelia. I am **Ophelia.** I am
Ophelia. I am Ophelia. I am **Ophelia.** I am
Ophelia. I am Ophelia. I am **Ophelia.** I am
Ophelia. I am **Ophelia.** I am Ophelia. I am
Ophelia. I am **Ophelia.** I am Ophelia. I am
Ophelia. I am **Ophelia.** I am Ophelia. I am
Ophelia. I am **Ophelia.** I am Ophelia. I am
Ophelia. I am **Ophelia.** I am **Ophelia.** I am
Ophelia. I am **Ophelia.** I am **Ophelia.** I am
Ophelia. I am Ophelia. I am Ophelia. I **am**
Ophelia. I am **Ophelia.** I am Ophelia. I am
Ophelia. I am Ophelia. I am **Ophelia.** I am
Ophelia. I am **Ophelia.** I am **Ophelia.** I am
Ophelia. I am **Ophelia.** I am Ophelia. I am
Ophelia. I am Ophelia. I am Ophelia. I **am**
Ophelia. I am **Ophelia.** I am Ophelia. I am
Ophelia. I am Ophelia. I am **Ophelia.** I am
Ophelia. I am Ophelia. I am **Ophelia.** I am
Ophelia. I am Ophelia. I am **Ophelia.** I am
Ophelia. I am Ophelia. I am **Ophelia.** I am
Ophelia. I am Ophelia. I am **Ophelia.** I am
Ophelia. I am **Ophelia.** I am **Ophelia.** I am

and lacking a center or hub, the rhizome is a model which may explore the relationships between art and life.[2] The Praxis Group sought to explore the rhizomatic quality of the text in performance, specifically in the multiplicity of venues, the decentered quality of the performance, and the intriguing character of Ophelia.

Section 2 **The Europe of Women**

Within the text of *Hamletmachine*, Müller defies the traditional plot development of conflict, rising action, climax, and denouement. The narrative functions, instead, as five distinct and autonomous sections, working from Shakespeare's tragedy, but not directly analogous to the events therein. The structure of *Hamletmachine*, then, becomes rhizomatic, lacking a center or tree/taproot linear development. Instead, various lines of flight connect passages within text like so many worm holes, or internet hypertexts, each point linking to several others throughout the section.

Of the several textual elements that function in a rhizomatic manner, the most fascinating for the project was Müller's Ophelia. In the introduction to his translation of the text, Carl Weber cites Müller as saying 'it was my intention to make Ophelia a character of equal importance. That could become an interesting aspect in the US.'[3] With that suggestion in mind, the Praxis Group production of *Hamletmachine* experimented with the idea of an *Opheliamachine* that opened the text to a contemporary, American historical situation.

One way the project approached the American Ophelia was through questions of technical mediation and projecting images of various kinds onto the performers. The production used a wide array of video sources that had in some way become re-defined by the specificity of their origination. A series of videos came from the University of Minnesota Clinic in Human Sexuality that specializes in transgender counseling and services. Many of the videos taken from that source are catalogued as 'Women's Health Videos' and articulate safe and healthy sexual practices. Suzanne Scholten, the video artist who worked on the project,

Ophelia. I am Ophelia. I am Ophelia. I am
Ophelia. I am Ophelia. I am Ophelia. I am
Ophelia. I am Ophelia. I am Ophelia. I am
Ophelia. I am Ophelia. I am Ophelia. I am
Ophelia. I am Ophelia. I am Ophelia. I am
Ophelia. I am Ophelia. I am Ophelia. I am
Ophelia. I am Ophelia. I am Ophelia. I am
Ophelia. I am Ophelia. I am Ophelia. I am
Ophelia. I am Ophelia. I am Ophelia. I am
Ophelia. I am Ophelia. I am Ophelia. I am
Ophelia. I am Ophelia. I am Ophelia. I am
Ophelia. I am Ophelia. I am Ophelia. I am
Ophelia. I am Ophelia. I am Ophelia. I am
Ophelia. I am Ophelia. I am Ophelia. I am
Ophelia. I am Ophelia. I am Ophelia. I am
Ophelia. I am Ophelia. I am Ophelia. I am
Ophelia. I am Ophelia. I am Ophelia. I am
Ophelia. I am Ophelia. I am Ophelia. I am
Ophelia. I am Ophelia. I am Ophelia. I am
Ophelia. I am Ophelia. I am Ophelia. I am
Ophelia. I am Ophelia. I am Ophelia. I am
Ophelia. I am Ophelia. I am Ophelia. I am
Ophelia. I am Ophelia. I am Ophelia. I am
Ophelia. I am Ophelia. I am Ophelia. I am
Ophelia. I am Ophelia. I am Ophelia. I am
Ophelia. I am Ophelia. I am Ophelia. I am
Ophelia. I am Ophelia. I am
Ophelia. I am Ophelia. I am Ophelia. I am
Ophelia. I am Ophelia. I am Ophelia. I am
Ophelia. I am Ophelia. I am Ophelia. I am
Ophelia. I am Ophelia. I am
Ophelia. I am Ophelia. I am
Ophelia. I am Ophelia. I am Ophelia. I am
Ophelia. I am Ophelia. I am Ophelia. I am
Ophelia. I am Ophelia. I am Ophelia. I am
Ophelia. I am Ophelia. I am Ophelia. I am
Ophelia. I am Ophelia. I am Ophelia. I am
Ophelia. I am Ophelia. I am Ophelia. I am
Ophelia. I am Ophelia. I am Ophelia. I am
Ophelia. I am Ophelia. I am Ophelia. I am
Ophelia. I am Ophelia. I am Ophelia. I am
Ophelia. I am Ophelia. I am Ophelia. I am
Ophelia. I am Ophelia. I am Ophelia. I am
Ophelia. I am Ophelia. I am Ophelia. I am
Ophelia. I am Ophelia. I am Ophelia. I am
Ophelia. I am Ophelia. I am Ophelia. I am
Ophelia. I am Ophelia. I am Ophelia. I am
Ophelia. I am Ophelia. I am Ophelia. I am

hand-selected videos that resembled, for many people, pornography. By showing women's sexual health videos, a process of titillation often blocked consideration of the projected bodies as anything other than porn. The decision to proceed in this direction was not naive. The Praxis Group wanted to explore the question of how, in America, Ophelia has become a machine – in this case, a product of the desiring machines programmed into the consciousness. While the provocative images were projected, the production's Ophelias delivered the text: one woman in a wheelchair, another woman standing behind her. The machine of sexual titillation then fought a battle against the Ophelia monologue.

Not surprisingly, audiences either loved or hated this section. One way the text became a powerful tool against the overriding video-image saturation was by establishing three different methods of delivering the monologue. The first way was by starting the text with the last line working towards the first line of the monologue:

Once the first line was reached, it was stated for a period of roughly four to five minutes.

The 'I am Ophelia' line became itself a machine-like gesture towards repetition and production. When the four to five minutes had elapsed, the actress saying Ophelia's lines then went back through the monologue to the end. By staging the text in this manner, the audience was presented with the history of Ophelia before it was named, the naming of the woman described in the text repeated as only a name and then the return to the history of oppression.

The space of the text as well as the history became a multi-entry point, rhizomatic threshold that for the purposes of this production became a way of stating that the *Opheliamachine* has, can, and will appear at any moment in traditional historiographical modes. The *Opheliamachine* becomes a historiographical tool that allows an entry and exit in multiple directions, velocities,

Ophelia. I am Ophelia. I am Ophelia. **I am**
Ophelia. I am Ophelia. I am Ophelia. I am
Ophelia. **I am Ophelia. I am Ophelia.** I am
Ophelia. I am Ophelia. I am Ophelia. **I am**
Ophelia. I am Ophelia. I am Ophelia. **I am**
Ophelia. I am Ophelia. I am Ophelia. I am
Ophelia. **I am Ophelia. I am Ophelia.** I am
Ophelia. I am Ophelia. **I am Ophelia. I am**
Ophelia. I am Ophelia. I am Ophelia. **I am**
Ophelia. I am Ophelia. I am Ophelia. I am
Ophelia. I am Ophelia. I am Ophelia. I am
Ophelia. I am Ophelia. **I am Ophelia.** I am
Ophelia. I am Ophelia. **I am Ophelia. I am**
Ophelia. I am Ophelia. I am Ophelia. I am
Ophelia. **I am Ophelia. I am Ophelia.** I am
Ophelia. I am Ophelia. **I am Ophelia.** I am
Ophelia. I am Ophelia. I am Ophelia. **I am**
Ophelia. I am Ophelia. I am Ophelia. **I am**
Ophelia. I am Ophelia. I am Ophelia.
When she walks through your bedrooms
carrying butcher knives you'll know the
truth.[4] Müller took the line from Manson
Family member Squeaky Fromme and
commented, 'I believe the sentence contains
a truth that wasn't necessarily known to that
girl.'[5] That truth, as Müller uses it in Section
5, suggests the emergence of a rather glum,
post-apocalyptic setting in which

ravage the social reality. The argument,
however, is not that the emergence of these
circumstances is inevitable (or not already
present) but a product of social conditions in
which the populace is manipulated.

The presence of Squeaky Fromme, as it
comes closest to representing European
terrorism in the US for Müller, attaches a
sense of contemporary urgency when
connected to the characters of Electra and
Ophelia used in the text. All three women
form a triangulation that focuses on a
destruction of the authority, real and
symbolic. As each of the these women is
produced by the social conditions in which
they live, the affinity for Müller lies in their
potential overthrowing of all existing
conditions.[7] Hyperbole, however, should not
pervade the read and use of these characters
so that a new, international Revolutionary
fervor is ascribed the global populace of
women. Müller critiques the conditions in
which the 'Europe of Women' stands through
three distinct female characters. Section 5
begins with the character of Ophelia, now
physically in a machine (wheelchair),
declaring herself to be Electra and speaking
the words of Fromme. While the
Opheliamachine character speaks

and times. The audiences were confronted
then by the shifting text of repeated
statements that often contradicted the
appearance of women's sexual health
videos. The question of a crisis between the
text and the video montage most certainly
appeared before many eyes in the audience.
The resolution of how that crisis evolved
really depended on how agile the viewer was
in disconnecting prior meanings associated
with sex, desire, and history. The separation
or lack thereof made the questions
presented to the audience, a deeper
examination of how it could mean to say,

The most provocative location to begin
reading the *Opheliamachine* code of the text
is in Section 5 with the last line of the text,

I am Ophelia. I am Ophelia. I am Ophelia.
I am Ophelia. I am Ophelia. I am Ophelia.
I am Ophelia. I am Ophelia. I am Ophelia.
I am Ophelia. I am Ophelia. I am Ophelia.
I am Ophelia. I am Ophelia. I am Ophelia.
I am Ophelia. I am Ophelia. I am Ophelia.
I am Ophelia. I am Ophelia. I am Ophelia.
'hate and contempt, rebellion and death'[6]
I am Ophelia. I am Ophelia. I am Ophelia.
I am Ophelia. I am Ophelia. I am Ophelia.
I am Ophelia. I am Ophelia. I am Ophelia.
I am Ophelia. I am Ophelia. I am Ophelia.
I am Ophelia. I am Ophelia. I am Ophelia.
I am Ophelia. I am Ophelia. I am Ophelia.
I am Ophelia. I am Ophelia. I am Ophelia.
I am Ophelia. I am Ophelia. I am Ophelia.
I am Ophelia. I am Ophelia. I am Ophelia.
I am Ophelia. I am Ophelia. I am Ophelia.
I am Ophelia. I am Ophelia. I am Ophelia.
I am Ophelia. I am Ophelia. I am Ophelia.
I am Ophelia. I am Ophelia. I am Ophelia.
I am Ophelia. I am Ophelia. I am Ophelia.
I am Ophelia. I am Ophelia. I am Ophelia.
I am Ophelia. I am Ophelia. I am Ophelia.
I am Ophelia. I am Ophelia. I am Ophelia.
I am Ophelia. I am Ophelia. I am Ophelia.
I am Ophelia. I am Ophelia. I am Ophelia.
I am Ophelia. I am Ophelia. I am Ophelia.
I am Ophelia. I am Ophelia. I am Ophelia.
I am Ophelia. I am Ophelia. I am Ophelia.
I am Ophelia. I am Ophelia. I am Ophelia.
I am Ophelia. I am Ophelia. I am Ophelia.
I am Ophelia. I am Ophelia. I am Ophelia.
I am Ophelia. I am Ophelia. I am Ophelia.
I am Ophelia. I am Ophelia. I am Ophelia.
I am Ophelia. I am Ophelia. I am Ophelia.
I am Ophelia. I am Ophelia. I am Ophelia.
I am Ophelia. I am Ophelia. I am Ophelia.

simultaneously for all three women, she's wrapped in gauze and left on the stage by men in white smocks. With an understanding of Müller's belief in making Ophelia the main character for Hamletmachine, we suggest that in this moment of gauze wrapped motionlessness, the ontology of a cyborg and HumanMachine politics is silenced – but not forever.

The *Opheliamachine* quite literally becomes a multiplicity of relational points, and as suggested in an earlier section of the essay, a rhizomatic space. The multiplicity of relational points, with the Opheliamachine as a conduit, opened the entire project to a series of entrances and exits that emerged through sound, lights, video, live performance, and machine. These free-floating rhizomatic pathways emerged within the text as well, with the location of certain 'Other Ophelias in Western history,' as Müller might call them.

I am Ophelia. I am Ophelia. I am Ophelia.
I am Ophelia. I am Ophelia. I am Ophelia.
I am Ophelia. I am Ophelia. I am Ophelia.
I am Ophelia. I am Ophelia. I am Ophelia.
I am Ophelia. I am Ophelia. I am Ophelia.
I am Ophelia. I am Ophelia. I am Ophelia.
I am Ophelia. I am Ophelia. I am Ophelia.
I am Ophelia. I am Ophelia. I am Ophelia.
I am Ophelia. I am Ophelia. I am Ophelia.
I am Ophelia. I am Ophelia. I am Ophelia.
I am Ophelia. I am Ophelia. I am Ophelia.
I am Ophelia. I am Ophelia. I am Ophelia.
I am Ophelia. I am Ophelia. I am Ophelia.
I am Ophelia. I am Ophelia. I am Ophelia.
I am Ophelia. I am Ophelia. I am Ophelia.
I am Ophelia. I am Ophelia. I am Ophelia.
I am Ophelia. I am Ophelia. I am Ophelia.
I am Ophelia. I am Ophelia. I am Ophelia.
I am Ophelia. I am Ophelia. I am Ophelia.
I am Ophelia. I am Ophelia. I am Ophelia.
I am Ophelia. I am Ophelia. I am Ophelia.
I am Ophelia. I am Ophelia. I am Ophelia.

Section 3 **Scherzo**

In performance, the Praxis Group took the rhizomatic quality of the text and complicated it. Their manipulation of audience expectations of conventional theatre venue allowed for individuals to experience the text of Müller's play in a different manner than in a traditional theatre space. The locations in which Praxis Group performed were sites of contestation, under various states of surveillance, each with a visceral history of the breaking of normalizing behavior.

For instance, one performance took place on a barricaded stretch of Nicollet Mall, a pedestrian mall in Downtown Minneapolis during a conference of the International Society for Animal Genetics (ISAG) the weekend of July 21-23, 2000. The area was a veritable site of martial law, with an enormous police presence, implying, as de Certeau would say, 'an appearance of stability.'[8] Those who happened upon this performance brought with them the compiled social and popular history of animal rights activism, recent rioting in Seattle, and the last week of reportage on the Minneapolis police's right to stop and search random pedestrians to determine if they had a legal reason to be in the vicinity.

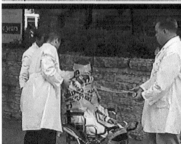

Section 4 **Pest in Buda/the Battle for Greenland**

It was during the genetics conference that the Hamletmachine project took a cue from Müller's Section 4: *Pest in Buda/the Battle for Greenland* with the lines,

'My drama, if it still would happen, would happen in the time of the uprising. The uprising starts with a stroll. Against the traffic rules, during the working hours. The street belongs to the pedestrians.[9] In the downtown area of Minneapolis that the conference was held, Minneapolis police were positioned (literally hundreds at a time) along the borders of concrete barriers with chain link fence that had been put in place. US Constitutional questions aside, what was more disturbing were the majority of people who simply allowed the creation of a Minneapolis Police state without questioning it. In order to test the limits of legal reasons for being on a street, the *Hamletmachine* project entered the blockaded section of downtown to perform section four of the text. Once downtown, the performers, dressed in white lab coats, walked through a an area set up for the summer's annual Sommerfest, a simulacrum of what people in Vienna apparently do while listening to classical music in beer gardens. In the urban map of downtown Minneapolis, the performers walked one-block through the Sommerfest to the policed area that blocked off the street to the genetics conference. A certain instability was already apparent even before the performers began saying,

Policemen, if in the way, are swept to the curb.[10]

Because of the group's slippery performance of their own identity, bystanders and press were quick to ascribe the performers into the category of animal rights activists: the local Channel Nine news reported on the event that evening (Friday, July 21) as a disappointing bit of theatricalism on the part of animal rights activists seeking awareness for their cause.

While the police presence in the space was a strategic maneuver to affirm and maintain the rules and regulations of the city, Praxis's presence was tactical: the *Hamletmachine* performance did not reciprocate nor contradict the police strategy, thereby giving them something to reinforce, and thus did not fulfill their expectations of how suspicious groups should act. While the Praxis Group's performance retained the notion of the contested space, it was the spectators who often made the site into a *place*, by categorizing the performers and practices into a normative, predictable, and thus consumable, event. Ultimately, the performance would not have been 'successful,' as participants understood this to mean, without the presence of the police. The success had less to do with the staging of the text than the way Praxis Group's presence and the use of the text pointed to and signified the police presence and enforced order. The notion of a 'legal reason' to be in the space was then conflated with additional layers of legitimacy of presence: the police did not fit into this environment, but instead reconstructed the environment to fit their presence. If the Praxis Group had not been performers of *Hamletmachine*, but rather animal rights activists, their presence would have been *more* legitimate in the necessitated binaries of legal/illegal, established by the police, the press, and bystanders.

Perhaps the most notable aspect of the Praxis Group's multi-venue production of *Hamletmachine* was the manner in which it toyed with, unpacked, and pointed to the omnipresence of surveillance in late-twentieth century America, especially in spaces of contestation or anti-normative behavior. In each of its venues, the group established a video camera as an intersecting element in the performative milieu. In downtown Minneapolis, for instance, the videographer circling the labcoat-wearing performers, negotiating the concrete barricades and the groups own 'police line—do not cross' tape, served not only as a documentarian of the event, but also as an indicator of the other modes of surveillance existing simultaneously in the space. On a macro-level, the police officers patrolling the vicinity were an example of regulation of behavior via surveillance *par excellence* On another level of surveillance, the media was there—the local Channel Nine news emblem distinguishing the cameraman from the praxis videographer and the bystanders' cameras.

In the performance at Gus Lucky's, a gallery in East Minneapolis, spectators watched as Müller's text was interwoven with images collected from multiple surveillance sources: from the videotape of the Nicollet Mall performance, from Channel Nine News' story about the performance, images from simultaneous, *Hamletmachine*-related performances in New York City's Times Square, Denver, and India—and the audience's own image, recorded by the three security cameras mounted in the corners of the room and trained objectively and permanently on the spectators.

With Praxis Group's incorporation of surveillance technology, the traditional spectator/performer relationship was disrupted. No longer could the gaze of the spectator consume the image of the performer with the comforting frame of the proscenium arch separating the two as an invisible fourth wall. The surveillance cameras' unblinking eyes, focused upon the seated spectators, showed their image back to them in garish security-booth lighting, projected on the back wall of the stage and even on the performers.

In the performance at Gus Lucky's (itself a site of police monitoring for drugs and prostitution by virtue of its location in the inner city East Lake Street neighborhood), the Praxis Group split, multiplied, and decentered the audience's image by splicing in footage from Columbine, Women's Health Videos (here we refer you to Section 2), previous, and simultaneous performances, changing both the way the audience interfaced with the production, and the way in which the spectators placed themselves in the world of the text. No longer autonomous voyeurs on the other side of the fourth wall, the spectator's image in the Gus Lucky's performance was on stage with the performers, and layered into the text of *Hamletmachine* and current events. Once the protective layer of the proscenium was erased, the spectator was forced to deal with a new vulnerability that disallowed willing suspension of disbelief.

Furthermore, with the concurrent performances beamed in from outside the venue, the spectators were made aware of a simultaneity outside of the space. They witnessed live webcast from Times Square interrupted by Police. From India, a collaborator stood with his back to the Indian Ocean embodying his own interpretation of Hamlet's line at the beginning of Müller's play

'I stood on the shore and talked with the surf BLABLA the ruins of Europe in back of me.' The webcast linked the formerly autonomous and intimate space of the auditorium-as-center-of-the-universe into one of many points of intersection in a rhizomatic field. Subjectivity was, thus, shattered and scattered.

Section 5
In conclusion, the locations in which Praxis Group performed were sites of contestation, under various states of surveillance, each with a visceral history of the breaking of normalizing behavior. The spaces functioned as what Michel Foucault would call heterotopias, which, in his essay 'Of Other Spaces' he defines as counter-sites to real sites, where the normal rules of society are recognized, but contested and reversed.[11] It was in these spaces that the Praxis Group sought to wrestle individual's expectations out of conventional systems, and even from their homogenized expectations of 'experimental performance' – black-box spaces in gentrified warehouse districts, featuring smoky atmospheres and rehashed performance art. By seeking these multiple points of contestation, and engaging in a rhizomatic mode of performance, the Praxis Group's production of *Hamletmachine* required, in Müller's words, 'fierce endurance.'

BlaBla BlaBla BlaBla BlaBla BlaBla
BlaBla BlaBla BlaBla BlaBla BlaBla
BlaBla BlaBla BlaBla BlaBla BlaBla
BlaBla BlaBla BlaBla BlaBla BlaBla
BlaBla BlaBla BlaBla BlaBla BlaBla
BlaBla BlaBla BlaBla BlaBla BlaBla
BlaBla BlaBla BlaBla BlaBla BlaBla
BlaBla BlaBla BlaBla BlaBla BlaBla
BlaBla BlaBla BlaBla BlaBla BlaBla
BlaBla BlaBla BlaBla BlaBla BlaBla
BlaBla BlaBla BlaBla BlaBla BlaBla
BlaBla BlaBla BlaBla BlaBla BlaBla
BlaBla BlaBla BlaBla BlaBla BlaBla
BlaBla BlaBla BlaBla BlaBla BlaBla
BlaBla BlaBla BlaBla BlaBla BlaBla
BlaBla BlaBla BlaBla BlaBla BlaBla
BlaBla BlaBla BlaBla BlaBla BlaBla
BlaBla BlaBla BlaBla BlaBla BlaBla
BlaBla BlaBla BlaBla BlaBla BlaBla
BlaBla BlaBla BlaBla BlaBla BlaBla
BlaBla BlaBla BlaBla BlaBla BlaBla
BlaBla BlaBla BlaBla BlaBla BlaBla
BlaBla BlaBla BlaBla BlaBla BlaBla
BlaBla BlaBla BlaBla BlaBla BlaBla
BlaBla BlaBla BlaBla BlaBla BlaBla
BlaBla BlaBla BlaBla BlaBla BlaBla
BlaBla BlaBla BlaBla BlaBla BlaBla
BlaBla BlaBla BlaBla BlaBla BlaBla
BlaBla BlaBla BlaBla BlaBla BlaBla
BlaBla BlaBla BlaBla BlaBla BlaBla
'I was Hamlet. I stood at the shore and talked with the surf BLABLA the ruins of Europe in back of me.'

Notes
1 Heiner Müller, 'Hamletmachine,' *Hamletmachine and Other Texts for the Stage*, trans. Carl Weber (New York: PAJ, 1984) 56.
2 See Deleuze's 'Rhizomes Versus Trees,' and 'Nomad Art,' *The Deleuze Reader*, ed. Constantin Boundas (New York: Columbia UP, 1993).
3 Müller 51.
4 *ibid* 58.
5 *ibid* 51.
6 *ibid* 58.
7 *ibid*.
8 Michel De Certeau, *The Practice of Everyday Life*, trans. Stephen Rendall (Berkeley, U of CA P) 117.
9 Müller 56.
10 *ibid 58*.
11 See Foucault's 'Of Other Spaces,' *Diacritics* 16.1 (Spring 1986).

Intervention 5
Say: 'Parsley'

Cathy Turner

Caroline Bergvall with Ciarán Maher, 24–30 November 2001, Spacex 2, Exeter

Say: 'Parsley', created by Caroline Bergvall with Ciarán Maher, was part of Spacex Gallery's multi-site art project, *Patterns*, which explored the relationship between Islamic and Western traditions of representation in the context of the city of Exeter. This exhibit touched the theme obliquely, taking its title from the Dominican Republic's 'El Corte' massacre of 1937, during which Creole Haitians were identified by their failure to pronounce the word 'parsley' ('perejil') with a rolling Spanish 'r'. Its positioning within *Patterns* invited connections between Trujillo's wish to 'purify' the nuances of speech and attempts to identify and contain the expression of Islamic and other minority traditions within the UK. Other connections became apparent as the range of works was experienced.

Exeter's Spacex 1 is tucked away in the back streets: it attracts virtually no passers by, but must be sought out deliberately. With *Patterns*, the curators have been determined to reach out to diverse communities within the city, with exhibits in Exeter Cathedral, The Islamic Centre, The Institute for Arab and Islamic Studies (University of Exeter), Willy's Designer Clothing and Spacex 2, the former Maritime Museum, itself a former warehouse.

Spacex 2, the site of this installation, may not attract large weekday audiences, yet is perfectly positioned to draw in weekend strollers and browsers. In terms of attracting a new audience to a potentially 'difficult' piece, the work couldn't have been much better placed. However, the specificity of the location also broadened its frame of reference. Exeter's Quayside is a contested space. The voice-overs of promotional tourist videos can be heard feet away from the clubs that spill out their blaspheming occupants onto the late-night riverside. Private apartments struggle to obtain silence among cafés and walkways that are deliberately, hungrily public. The river itself, like so many English rivers, divides the more prosperous parts of town from the poorer areas, the centre from the margins.

These characteristics might, if only in a gentle way, invite the viewer to make links between the patrolling of Exeter's municipal spaces and the

Performance Research 7(2), pp.129–131 © Taylor & Francis Ltd 2002

more extreme circumstances at the Massacre River, the Dominican Republic's Northern border, where the word 'parsley' became the key to identity. This Dominican–Haitian border was a bilingual space – one where subtleties of accent were almost impossible to identify. *Say: 'Parsley'*, created by a poet and a composer, spoke to us through the half-heard and the half-recognized.

The first gallery was the most daringly minimal, containing only a whisper of white 'r's on a white wall. In the next, a sequence of voices repeated the same phrase, 'rolling hills', evoking the rolling 'r' of 'perejil', the rolling hills of Devon – and, perhaps coincidentally, the name of the last trade ship to navigate the Exeter Canal (Exeter's sludge ship, later renamed SW3). The pronunciations were close enough to require attentive listening. The sound of environmental noise tantalized – I found myself struggling to identify the literal 'background' to each voice. Text on a white wall again required close attention, as it incorporated almost invisible, whited-out phrases:[1]

> Speech mirrors ghosts speak as if
> appeased by the evidence of this
> when I speak I hold at least two
> or as if intensely preoccupied
> when I speak up I am held to one.

This part of the installation seemed an enactment of de Certeau's expression of the relationship between written and oral speech: 'the illegible returns of voices cutting across statements and moving like strangers through the house of language, like imagination' (de Certeau 1984: 159). Not only was the speaking 'I' made almost illegible (whited out), cutting through the cryptic statements of plurality, hauntedness, preoccupation (the 'returns' of 'strangers'), but the accompanying recorded voices provided sonic evidence of the way the body haunts language, through accent and timbre. The violence of the 1937 massacre was a punishment of the body for its foreignness – the suppression of a haunting presence that threatened the 'writing' of a 'pure' Dominican culture.

The two syllables of 'Mis-lead' framed the staircase to the upper level where a grid of lead pendulums suggested bullets, the 'lead' of 'mislead', tears, water drops, grains, plumb lines, fishing lines, punctuation marks that skittered and swung across the floor: the text's 'ambiguous depth in which sounds . . . move about'? (de Certeau 1984: 162). On the floorboards, beneath each weight, was a trace of erased writing – a letter, a quotation mark. A solitary gold weight gleamed under an archway, talismanic, singled out.

The grid, emblem of a man-made ideal, an organizing and unifying schema, imposes stasis. In *Say: 'Parsley'* the grid of pendulums was set in motion by the slightest touch or draft. As it trembled and swayed, traces of language were revealed. Among these letters, pieced together, we could read 'VOICES', or perhaps '("VOICES?")', as if by mobilising the grid, creating new currents through the organization of culture, or language, we discovered the lost voices of the dispossessed. A stray 'i' seemed adrift among colons, suggesting, with the 'I' in 'VOICES, the silenced half of the bilingual voice, which is 'held to one.' Or perhaps, 'VOICI'.

This use of the grid set up connections with the dismantled grids of letters in Bergvall's *Goan Atom* (Bergvall 2001) and with the other *Patterns* exhibits. In the cathedral, Samta Benyahia produced mirrors on which were marked patterns resembling the lattice work of the 'moucharabieh' or carved wooden screen that traditionally divides Berber women from outside the world. By looking at the cathedral through this screen, we could both observe how the building's patterns echo those of Islamic and Arab cultures, and gain a sense of 'the experience of always looking through an obstacle', which, according to Benyahia, 'renders women blind' (Heartney 1996: 2).

Introducing this work, Keith Jones, the Dean of the cathedral writes:

> Regular geometric patterns, subtly modulated and intricately reflecting each other, have for Christians and Muslims, reflected the shared belief that God takes pleasure in reason, created by law, and lays down straight

lines of wisdom across the folly and evasions of our
human life. (Jones 2001)

He goes on to quote Thomas Browne, writing of
'the mystical mathematics of the Kingdom of
Heaven'. But although Benyahia's work did draw
parallels between Islam and Christianity (as did
Zineb Sedira's *Self-Portrait or the Virgin Mary*, a
ghostly photograph of a veiled woman), it also
implicitly questioned the universalism of a patriar-
chal religious code in both cultures.

Bergvall and Maher's work took up the theme of
a universal geometry and applied it to language,
where any deviation from the accepted 'patterns' of
speech can be a cue to violence. Across from the
grid of pendulums, between two speakers,
Bergvall's (French-Norwegian) voice demanded the
pronunciation of different words, framed by a stut-
tering introduction. Here, language fragmented ('s
wallow') among images of 'the gate of the law',
teeth being pulled, 'the big mouth' which has a
'rock in the throat' – as if, this time, the mouth
itself was imagined as the 'ambiguous depth', the
border river, the gateway to language. Heard from
close up, it was possible to catch the incidental
sounds of mouth and breath. Moving away, the
voice was faintly heard across the room. Distant or
close, the listener strained to hear.

Even from the ground floor, visitors to the
installation would have been aware of sound
bleeding through from the fourth and last space.
Here, four speakers were positioned in pairs. The
repetitive, looped sound gradually revealed itself
as language. 'Nothing', 'Certain', 'Speak',
'Freely', 'Standard', 'English', 'At' and 'Home'
bounced off each other as units of sound: the shrill
soundtrack to persecution or the insistent music
of rejected voices?

These planes of sound were reminiscent of the
ululation of Zineb Sedira's *A Scream for Liberation*
which filled Spacex 1. Here, as in Bergvall and
Maher's work, the cry was enigmatic: was it a wail
of grief or a shout of triumph? A video showed only
the woman's mouth, so that her identity was
hidden, or perhaps veiled. In *Say: 'Parsley'*, the

voices were only heard clearly as we moved closer
to stand between the speakers. The anonymity, the
'foreignness' of the sound fragmented on close
listening.

The beauty of this installation was in its
apparent sparseness, the subtle layering of linguistic textures, the way it made us listen carefully to
what was beyond absolute identification. Back in
Spacex 1, Benyahia's *Night of Destiny*, a sound
piece, re-told popular Arabic and French poetry.
These poems were once recited by groups of
women who met late at night when the men were
asleep. The recitations of *Say: 'Parsley'* were also
quietly subversive; the work was similarly disin-
clined to declare itself in slogans. It was worth a
second visit and time spent silently moving through
its murmuring spaces. The writing may have been
on the wall, but it was written in white.

NOTE
1.   Here I should acknowledge cris cheek's extensive
commentary on *Say: 'Parsley'*, posted to the liveart
mailbase 10 December 2001. I have adopted his method
of representing Bergvall's text here, and this review owes
a debt to his observations.

REFERENCES
Bergvall, Caroline (2001) *Goan Atom*, San Francisco:
     Krupskaya.
De Certeau, Michel (1984) *The Practice of Everyday Life*,
     London: University of California Press.
Heartney, Eleanor (1996) 'Samta Benyahia: Interview
     with Eleanor Heartney', in *Samta Benyahia* (Exhi-
     bition Catalogue), New York: Art in General.
Jones, Keith (2001) *Patterns* (Information Leaflet),
     Exeter: Spacex Gallery.

Translating John Malkovich

Lynn Turner

Did you just call me 'Lotte'?

(Being John Malkovich)

[Voice] is part of the body but because it traverses
the body, because it disposes of it, it retains almost
nothing of it, comes from elsewhere and goes
elsewhere, and in passing it may give to this body
a locus but does not depend upon it [. . .] insofar as
'its own place' is sexually determined [. . .] Voice
can betray the body to which it is lent, it can make
it ventriloquize as if the body were no longer
anything more than the actor or the double of
another voice, of the voice of the other, even of an
innumerable, incalculable polyphony.

(Derrida 1995a: 161)

'God weeps over his name' (Derrida 1985: 184).
Forbidding the translation of his own proper name
he also demands it, cries out for it. From the covert
sale of 15 minutes of being someone else, to the
group possession of the ripe vessel, the one who
should be stable, discrete and proper, who should be
capable of *authoring* exchanges, John Malkovich, is
himself put into circulation as a commodity. *Being
John Malkovich* sets forth this circulation through
the yarn of the body as vessel accessed by an
unlikely portal – a portal without sexual discrimi-
nation – hidden behind a filing cabinet in one of the
nondescript offices of the equally unlikely 7½th
floor of the Mertin–Flemmer building. Claims upon
this vessel occur via the name. *Malkovich* undoes
Malkovich. Malkovich undoes Malkovich, willingly,
and repeatedly, and without knowing that he does
so. Craig Schwarz (John Cusack) projects himself

into the Malkovich vessel in the erroneous belief
that he can instrumentalize it, overcome it with his
own signatorial force only to be himself sublated.
Desiring to have the vessel as just one more puppet
in his workshop, Craig ends up following his own
description of puppeteering as 'the idea of becoming
someone else . . . Being inside another skin. Moving
differently, thinking differently, feeling differently',
but for rather more than his calculated 'little while'.
I want to think of the *movement* at stake here as a
translation. This translation, following Walter
Benjamin's idiosyncratic use of the term, bears
upon the working of metaphor, *translates* the
workings of metaphor such that its smooth claims
for natural resemblance are uprooted and therefore
disarticulated. The disarticulation that interests me
is the erotic one occurring in this film to contrasting
degrees when Malkovich and Maxine (Catherine

Performance Research 7(2), pp.132–137 © Taylor & Francis Ltd 2002

Keener) have sex, firstly with Lotte (Cameron Diaz) 'inside' the vessel, and secondly with Craig bent upon pulling the strings.

Puppet-man, dog-boy, doll-face: these are the less than flattering portmanteau names with which Maxine addresses Craig, names that mark his auteurial decay. She only bothers to use his given name at the height of her manipulation of him – coincidental with the necessity to retain (her) control over the Malkovich vessel. (Whereas Lotte keeps her name for Maxine even when she is being John Malkovich.) But Craig's name has been in shreds ever since he left the fictional sanctuary of his private puppet theatre.

If Craig attempts mastery through practising puppetry as an art form, performing a desire to be recognized as a Puppeteer, the banality of his existence is thrust upon him as he hangs up his puppet following the puppet show which opens *Being John Malkovich*. In voice-off a woman's voice calls Craig out of his reverie: 'Craig, honey, time for bed'. He does not respond. The screen fades to black. Before the next scene fades up the dull familiarity of the previous voice-off is parroted by another: 'Craig, honey, time to get up, Craig, honey, time to get up. . .'. A cockateel perched on Craig's head is visually remarked as its source. Truly regardless of intent, yet, insofar as it *is* morning, felicitously, it really is time to get up. Craig Honey is unresponsive. This is only one of many instances in the film where speech is shown to function through conventionality not intentionality. The *coup de théâtre* of entering the uncanny environment of the 7½th floor, after which all scenes become a puppet theatre of some description, simply marks an acceleration of these idiosyncrasies of communication and perspective. It also marks the point at which Craig's fantasy of controlling the theatrical scenes that he would author begins to come undone. Stepping into the corridor of the 7½th floor, he is obliged to bend almost double since the whole environment is radically scaled down. As the viewer knows, Craig already has a double in the form of his puppet. Only for him is this floor uncanny: he is used to manipulating

movement within small spaces rather than having his own movements determined by them. Everyone else accepts it at face value. On arrival at *Lester Corp* for his job interview, having succumbed to the pedestrian necessity of work, Craig's name is the first thing to be subjected to the violent repetitions of the secretary, Floris: my name is Craig Schwartz, he says, have a seat Mr Juarez, comes the reply.

Having sex with Malkovich/Craig is filmed in marked contrast to that with Malkovich/Lotte. Maxine collects Malkovich from a dress rehearsal of *Richard III*, where his lines again converge with the direction of the main narrative in the form of a literal prediction. Richard/Malkovich, having seduced Lady Anne through the force of his wit alone (overcoming having recently murdered her husband and father, as well as his own notorious physical deformity) crows

Was ever woman in this humour woo'd?
Was ever woman in this humour won?

Interrupting himself at the arrival of Maxine, he breaks off. Had he continued, the next line would have declared 'I'll have her; but I will not keep her long!' This speech act, albeit a 'pretended' one, nevertheless predicts exactly what will transpire for Malkovich/Craig vis-a-vis Maxine – but for reasons quite at odds with those enforced by Richard, then Duke of Gloucester. *Malkovich* cuts to a two shot of Malkovich/Craig and Maxine fucking on the couch. Like the scene with Malkovich/Lotte and Maxine (below), it is clearly framed as the passionate afternoon sex of new lovers but here their bodies are in full frame, given emphasis since both have bare legs. The film foregoes an easy and habitual breast shot even as Craig mechanically and repetitively instructs Malkovich to 'Move right hand across left breast now' in a scene framed similarly to a pornographic come shot. The film does not employ any music to weight the scene, for example as romantic or sexy. Craig's mutterings are directed to himself and to (controlling) Malkovich rather than to Maxine who remains unaware of the substitution. Craig's voice begins as a variety of stage whisper, both quiet as if not to be overheard, and loud since his voice is miked up much more prominently than that of Maxine, who consequently seems very distant. Unlike Lotte, Craig does not call out Maxine's name at all, and when he subsequently informs Lotte of his success this is framed entirely in terms of his pleasure in gaining motor control over Malkovich. The strength of Craig's delight in manipulating Malkovich spills over into speech: exclaiming 'Holy shit, yes!' as he moves Malkovich's hand, Malkovich in a strangled squawk repeats his words. Recognizing that Malkovich is not himself, Maxine assumes that Lotte has been able to ventriloquize him. Craig attempts to extend his articulation of Malkovich and to use his body as a convenient mask, obliging Malkovich to claim to be Lotte, albeit still through a speech which contorts his face and his voice. Again Malkovich interrupts himself – this time from a role that he was not aware of inhabiting. As Maxine attempts to placate his panic, Malkovich seizes the term with which she casually addresses him, '*doll-face*', recognizing its implications, and leaves the scene.

At first Lotte misrecognizes the experience of the vessel, of being John Malkovich, as telling her something about the truth of her own 'being' (saying 'I've decided I'm a transsexual'). Malkovich, however, soon becomes the vehicle, the point of articulation, for her sexual relationship with Maxine. Seduced by the shock of Maxine's flirtation, a shock derived from her change of context – her contingent inhabitation of Malkovich enabling her to become the recipient of another woman's address, Lotte accepts the limited terms of her prosthetic contact with Maxine and arranges a date *with* her and *via* Malkovich. Being John Malkovich gets Lotte translated.[1] Being John Malkovich lets Lotte have Maxine. It is Maxine's attention (an interpellation from without) that clinches Lotte's obsession with being Malkovich above and beyond the sensations of the body of the other: Maxine mediates her experience of being him.

Opening the door of his apartment to Maxine, Malkovich assumes that they will go straight to bed. She has after all, as far as he can be aware, been behaving like a groupie, soliciting a famous name for sex. As he runs his hand up to her breast, Maxine checks his watch and declares herself early. An extremely awkward and inane conversation on the sofa ensues. They sit far apart. No point-of-view shots are given. When the clock turns 4.11pm exactly, the time of her date with Lotte rather than Malkovich, Maxine's behaviour dramatically alters. She turns towards Malkovich, showing interest in 'him' for the first time and coyly says 'hi' waving in 'his' direction. He, unsurprisingly, appears a little mystified but plays along, saying 'hi' back to her. As she moves towards him romantic music codifies their encounter. Two types of shot are used – either the two-shot with the pair of them in frame at varying distances, or the point-of-view shot connotative of Lotte's viewpoint and her perceptions to the exclusion of those of Malkovich. At no time does the film approximate Maxine's viewpoint, thus the audience is never aligned with her in terms of spectatorial identification and is obliged to take Maxine's word for it that Lotte's 'feminine presence' can be sensed behind Malkovich's 'too prominent brow and male pattern baldness'. In distinction to the first time Lotte inhabited Malkovich, where her voice-over was coded as the repetition of his lines (though the authority of his voice was being supplemented by Chekhov's script), here his speech unconsciously and ironically follows hers in the adoring repetition of Maxine's name. Maxine kisses Malkovich, moving to sit astride him as he reclines on the sofa, putting himself into her hands. Through the oval framing of Lotte's hidden viewpoint we see Maxine's smiling face as she and Malkovich begin to caress each other. Lotte giggles nervously but with pleasure, murmuring 'Oh Maxine, my sweet Maxine'. As if in direct response, Maxine addresses Lotte by name, telling her she loves her. Briefly the scene continues, but then it breaks, cutting to the two-shot, dropping the music, and, although Maxine continues to kiss Malkovich's neck, he looks perplexed and asks her whether she did in fact just call him 'Lotte'. Switching back to Lotte's viewpoint, she is silent as if afraid of being found out. Maxine smiles and asks him whether he minds. In close-up, though still in profile, he pauses and then replies in the negative: *he accepts her name.* Lotte's viewpoint resumes and henceforth the romantic music signifying their enjoyment of the scene is associated only with her perspective – arguably it also informs Maxine's participation through their verbal address to each other, using each other's names. Since Lotte remains hidden this is the only way the film can present her as part of the scene – by calling her into it. Since the notional perspective of Lotte within Malkovich is also aligned with that of the audience – we see what she sees and, like her, we cannot see ourselves – the repetitive use of her name both names the audience as 'Lotte' rather than 'Malkovich' and remarks on the apparatus of identification that it choreographs: the postal address of the look is shown as that of a contingent apparatus. Slipping over to a different point in the circuit of this apparatus, the picture changes for Lotte. Malkovich, unwittingly sandwiched between the two of them, is reduced to his use value as a point of mediation which manages to vehicle an erotic intensity without particular emphasis upon distinct bodies.[2] Unusually for cinematic sex, both visible parties remain fully clothed, even when we see Malkovich's hands caressing Maxine's breasts he does so through her dress. Although Maxine dazzles both Lotte and Craig she never becomes contained by spectacle. Maxine crafts the narrative, though her look, desired by both Lotte and Craig, is never inhabited by the camera/the audience. Although it is clear that Maxine has straddled Malkovich, none of the shots emphasize the movement of fucking; instead they concentrate upon the verbal exchange framing this scene. Language – or more specifically the incantation of the proper names hovering at the edges of language – directs the cinematic rendition of this sex. That this exchange occurs mainly through the illocutionary repetition of their names contributes to the construction of Malkovich as a vessel that can transport any contingent relation. Though this sequence ends before any indication of

orgasm for Maxine or Malkovich, when Lotte is expelled she falls on her back and remains lying on the grass verge, her face shiny, elated by her experience, her sexual pleasure strongly implied.

Does Malkovich cry out for translation?[3] He cries out for Maxine, readily giving up his name. Accepting the substitution of a seemingly random woman's name pulled from the air, he colludes in his own effacement. Even his cries repeat those of Lotte. This substitution is not a metaphor insofar as Lotte bears no necessary resemblance to Malkovich: she is not *like* him. They do not match. In this contiguity of subjects who look – Malkovich; Lotte; the audience – anyone can step into Malkovich's shoes. In the vein of allegory, 'any person, any thing, any relationship can mean absolutely anything else' (Benjamin 1998: 175). But following in his footsteps, they/we incorporate his mode of signification, following him in every detail. The only similarity linking 'Malkovich' and 'Lotte' is their subscription to the set 'proper names', the subdivision of gender or genre sets them apart, as does given name and surname. The symbolic status of the patronym 'Malkovich' marks out the name that he has made for himself (a phrasing which gives the sense of the name yet requiring to be *made*), the name that he trades upon as a celebrated actor, and the name that signs any and every performance maintaining a borderline between the character he assumes and the artistic authority sketching that character. Star-billing rests upon the marketing of originality, Malkovich has to be the one and only auratic John Malkovich, assumed to be his own author, abysmally marked by *Malkovich* in that he plays 'himself', and that he is destined within *Malkovich* to be his own copy first by Lotte, then by countless strangers, then by Craig, and ultimately by Lester and all his friends.[4] Moreover, even as the film flags his name in its title, its successful transmission is continually mocked. When Craig parasitically inhabits Malkovich for the first time, he is shown as anything but successfully self-authoring and incapable of obtaining more than the vaguest recognition from his taxi driver, who can barely remember his name, let alone any films in which he has actually starred. Lotte is *translated* into Malkovich insofar as she *moves across* into him. Her point of view supplants his (when the vessel is occupied all point-of-view shots are connotative of the inhabitant). Truly the original – Malkovich – is understood through the apparently secondary translation (to, again, recall Benjamin). From here the proper name as place name becomes a stage, a theatre. It becomes uncanny. The name shakes.[5]

Taking advantage of the instability in the name, Lotte and Maxine shake it loose a little more. This is not to say that their own (first) names are unshakeable or sealed, made watertight in some way; far from it. But that it is the patronym, culturally called upon as the guarantee of the patriarch, the patri-*arkhē*, the 'patriarchive', the origin of the father's name, the house of the father's name, the conservatory of his seed, that they shake (Derrida 1995b: 4, n.1). And the insemination that occurs in this scene will be a dissemination. Necessarily,

> The movements of deconstruction do not destroy structures from the outside. They are not possible and effective, nor can they take accurate aim, except by inhabiting those structures. Inhabiting them *in a certain way*, because one always inhabits, and all the more when one does not suspect it. Operating necessarily from the inside, borrowing all the strategic and economic resources of subversion from the old structure, borrowing them structurally . . .
>
> (Derrida 1976: 24)

Elsewhere I have had cause to critique Derrida's work on translation – as it is figured in 'Des Tours de Babel' as a marriage contract signed by the proper names of the author and translator across the translation with a promise of the reconciliation of languages – in order to question the heteronormativity of this contract, the contract of contracts guaranteeing all subsequent contracts.[6] Here, however, up against the proper name, I want to change tack slightly and suggest that *Being John Malkovich*, if it does not terminate this contract, nevertheless does insist upon a suppleness within

its terms even as it plays them out. Playing them out, in the writing of this translation, the orderliness of the law that requires a signature and a countersignature, is precisely what is in question. The philosophical question regarding point of view – 'who speaks?' – becomes a legalistic 'who signs?' Instead of the copulation of the two names at the edge of the tongue, at the edge of the lip, being those of the author of the original text and the translator, in this scene the authority of the original is wholly expropriated. Teased out from two sides, two translators, *traducteuses*, manipulate the text, and manipulate a text (the patronym) conventionally assigned especial authority but now shown to remain frayed at the (selv)edges (Spivak 1995: 180).

The performative repetition of their names, each calling to the other, demonstrates their need for repetition, that the name does not quite succeed in capturing or contracting a property. The interpellation of the name, fired through the Malkovich vessel, shatters it, or perhaps reveals it to be always and already shattered, reminiscent of the manner of the fragmentation of the vessel to which Benjamin compares the making of a translation (Benjamin 1992: 79). Maxine and Lotte pervade each other with their names. Their names resonate, vibrate. If Benjamin compared the relation of the translation to the original as that of a royal robe only loosely enfolding its 'meaningful' content, then, underneath the *royal cloaking device* of the Malkovich vessel there is plenty of space for the women to have sex. And in this space, this spacing, 'where there is voice, sex becomes undecided' (Derrida 1995a: 161). While this cloak (directly compared to 'an expensive suit' later in the film) may fit Malkovich, truly it does not 'cling strictly enough to the royal person' to prevent others slipping under its hem (Derrida 1985: 194). This cloak will turn out to be sufficiently expansive to accommodate quite a crowd. For truly 'what counts is what comes to pass under the cape' (194). And this cape, this cloak, this *Königsmantel*, joined in the metonymic train of thought of 'Des Tours de Babel' to a wedding dress and thus to a hymeneal narrative, turns upon the trope of virginity. The virginity of John Malkovich turns out to devolve upon a forgotten orifice or portal, or the forgetting of an originary spacing which nevertheless opens a passage to his name from outside. If Jacques Derrida once critiqued Jacques Lacan's analysis of *The Purloined Letter* on grounds of that letter being found, *as expected*, in its proper place between the legs of the giant female body that was the *mantelpiece* (Derrida 1987: 440), here, the generous folds of the *Königsmantel* of John Malkovich cannot be reduced to a '*Königsmantel*-piece,' encompassing a content foretold.

NOTES
1   As Barbara Engh pointed out to me, famous names get translated.

2   Referring to the intoxication of this situation Maxine later describes it in terms of having two people looking at her 'with total lust and devotion through the same pair of eyes' rather than any acknowledgement of sex or gender. *Malkovich* renders the complexity of this sexual encounter in a much more interesting way than, say, *Ghost* (Dir. Jerry Zucker, US, 1990) – in which the medium (Whoopi Goldberg) allows herself to be temporarily possessed by the titular ghost (Patrick Swayze) in order that he might kiss his lover (Demi Moore). However, the mediation is homophobically erased at the point of the kiss when Goldberg is visually substituted by Swayze. This is indeed the tyranny of metaphoric substitution, resemblance in the service of homophobia.

3   I make the link between God's name and that of Malkovich not in simple disregard for their divine/human difference but bearing in mind the purported star status for which Malkovich is cast and the marketing of the 'star' as substitute for aura.

4   This is further remarked by the film since all of its major characters are cast against type.

5   'The name itself is the cry of naked lust' (Benjamin, cited in Hansen 1987: 219, n.66).

6   And right here, significantly, is the spot, marked with an 'x', upon which the heteronormative breaches the public and private spheres: it is the union of copulation and contract. See my unpublished paper 'Line of flight > line of plight'.

REFERENCES
Being John Malkovich, dir. Spike Jonze, US, 1999.

Benjamin, Walter (1992) 'The Task of the Translator', in Harry Zohn (trans.) *Illuminations*, London: Fontana.

—— (1998) *The Origin of German Tragic Drama*, trans. John Osborne, London: Verso.

Derrida, Jacques (1976) *Of Grammatology*, trans. Gayatri Spivak, Baltimore, MD: Johns Hopkins University Press.

—— (1985) 'Des Tours de Babel', in Joseph Graham (ed. and trans.). *Differences in Translation*, Ithaca, NY: Cornell University Press.

—— (1987) *The Postcard: From Socrates to Freud and Beyond*, trans. Alan Bass, Chicago: University of Chicago Press.

—— (1995a) *Points . . . Interviews 1974–1994*, Stanford, CA: Stanford University Press.

—— (1995b) *Archive Fever: A Freudian Impression*, trans. Eric Prenowitz, Chicago: University of Chicago Press.

Hansen, Miriam (1987) 'Benjamin, Cinema, & Experience: "The Blue Flower in the Land of Technology",' *New German Critique* 40.

Spivak, Gayatri (1995) *Outside in the Teaching Machine*, London & New York: Routledge.

Performance Review
Facing Pages

Joanna Roche

Did they remember who we were?
Did they remember what we said?
Maybe someone else came along and said pretty
    much the same thing.
Did anybody notice?

Did we speak the same language?
Did it rain?
Was there a wedding?
Did we have parents?

Did we have to go to work every morning?
What kind of cars did we drive?
What sort of houses did we live in? Cities, I
    remember.
What did we wear?

Did we mean well?
Did we think that life was sacred?
Did it matter?
Do we matter?

(It's an Earthquake in My Heart)[1]

Is this the space where we seek the whirring heart of the 'impossible problem' posed to us by Goat Island – here, in the closing monologue spoken by Matthew Goulish of *It's an Earthquake in My Heart*? I am not sure, but as a closing, it points (indexically) to where we have come in the preceding hour and 40 minutes: the *running* time of Goat Island's most recent performance. Through gestures, spoken words, music, motions, objects and the infinite recombination of these and other elements, *Earthquake* keeps us in suspension within the very process of understanding itself.

In poetry, I look for facing page translations. I still prefer this format to those that show just half the process. Half writings let us forget the difficulties (among other beauties) faced by the translator. In the facing form, we can cross at will between spaces – authors' and translators' – finding pleasure in difference.

The facing page – as space, as process – is somehow familiar to viewers of Goat Island. My own response to *Earthquake* over the last months has been a back and forthing, a perpetual movement across the spine from Goat Island's work to my own. My 'work' has revised itself countless times since my initial experience of *Earthquake* at Dartington this past October, changed/charged through memory – as anyone familiar with the collaborations of this group of six knows. To make our own facing pages, as audience/author, is to continue the 'slow thinking' of Goat Island which is at the basis of *Earthquake* (each of the seven works Goat Island has made since 1987 takes two years' work). In the afterwards

Performance Research 7(2), pp.138-140 © Taylor & Francis Ltd 2002

of interpretation, we replicate the process of the collaborative ensemble: looking across the page back to Goat Island's/ our previous thinking, then reworking what was just made, which continues to face Goat Island's/our next draft. Pages proliferate. My understanding faces itself on a new page an hour after *Earthquake*, a day, a week, a month. . . .

At Dartington, I sought the privacy of my own response to *Earthquake*, and the possibility of a memory formed in isolation. This brief work begins another facing page.

NOTE
The left-hand column consists of three performance maps/drawings created for Earthquake by Lin Hixson, Matthew Goulish and Karen Christopher.

When did *logos* become logo
(did somebody say this already while I slept?)
because here we are, America,
back in that Chevy saddle.
'Pony up boys & let's get down & suck that waterhole dry,
before the rest of the world shows up.'

Goat Island doesn't ride a horse,
or even a car, just an *Earthquake* that begins and ends
with resolute flesh made strong
through collisions of motion and emotion.
Their gift transports the signifiers of daily life
from Wellington Ave. to Prague and back,
made from hymns and shoes and chairs that rhyme
with four sides of a single question:
*What would your family do
if you did not come home last night?*
What would you do if your heart
stopped flaming and became a machine
whose motor forgot to spark, to ignite?

I leave on feet that were once trees
that now can walk *(clop clop)*
behind the prick of yellow plastic
birdy feet *(clipclip clipclip clipclip)*.
Even when trees walk
they can't keep up with the birds.
Names uttered as words, as lists
whose quiet speaking might heal,
or soften death.

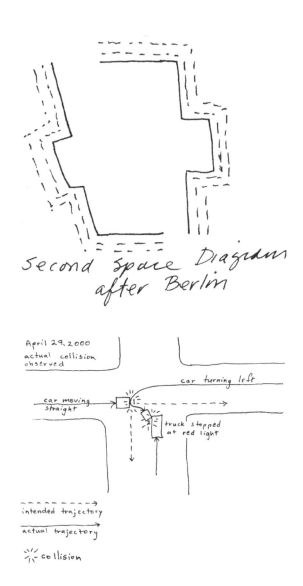

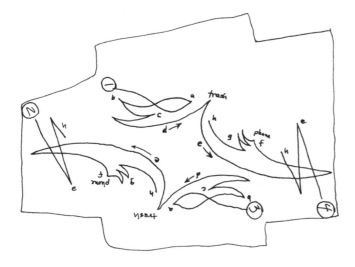

Oak.
Cedar.
Tulip, the lumbermen call it yellow poplar.
Sycamore.
Gum, both sweet and sour.
Beech.
Black walnut.
Sassafras.
Willow.
Butternut.
Cypress.
Larch.
Box elder.
Yew.
Catalpa.[2]

Facing pages entwine over time. Faulkner wrote of wisteria (and memory) that it grows 'by secret and attritive progress from mote to mote of obscurity's myriad components' (*Absalom, Absalom*). Goat Island's performances remind me of Faulkner's writing about wisteria. Perhaps in his fantastic sentence we can understand the beauty that overwhelms us when we watch Goat Island perform. The bloom hints at what the vine has been doing. Wisteria and the making of pages take years. The elusive space of *Earthquake* contains both joy and pain, inviting us to *be* within the instant of experience as it vanishes. 'Did anybody notice?'

NOTES
1 From *Book of Life*, Hal Hartley (1999).
2 This final list of trees is from the performance text of *It's an Earthquake in My Heart* (draft 11/1).

Performance Research: Translations

Notes on Contributors

THE EDITORS

Ric Allsopp is a founding editor of *Performance Research* and Reader in Performance Research at Dartington College of Arts, UK. He is co-founder of Writing Research Associates, an international partnership organizing, promoting and publishing contemporary performance projects including *Migrations* (2000); *In the Event of Text* (1999) and *Performance Writing* (1996).

Richard Gough is general editor of *Performance Research*, a Senior Research Fellow at the University of Wales, Aberystwyth, and Artistic Director for the Centre of Performance Research (CPR). He edited *The Secret Art of the Performer* (Routledge, 1990) and has curated and organized numerous conference and workshop events over the last 20 years as well as directing and lecturing internationally.

Claire MacDonald is a founding editor of *Performance Research* and a Visiting Assistant Professor in the College of Visual and Performing Arts at George Mason University in Northern Virginia. She teaches theatre and writing for performance and has held curatorial positions and fellowships in Britain, the USA and Holland. Her recent publications include 'Writing Outside the Mainstream' in *The Cambridge companion to Modern British Women Playwrights* (2000).

ISSUE CO-EDITOR

Caroline Bergvall is a French-Norwegian poet and mixed-arts writer based in England. Her work is frequently concerned with issues of cultural belonging, multiple languages and sited text. She has published her poetic and critical texts internationally and has developed a number of performance and installation projects, frequently in collaboration with other artists, some of which are: *Ambient Fish* (Hull Time Based Art, 1999), *About Face* (Berlin, 2000 & NY, 2001), *Say Parsley* (Spacex Exeter, 2001). Her books include: *Eclat* (Sound & Language, 1996), *Jets-Poupee* (RemPress, 1999), and *Goan Atom* (Kruspkaya, 2001). She was the Director of Performance Writing, Dartington College of Arts, England (1994–2000).

CONTRIBUTORS

Charles Bernstein is the Director of the Poetics Program at SUNY-Buffalo, where he is David Gray Professor of Poetry and Letter. His most recent books are *With Strings* and *My Way: Speeches and Poems* (both University of Chicago Press).

cris cheek is a writer, artist and sound composer working on interdisciplinary and hybrid poetic textualities/performances.

Scott deLahunta specializes in the relationship between performing arts and emerging technologies and has co-organized and participated in projects in over a dozen countries. For more material and on line articles and reports, visit: http://huizen.dds.nl/~sdela.

Arnold Dreyblatt has lived in Berlin since 1984 and is currently a guest professor at the College of Fine Arts in Saarbrücken. His works take a variety of forms; contemporary opera, interactive performance and installation as well as books and digital media.

Allen Fisher currently edits *Spanner*, lives in Hereford and is Head of Art at the University of Roehampton Surrey, where he is Professor of Poetry & Art.

Rainer Ganahl is an artist living and working in New York. He has exhibited work internationally since 1989 in one person and group shows including exhibitions in New York, Paris, Vienna, Tokyo, and the Venice Biennale (1999). For further information see: www.ganahl.info.

Adrian Kear is Programme Convener for Drama & Theatre Studies at University of Roehampton Surrey. He is the author of numerous articles on the relationship between critical theory, cultural politics, performance and ethics.

Anya Lewin is an artist, organizer of events, and educator. She was the founder and programmer of Cornershop, a cross arts gallery and performance space in Buffalo NY that ran from 1997–2000. She is currently a lecturer in Art & Performance at Dartington College of Arts.

Scott Magelssen is a PhD candidate in Theatre History Theory at the University of Minnesota. He is currently finishing his dissertation on touristic space and performance of the past at living history museums in the US. He served as dramaturg for the 2000 production of *Hamletmachine* in Minneapolis.

Rod Mengham is a Senior Lecturer in the English Faculty at Cambridge University where he is also Director of Studies in English at Jesus College. He is the author of books on Charles Dickens, Emily Bronte and Henry Green, as well as of *The Descent of Language* (1993).

Clare Moloney is a performer and theatre maker based in London and is enrolled in post graduate research at Dartington College of Arts.

Erin Mouré, poet and translator, also known as Eirin Moure and Erín Moure, lives in Montréal. Her translation

Sheep's Vigil by a Fervent Person: a Translation of Alberto Caeiro/Fernando Pessoa's O Guardador de Rebanhos appeared in 2001, and a new book of her own poetry, *O Cidadán*, in 2002.

Morgan O'Hara lives and works in New York and Europe. Her *Live Transmissions* render normally unremarked movement visible through the pulse of life-vitality carefully observed and simultaneously tracked with two or more pencils.

Redell Olsen is a poet. Her publications include *Book Of The Insect* (London: Allsingingalldancing press, 1999) and *Book of The Fur* (Cambridge: REMpress, 2000). She is currently completing a Phd on the relationship between image and text in poetry and the visual arts at Royal Holloway, University of London, where she also teaches.

Alain Platel is a director and choreographer whose prize-winning work with Les Ballets C. de la B. and Victoria has been produced throughout Europe and internationally. In 2001 he received the VIIth Prix EuropeNouvelles Théatrales in Taormina (Italy) and the title of Chevalier de Ordre des Arts et des Lettres de la République Française from the French Ministry of Culture.

George Quasha is a poet, artist (performance, video, installation, stonework), and publisher (Station Hill/Barrytown Ltd.) in Barrytown, NY. See: www.quasha.com.

Joanna Roche is Assistant Professor of Contemporary Art History at California State University, Fullerton. She is currently working on a book that examines the processes of memory practiced by Joseph Cornell and Goat Island.

Monica Ross is an artist. She is an AHRB fellow in the Creative and Performing Arts in the Department of Fine Art at the University of Newcastle upon Tyne. Her notebook on current work can be seen at: http://www.justfornow.net.

Zineb Sedira has exhibited extensively in the UK and internationally. Her exhibitions include 'Authentic/excentric: Africa In and Out Africa', 59th Venice Biennale. She has won the AfAA's Laureat 2001 at 'Les Rencontres Photographique de Bamako', Mali.

P. A. Skantze is an independent scholar and director working in Rome. She received her PhD in Literature and Drama from Columbia University. Her book *'Still in Motion': The Paradox of Movement and Stasis on the 17th Century Stage* is under contract to Routledge.

Charles Stein is a poet and artist (photography, drawing, performance), author of 11 books of poetry, philosophical and literary essays including a critical study of Charles Olson and C. G. Jung.

Anne Tardos is a poet, a visual artist, and a composer. She has lectured and performed her works widely in the US and Europe. Her books of polylingual poems and graphics are *Cat Licked the Garlic* (Vancouver, BC: Tsunami Editions, 1992) and *The Dik-dik's Solitude* (New York: Granary Books, 2002).

John Troyer is currently a PhD student at the University of Minnesota. He directed the 2000 production of *Hamletmachine* in Minneapolis. He researches 19th Century embalming technologies and the invention of the corpse. The Praxis Group is located at: http://www.waste.org/praxis.

Cathy Turner, PhD, is a Research Fellow in the Creative and Performing Arts at Exeter University Drama Department. She is a core member of Wrights & Sites, creating performance-based and cross-art-form site-specific work.

Lynn Turner is Lecturer in Art History at Goldsmith's College, London. She has recently completed her PhD, *With Reservation: choreography reading sexuality*, at the University of Leeds. She was an editor of *Parallax* (2000–2002).

Bronwyn Tweddle is a theatre director and Lecturer in Theatre at Victoria University, Wellington, NZ, with research interests in multi-lingual theatre, 20th century German-language performance, cabaret and puppetry.

Lawrence Venuti's books include *The Translator's Invisibility: A History of Translation* (1995), *The Scandals of Translation: Towards an Ethics of Difference* (1998), and *The Translation Studies Reader* (2000). He has translated, most recently, Juan Rodolfo Wilcock's *The Temple of Iconoclasts* (2000) and Antonia Pozzi's *Breath: Poems and Letters* (2002). He is currently professor of English at Temple University.

Claudia Wegener works as an artist and writer in London. She completed a PhD in visual arts at Goldsmith's College in 1998, is a visiting lecturer at the Royal Academy schools and founding member of Foreign Investment, a London-based artist performance group.

Sean Wu Shih-hung has practiced arts criticism since 1994 and exhibited regularly his works integrating texts/photos/videos and performance installations in England. He is completing a MPhil on Minimalist performance (University of Surrey).

Performance Research

PR CONSORTIUM:

T - #0199 - 270225 - C0 - 269/210/8 - PB - 9780415289412 - Gloss Lamination